T0261496

Marketing Automation and Decision Making

In memory of Marisa Bezzini, my mom,
grateful for what she taught me,
and who is always alive in my heart.

Marketing Automation and Decision Making

The Role of Heuristics and AI in Marketing

Simone Guercini

Full Professor of Marketing and Management, Department of Economics and Management, University of Florence, Italy

Edward **Elgar**
PUBLISHING

Cheltenham, UK • Northampton, MA, USA

Published by
Edward Elgar Publishing Limited
The Lypiatts
15 Lansdown Road
Cheltenham
Glos GL50 2JA
UK

Edward Elgar Publishing, Inc.
William Pratt House
9 Dewey Court
Northampton
Massachusetts 01060
USA

A catalogue record for this book
is available from the British Library

Library of Congress Control Number: 2023946640

This book is available electronically in the **Elgar**online
Business subject collection
http://dx.doi.org/10.4337/9781035312870

ISBN 978 1 0353 1286 3 (cased)
ISBN 978 1 0353 1287 0 (eBook)

Printed and bound by CPI Group (UK) Ltd, Croydon, CR0 4YY

Contents

Figures

Tables

About the author

Simone Guercini is a Full Professor of Marketing and Management at the Department of Economics and Management of the University of Florence. He received a Ph.D. in Economics at Sant'Anna School of Pisa, and a TAGs at SPRU, University of Sussex in Brighton. His research interests include business marketing, international business, marketers' decision making and heuristics, and qualitative research in marketing and management. He has been a Visiting Scholar at primary universities and research institutes, including Max Planck Institute for Human Development in Berlin (Germany), GSU-CIBER in Georgia State University and Kelley School of Business at Indiana University in Bloomington (United States), and ISEM in the University of Navarra (Spain). He has given courses and talks on the results of his research at many universities, including Stockholm Business School, Manchester Metropolitan University, Hong Kong Polytechnic University, University of Navarra, and Grenoble School of Management. He is a member of national and international academies and research groups. He has been a Ph.D. thesis evaluator for universities in Italy, the UK, Switzerland, Australia, Spain, Netherlands, and India. He is a Senior Associate Editor of Management Decisions and a member of the editorial board of other academic journals in the field of marketing and management. He has authored, written chapters in books and been editor of books in the field of international and cross-cultural business, marketers' behavior and cognition, entrepreneurship and marketing. He has published more than 80 articles in journals including *Industrial Marketing Management, Global Strategy Journal, Journal of Business Research, Management Decision, Organization Theory, Journal of Business and Industrial Marketing, European Journal of Marketing, International Business Review, International Marketing Review, Journal of Cleaner Production, Mind & Society, Journal of Service Theory and Practice, Journal of Global Fashion Marketing,* and *Journal of Fashion Marketing and Management.*

Abbreviations

AD:	advertising
AEES:	adaptive extended exponential smoothing
AI:	artificial intelligence
AI/ML:	artificial intelligence / machine learning
APIs:	application program interfaces
ATD:	advertising trade desk
B2B:	business-to-business
B2C:	business-to-consumer
CBC-HB:	choice-based conjoint hierarchical Bayes
CCT:	consumer culture theory
DL:	deep learning
DMPs:	data management platforms
DOC:	disjunctions-of-conjunctions
DSP:	demand side platform
DSPs:	demand side platforms
DSS:	decision support systems
GDPR:	general data protection rules
HINoV:	heuristic identification of noisy variables
MAX:	maximum decision heuristic
MDPs:	Markov decision processes
MIN:	minimum decision heuristic
ML:	machine learning
NBD:	negative binomial distribution
NORMCLUS:	approach for the construction of market segments for particular applications
NPTB:	next product to buy
PA:	programmatic advertising

PQE:	price-quality effect
PROSAD:	profit optimizing search engine advertising
RFM:	recency, frequency and monetary
RPD:	recognition-primed decision
RTB:	real time bidding
SDRs:	sales development representatives
SMEs:	small and medium enterprises
SSP:	supply side platform
SSPs:	supply side platforms
STP:	segmentation-targeting-positioning
VLNS:	very large neighborhood search
WTP:	willingness to pay

1. Introduction to *Marketing Automation and Decision Making*

1.1 THE IMPACT OF NEW MARKETING TECHNOLOGIES

The application of new technologies to marketing, the way in which this impacts on the decision-making processes of marketers, and the problems associated with the use of simple, intuitive decision-making models, are issues experienced by all those managers and entrepreneurs who are incorporating new technologies into their marketing activities and to address which satisfactory models are still lacking.

When we speak of new technologies for marketing we mean to refer primarily to the processes of digitalization that have not only seen the rise of such topics as search engine marketing or social media marketing, but also the development of all those hardware and software systems and especially those applications that have revolutionized traditional areas of marketing such as customer database management and direct marketing, marketing research and information system, customer communication, forms of programmatic or real-time advertising with implications in strategic marketing for the segmentation-targeting-positioning process, often summarized in the acronym STP. Technological change has produced increasing data-driven marketing, with technology solutions replacing the activities of human operators in many activities, both of augmentation of marketers' capabilities.

The emergence of new marketing technologies can lead to a change in the processes and skills required to perform marketing tasks, as is evident, for example, in the case of communication with the rise of programmatic advertising (Busch, 2016; Malthouse, Maslowska, and Franks, 2018) and more generally of artificial intelligence in marketing (Agrawal, Gans, and Goldfarb, 2018; Davenport, Guha, Grewal, Bressgott, 2020). At the same time, it is recognized that there is extensive use of simple rule-based, decision-making models or heuristics in marketing (Merlo, Lukas, and Whitwell, 2008), and the discipline has been authoritatively described as the first form of behavioral economics (Kotler, 2016). In the behavioral and cognitive sciences, references to marketing as a field of application are frequent (Kurz-Milcke and Gigerenzer 2007;

Thaler, 1985). A negative view takes up strands of research on the biases associated with the use of heuristics (Tversky and Kahneman, 1974; Kahneman, 2003), while a positive view sees heuristics as decision-making models that can offer advantages in terms of speed, simplicity, frugality, and transparency (Gigerenzer et al., 1999; Todd and Gigerenzer, 2012). With references to these views about the effectiveness of heuristics, the application of artificial intelligence tools to marketing raises further questions about the decision-making models to be adopted. Where we have tools to collect data in large volumes and make complex calculations, what about traditional decision-making models? In other words, now that we have artificial intelligence, what is the point of using heuristics in marketing?

The thesis that is proposed in this volume is that heuristics are still important, and that in the new context, a greater awareness of their use and greater legitimacy precisely as a function of the integration of new technological tools becomes essential (Gigerenzer, 2022). This is so that a conscious use of heuristics can integrate artificial intelligence itself into the enterprise in a way that does not replace human capabilities but sees machine capabilities as an element of support and augmentation of the capabilities of human actors.

Addressing the issue of heuristics means posing a definitional problem that in a first approximation associates them with simplicity, speed, and transparency (Katsikopoulos, Şimşek, Buckmann and Gigerenzer, 2021). There are different types of heuristics proposed by different authors (Guercini and Lechner, 2021). Heuristics are seen as "simpler methods", often associated with the idea of "rule of thumb", which can be compared with "more complex methods", where, however, the boundary between the two contexts does not always appear clear, which mimics dual system approaches in some respects. The problem of the definition of heuristics has been critically posed in philosophy (Chow, 2015) and is intertwined with that of their origin and the reasons for their widespread adoption, on which there seems to be a consensus, however, even among authors who propose conflicting theses about their effectiveness. Indeed, it is important to be able to test heuristics as models competitively against other models (Gigerenzer and Todd, 1999), not assuming a priori that the best outcome is always of one type of decision-making model over another. However, defining the amount of complexity below which we are in heuristics and above which we are in the realm of "more complex methods" is not simple and makes the placement of some models of judgment and choice formation questionable, posing a difficult problem to address in rigorous terms. It is not only necessary to take into account different aspects, as much as recognizing the different features of the concept (Atanasiu, 2021; Cavarretta, 2021; Guercini and Lechner, 2021), but to offer a useful definition for research that wants to test whether heuristics have potential for integrating human and artificial intelligence.

Heuristics can be seen as algorithms that can be executed by most people quickly and transparently. For example, transparency of classifications is important in several respects (Katsikopoulos, Şimşek, Buckmann, and Gigerenzer, 2020). The perspective we adopt is that it is the ease for people, detectable subjectively with respect to the actor, that makes heuristics so. For this to happen, typically the algorithm is simple, but the simplicity is relative to people, so the simplicity is not absolute but relative to the characteristics of our cognitive abilities. This means that heuristics executable by people are not always replicable by machines. For reasons including the morphology of our bodies and our biological characteristics as an organism, which provide support for our cognitive abilities, offering us, for example, bases for metaphors and experiences different from those of actual machines. Thus in these characteristics, and consequently in the heuristics that are possible to us given these characteristics, reside elements that our intelligence has to offer in interfacing with artificial intelligence anyway. The fact that heuristics must be rigorously defined does not mean that it is not a fundamental advance to evaluate decision models for their performance, instead of using their low complexity as a proxy for wide error due to bias (Geman, Bienenstock, and Doursat, 1992). Heuristics are easy not in absolute terms but with respect to the capabilities inherent in human cognition, an aspect that makes them so widely adopted. What is simple for our bodies is not necessarily less accurate and effective than what is more difficult and complex for us. We simply have to be able to adopt the most convenient strategy, and to do this, now that our possibilities have increased thanks to machines, we must not forget to value even the simplest strategies when they are accurate and effective.

1.2 THE ROLE OF REPRESENTATIONS FOR DECISION MAKING

This volume examines the changing environment brought about by the arrival of new tools that enable marketing automation processes and how this impacts marketing decision models. The approach taken is partly descriptive, in that an attempt is made to define the patterns of behavior adopted through the description of those observed. In part, however, it is also prescriptive, in that it seeks to propose a point of view on the importance if not the necessity of maintaining the use of "certifiably human" judgment formation systems (Thaler and Sustain, 2008, p. 18) precisely when automation proposes in fact an increasing reliance on data-driven marketing automation models (Davenport, Guha, Grewal, Bressgott, 2020).

The idea being proposed is that as these new tools make their way into adopted decision-making models, it becomes important to maintain other tools that can balance out any errors in these new systems, if only at a stage when evolved systems such as those based on machine learning are still being tested. There are areas in marketing, such as programmatic advertising systems (Busch, 2016), where automation processes are strongly pushed.

The perspective of this book starts from the observation of changes in technology that bring the issue of decision making, particularly though not only from a marketing perspective, to the center of attention again today. The spread of artificial intelligence and its establishment in a growing number of domains, already now but even more so in the future, triggers processes of replacing human actors in specific tasks, augmentation through the use of the tools at their disposal to make decisions, or otherwise changing the decision-making model, which requires great attention. Artificial intelligence arrives in businesses and in any case in the marketer's perspective in the form of the adoption of new software and services that represent tools to perform tasks, sometimes operational in nature but often with strategic implications, resulting in a change in the way forecasts are made or behaviors are evaluated. What impact should we expect on decision making from new marketing technologies? It is understood that similar questions arise for other activities as well, but in marketing such effects are particularly relevant not only because of the implications of the development of marketing for the economy and society, the marketing context being of interest to the behavioral and cognitive sciences as well (Kurz-Milcke and Gigerenzer, 2007; Thaler, 1985).

New technologies intervene in a cultural context that has been attentive to models of cognition and behavior for years in a broader but also relevant field for marketers, as pointed out by Kotler (2016), and by writings such as those by Thaler in marketing journals in the 1980s (Thaler, 1985). Artificial intelligence comes in a context in which research has associated systematic errors (biases) with human behaviors, at least those that do not make use of large databases and more complex processing models. The realization of these limitations may encourage the push for replacement of the human actor through processes of pushed automation, when it was felt that channeling the possibilities of artificial intelligence to a final decision of the human actor is not sufficient to avoid the risk of biased judgments (Kahneman, 2003).

The assessment that the human mind can systematically go wrong must also confront some misunderstandings that arise from the very examples that are supposed to highlight the fact that the human mind "systematically goes wrong". At the beginning of the first chapter of the book *Nudge*, Thaler and Sunstein offer a very effective example of the kind of errors to which the human mind is thought to be subject (Figure 1.1.). Consider this figure adapted from Shepard (1990).

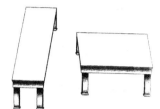

Figure 1.1   The Shepard tables

Thaler and Sunstein write:

> What would you say are the dimensions of the two tables? … Typical guesses are that the ration of the length to the width is 3:1 for the left table and 1.5:1 for the right table. Now take out a ruler and measure each table. You will find that the two table tops are identical. Measure them until you are convinced because this is a case where seeing is not believing … If you see the left table as longer and thinner than the right one, you are certifically human. (Thaler and Sunstein, 2008, pp. 17–18)

After taking measurements, one cannot help but agree that the two figures on paper are the same size and that, as the two authors point out "both the legs and the orientation facilitate the illusion that the table tops are different" in the figure, "so removing these distracters restores the visual system to its usual amazingly accurate state". Thaler and Sunstein's approach is formally kind toward human capabilities, emphasizing the fact that one should not see in this that the human mind is wrong, and even pointing out that the authors them-selves needed to verify the actual measurements of the two figures on drawing. Yet these respectful considerations result in the following conclusion: "that does not mean something is wrong with us as humans, but it does mean that our understanding of human behavior can be improved by appreciating how people systematically go wrong" (Thaler and Sunstein, 2008, p. 19). The effec-tiveness of the example is fascinating, and if you look closely at the two tables in the figure, you can see that the arrangement not only of the table surface, but also of the legs, can play a role in generating the effect described. However, I think it is interesting to ask this question: what is required of the cognitive abilities of the observer of the first figure? What is the surface area of the two rectangles on paper or what is the surface area of tables that should appear in the real world as depicted in the drawing? On paper the surface area of the two rectangles is the same, but evidently our cognitive abilities are selected to work in the real world (in the wild), rather than in representations such as that offered by the drawing. Because the two questions, as the study of perspective in drawing teaches us, have different answers (Figure 1.2). See this drawing:

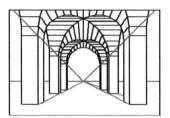

Notes: We thank the rights holders of this image for allowing access and free use under the terms of the license at this website: https://creativecommons.org.licences/by-sa/3.0/deed.en. No change has been made.
Source: https://commons.wikimedia.org/wiki/File:Zentralperspektive.png.

Figure 1.2   Representations and perspective

Six columns can be recognized, three on the right side and three on the left side. Let us take the three columns on either side, for example on the left side. Is the distance between the first and second columns equal to the distance between the second and third columns? If we measure these distances along the line at the base of the columns, we will find that the distance between the first and second columns is much greater than the distance between the second and third columns, yet our mind suggests that the two columns, in reality, not in the drawing, are probably equal distances apart. Our mind interprets images as derived from a representation of the real world, and bases its evaluations not on the distances measurable in the drawing, but on how we expect things to be in the real world of which this is supposed to be just a representation. According to the laws of perspective, one of the great achievements in Renaissance drawing and painting in the West (Andersen, 2008; Kubovy, 1986), different dimensions on paper correspond to the perception of equal dimensions in the real, and so if the dimensions are equal on paper, it is important to be aware that they are different in the real. It is no coincidence that Shepard's two tables are interpreted as being of different size by the human mind: if what we see were a representation of the real world, in the representation the two tables would be equal, but in the real they would be different. Does our mind make mistakes or does it answer a different question? And what becomes in human experience more important to evaluate, the drawing as such or the drawing as a representation of the real? Let us take the experience of driving a car and the image of the road (Figure 1.3) that appears to the driver:

Source: Author's elaboration.

Figure 1.3   Road representations and driving experience

What are the measurements that matter and how should distances be esti-mated? By measuring the distances between points on the flat photograph? Or by relying on our mind's intuitive perception of perspective, which leads us to assume that the distance between the first two columns is equal to the distance between the second and third columns in the drawing above? Is evaluating dif-ferent distances in the real from equal distances in the drawing a bias or a skill?

You may now be wondering if this is a marketing book, since this long digression has highlighted more. But let us now imagine that the driver of the car is the marketer and the road the market context on which judgments and choices must be formed and you will see the reason for this digression. The phase of change associated with the advent of artificial intelligence leads to the spread of forms of possible replacement of human actors for some tasks, augmentation of the elements underlying marketers' judgments in other cases, and in general to a possible change in decision-making processes not only with reference to operational activities but also to strategic marketing issues. Pursuing a descriptive intent, one can recognize the spread of decision making based on the use of systems such as the one that generates the perception that the two tables are different, and that corresponds to the adoption of heuristics, which have been described as a source of bias (Tversky and Kahneman, 1974) or as models that can be smart as they are fast and frugal (Gigerenzer, 2007).

Critical to their evaluation is the context in which they are used (Guercini, 2022). In the example described earlier, there is no doubt that Shepard's two table tops correspond to two equal rectangles, but if we understand them as representations of real tables, our intuition is probably right in thinking they differ in proportion, because there are conditions, such as those described by perspective, whereby equal measurements in what appears correspond to different measurements in the real world.

1.3   ORIGIN AND FRAMEWORK OF THIS VOLUME

New technologies are impacting on marketing activities to such an extent that new models and tools are emerging, which seem to propose a new marketing orientation, as it is in many respects different, albeit culturally connected to a pre-existing marketing concept. In particular, new technologies based on digital tools and big data are at the basis of the emergence of automated marketing systems (data-driven marketing automation), which appear to be able to significantly condition the skills required of those who take on marketing roles in companies, and more generally the activities of marketing in organizations. In this volume we focus on the role of the marketer, both at the operational and strategic level, to investigate the impact of these new technologies on decision-making processes. This is a particularly topical and important issue for the marketing of contemporary actors and in the object of this book. Knowledge of marketers, their market understanding and their behavior has been based on models using information for decision-making processes. The theme of the impact of marketing automation on the marketing context and on the work of the marketer is therefore dealt with starting from the relationship between heuristic rules used in marketing and automatic systems, including those that make use or may make use of artificial intelligence systems.

The book is divided into eight chapters, including this first introductory chapter and a final chapter of conclusions. Here in the first chapter we present the reasons for interest in the topic, the purpose of the work, together with notes on the main issues addressed and the structure of the volume. The next three chapters, the second, the third and the fourth, examine the issue of decision-making processes based on heuristic rules in contemporary marketing, with respect to the use of decision-making processes that make greater use of information, based on decision models that take into account many parameters. More precisely, the second chapter examines the relationship between marketing and decision-making heuristic rules in the marketing literature. We look at this relationship from the point of view of the marketer, noting how this figure is originally essentially referable to entrepreneurial and managerial roles, to be today for many reasons less and less distinguishable in terms of the characteristics of decision-making processes from consumer roles. The third and fourth chapters, on the other hand, consider the toolbox emerging from the marketing literature, making an examination of the heuristic rules diffused in the marketing literature and from there taken into consideration, commenting on the decision-making behavior and cognition of the marketer, both as decision maker and as choice architect. These chapters allow us to take stock of the role of heuristic rules used by the consumers and marketers for the marketing decision maker in a phase preceding the advent of automatic forms of marketing. This represents also in some respects an antecedent, given the role that heuristic rules may have had with respect to the formation of automatic systems of evaluation and choice.

The fifth and sixth chapters of this volume aim to see the characteristics and impact of the new forms of automatic marketing and artificial intelligence in forming judgements and choices. These judgements and choices impact the processes of analyzing the market, defining the strategy and setting the lines of action on the operational level. Automated marketing sees on the one hand a substitution or flanking of automated systems to human marketers, on the other hand it sees the emergence of the need for the latter to train new skills. More precisely, the fifth chapter is the one in which the concept of automatic marketing is examined, in itself as automatic support for marketing decisions in relation with digitalization and artificial intelligence, and in relation with the evolution of the marketing orientation. In the sixth chapter the current state and potential of the relationship between artificial intelligence and contemporary marketing is seen. The aim of this part is to see how the new automatic marketing systems affect the work of the marketer and how the role of artificial intelligence fits into this context.

The last two chapters of the book finally examine the relationship between heuristic processes and the adoption of new automatic marketing systems, taking into account the results of research conducted in recent years and the results of the analysis of specific automatic marketing tools proposed to companies by system providers. More precisely, in the seventh chapter we examine the heuristic rules adopted by marketers, which have long been widespread in marketing processes emerging from a field research realized in the last five years; then the chapter develops the idea that in parallel to the traditional distinction between industrial and consumer markets, an emerging differentiating factor in marketing is given by the degree of automation implicit in the use of artificial intelligence tools, as an alternative to the dimension of the human actor and the processes of personal interaction. Some areas to which we will give particular attention are those of customer clustering, targeting by recommendation systems and programmatic advertising, where artificial intelligence is already established in the context of data-driven marketing automation systems.

Finally, in an eighth and final chapter, we make some assessments of the place heuristic rules may have in the future, the implications for marketing theory and practice, as well as avenues for future research. It can be assumed that where decisions must be based on the use of data, the greater the potential role of artificial intelligence for automated forms of marketing. When decisions cannot be based on data alone, the human decision-maker and the heuristic processes involved in forming their judgments and choices may continue to play an important role. This fuels an emerging dichotomy between more or less pronounced forms of automation in marketing processes. The approach to the topic of heuristics in the volume looks at the effectiveness of research but assumes the relevance of the topic essentially because of the widespread use of such rules in actors' behavior.

This book is the result of a long journey based on some strong motivations. First, the conviction that the technological changes affecting marketing so strongly over the past decades require not only the addition of specialized topics (such as "digital marketing"), but a reorganization of the paradigm of the discipline as a whole (in the sense of rethinking the marketing paradigm). This text seeks to make a contribution to this second approach by focusing on the decision-making models of marketers. A second consideration concerns the role of new technologies, and in particular artificial intelligence, with respect to the topic of decision making, where alongside the idea of automation as the replacement of the human actor by artificial intelligence on various tasks, there is the idea that it is preferable to integrate the new tools with the contribution of decision makers and more generally of human actors. One aspect therefore to be evaluated are the limitations and errors that can result from the use of automation systems, including those that assume the use of artificial intelligence. Artificial intelligence applied to data-driven forms of marketing automation are not error-free. Given the increasingly important capabilities that algorithms can bring to bear even in creative tasks such as word processing (copywriting), not to mention all tasks that require processing on large databases. Finally, it is legitimate to ask what distinctive contribution human actors can bring to an integration with artificial intelligence. In this book we develop the idea that this distinctive contribution largely includes heuristics with their ease of use and "ecological rationality". To do this, the volume confronts different perspectives, seeking to integrate descriptive and prescriptive aspects and taking a positive approach toward the possibilities of human decision making.

At the end of this introduction, we recall some of the stages of the research journey completed, as well as some of the limitations of this ambitious work. Starting with the latter, the volume addresses a topic whose treatment is often difficult partly because it occurs at the intersection of behavioral, technological and social science disciplines, with respect to which a marketing perspective is nevertheless proposed. This makes one sometimes feel that themes we pose have a more general significance and are difficult to confine to marketing. The section on marketing technologies is in flux and is likely to see evolutions that may test the hypotheses proposed in this work. At various passages in this volume, it was not easy to choose between a descriptive or prescriptive slant. Turning instead to the accomplished research path, the interest in the topic of heuristics goes back to readings at the time of doctoral studies in the 1990s. I benefited from repeated periods as a visiting fellow between 2011 and 2015 at the Adaptive Behaviour and Cognition Group of the Max Planck Institute for Human Development in Berlin, coordinated by Gerd Gigerenzer. Konstantinos Katsikopoulos was the first interlocutor during periods as a visiting fellow at the Max Planck in Berlin. Other maturing stages of activity around the topic of heuristics for marketing decision making were accomplished by organizing a special track as part of the Industrial Marketing and Purchasing (IMP) Annual Conference in 2012, stimulated by Ivan Snehota. Other important occasions were the realization of a workshop in Prato in 2014, participation in annual conferences of the European Group for Organisational Studies and the Herbert Simon Society also in 2018 and 2019, up to a workshop of the Max Planck in Berlin in June 2022 (Guercini, 2022). Over the years, I have exchanged many ideas on the topic with Andrea Runfola, Matilde Milanesi, Susan Freeman, Christian Lechner, Julian Marewski, Antonella La Rocca, Ivan Snehota, and Arch Woodside. Writing the volume was exciting and answered a need felt by the author to take stock of an important part of his personal research program. The hope now is to share it with readers interested in the relationship between the evolution of marketing technologies and marketers' decision-making processes.

REFERENCES

Agrawal, A., Gans, J., & Goldfarb, A. (2018). *Prediction machines. The simple economics of artificial intelligence*. Harvard Business Review Press, Boston, Mass.

Andersen, K. (2008). *The geometry of an art: the history of the mathematical theory of perspective from Alberti to Monge*. Springer Science & Business Media.

Atanasiu, R. (2021). The lifecycle of heuristics as managerial proverbs. *Management Decision*, 59(7), 1617–1641.

Barnard, C. I. (1938). *The functions of the executive*. Harvard University Press, Cambridge, Mass.

Busch, O. (2016). The programmatic advertising principle. In Busch, O. (ed.) *Programmatic advertising*. Springer, Cham, pp. 3–15.

Cavarretta, F. L. (2021). On the hard problem of selecting bundles of rules: a conceptual exploration of heuristic emergence processes. *Management Decision*, 59(7), 1598–1616.

Chow, S. J. (2015). Many meanings of 'heuristic'. *The British Journal for the Philosophy of Science*, 66(4), 977–1016.

Davenport, T., Guha, A., Grewal, D., & Bressgott, T. (2020). How artificial intelligence will change the future of marketing. *Journal of the Academy of Marketing Science, 48*(1), 24–42.

Geman, S., Bienenstock, E., & Doursat, R. (1992). Neural networks and the bias/variance dilemma. *Neural computation, 4*(1), 1–58.

Gigerenzer, G., & Gaissmaier, W. (2011). Heuristic decision making. *Annual Review of Psychology, 62*(1), 451–482.

Gigerenzer, G., & Todd, P. M. (eds.) (1999). *Simple heuristics that make us smart.* Oxford University Press, USA.

Gigerenzer, G. (2008). Why heuristics work. *Perspectives on Psychological Science, 3*(1), 20–29.

Gigerenzer, G. (2022). *How to stay smart in a smart world: Why human intelligence still beats algorithms.* Penguin UK.

Guercini, S., & Lechner, C. (2021). New challenges for business actors and positive heuristics. *Management Decision, 59*(7), 1585–1597.

Guercini, S. (2022). Scope of heuristics and digitalization: the case of marketing automation. *Mind & Society, 21*(2), 151–164.

Kahneman, D. (2003). Maps of bounded rationality: Psychology for behavioral economics. *American Economic Review, 93*(5), 1449–1475.

Katsikopoulos, K. V., Şimşek, O., Buckmann, M., & Gigerenzer, G. (2021). *Classification in the wild: The science and art of transparent decision making.* MIT Press, Cambridge, UK.

Kotler, P. (2016) Why Behavioral Economics Is Really Marketing Science, *Evonomics,* https://evonomics.com/behavioraleconomics-neglect-marketing/.

Kubovy, M. (1986). *The psychology of perspective and Renaissance art.* CUP Archive.

Kurz-Milcke, E., & Gigerenzer, G. (2007). Heuristic decision making. *Marketing: Journal of Research and Management, 3*(1), 48–56.

Malthouse, E. C., Maslowska, E., & Franks, J. U. (2018). Understanding programmatic TV advertising. *International Journal of Advertising, 37*(5), 769–784.

Merlo, O., Lukas, B. A., & Whitwell, G. J. (2008). Heuristics revisited: implications for marketing research and practice. *Marketing Theory, 8*(2), 189–204.

Shepard, R. (1990). *Mind sights: Original visual illusions, ambiguities, and other anomalies, with a commentary on the play of mind in perception and art.* New York, Freeman.

Simon, H. A. (1979). Rational decision making in business organizations. *The American Economic Review, 69*(4), 493–513.

Thaler, R., & Sunstein, C.R. (2008). *Nudge: Improving decisions about health, wealth, and happiness.* Yale University Press.

Thaler, R. (1985). Mental accounting and consumer choice. *Marketing Science, 4*(3), 199–214.

Todd, P. M., & Gigerenzer, G. E. (eds) (2012). *Ecological rationality: Intelligence in the world.* Oxford University Press, Oxford.

Tversky, A., & Kahneman, D. (1974). Judgment under Uncertainty: Heuristics and Biases: Biases in judgments reveal some heuristics of thinking under uncertainty. *Science, 185*(4157), 1124–1131.

2. Decision making based on heuristics in the marketing literature

2.1 CONTEXTUAL UNCERTAINTY AND DECISION MAKING IN MARKETING

Marketing actors have always used problem solving tools such as those that go by the name of heuristics. Introduced into the contemporary literature by problem solving research (Polya, 1945; Simon, 1978), heuristics are also present in mainstream marketing as an alternative decision-making model to the optimizing model, based on finding reasonably good and possible solutions given the resource and contextual conditions under which marketers must operate (Kotler, 1967, pp. 226–227). Heuristics have been associated with forms of "rule-based decision making" (March, 1994) and identified with "simple rules" learned from experience (Sull and Eisenhardt, 2015), resulting in an essential part of research programs whose economic relevance has been widely recognized (Simon, 1979; Kahneman, 2003; Gigerenzer and Selten, 2002).

A more widespread definition of "heuristics" in psychology is that of cognitive shortcuts that emerge when information, time, and process capacity are limited (Newell and Simon, 1972). The study of heuristic processes is of interest to the cognitive sciences and has found particular attention in experimental psychology, turning out to be related to the themes of "bounded rationality" and "cognitive limits" (March, 1994; Miller, 1956). Approaches with opposing positions confront each other on the issue of the value of heuristics for the formation of judgments and choices (Kelman, 2011). These differing views emerge from authors such as Polya (1945), Simon (1957; 1979), Tversky and Kahneman (1974; Kahneman, 2003), Chaiken (1980), Thaler (1985; Thaler and Sustein, 2008), Klein (1998; 2015), Gigerenzer (2007; Gigerenzer and Todd, 1999; Gigerenzer and Selten, 2002) and are also relevant to research that sees heuristics in the specific domain of marketing. Indeed, the role of heuristics in decision making of managers and entrepreneurs is at the center of a multifaceted scholarly debate with differing positions comparing their effectiveness with that of other models for decision making (Artinger, Petersen, Gigerenzer, and Weibler, 2015; Guercini, 2012).

Despite this attention and wide use in cognitive science and behavioral economics, the term "heuristics" is associated with rather different methods, procedures, and decision-making models, for example, on the level of formalization (Gigerenzer and Todd, 1999), to the point that the debate over the accuracy and conditions of the use of heuristics could be traced in part to a problem of definition. Indeed, the term heuristics is employed by several disciplines (psychology, philosophy, etc.) where it is associated with often ambiguous and heterogeneous meanings (Evans, 2009; Chow, 2015). Albeit briefly, let us examine these features of ambiguity, which in some cases take on almost paradoxical traits. A first ambiguity resides in the fact that on the one hand heuristics are seen as a source of bias, while on the other hand there is agreement that is widely adopted in our behavior, to the point that different names, such as the Econs and Humans described by Thaler and Sustein (2008), are found to qualify those who can refer to models of other kinds. A second character of ambiguity lies in the fact that decision makers seek procedures that can offer guarantee-correct-outcomes, on the other hand, however, we confront ill-defined-problems, which have undefined or indeterminate states or goals (Simon, 1973; Hatchuel, 2001). A third ambiguity relates to the fact that heuristics can be seen as an approach that is able to simplify decision making by relating to the structure of complex problems as making predictions (Green and Armstrong, 2015). A fourth aspect of ambiguity, on the other hand, concerns the fact that under the same term of heuristics are recognizable both stimulus-driven behavior, which responds to the behaviorist idea of stimulus-response shared with animal behavior (Hutchinson and Gigerenzer, 2005), and heuristic-produced behavior, which is characterized by a more conscious processing, which sees the relationship between stimulus and behavior mediated by conceptual processing and as such studied only in human behavior (Chow, 2015). A fifth ambiguity concerns the use of heuristics at the perceptual, cognitive, or computational level. At the perceptual level, the human perceptual system (visual, auditory, olfactory, etc.) is too often deficient and imprecise to produce an output that can be relied upon (Miller, 1956), so heuristics are used in order to construct approximations. At the cognitive level, one can identify heuristics that serve for the construction and representation of concepts. At the computational level, on the other hand, we simply refer to processes that serve to make calculations and assign to classes without going through a more complex representation of a cognitive architecture (Chow, 2015, p. 996). Finally, a sixth character of ambiguity relates to the fact that the term heuristics finds use both on a methodological ground and on the ground of forming judgments and choices. In the methodological dimension, the term heuristic, consistent with its etymology, pertains to methods of discovery, the methodological approach to be followed in research (Moustakas, 1990) and strategies typically useful for problem solving (Polya, 1945). However, the heuristics being studied in psychological research, starting with satisficing (Artinger, Gigerenzer and Jacobs, 2022), as well as the heuristics popularized by Tversky and Kahneman (1974), are not methods of discovery, but principles that guide the formation of judgments and choices, so they have been referred to as inferential heuristics (Chow, 2015, p. 997). This is compounded by different levels of processing of heuristics (Cavaretta, 2021), different origins (Atanasiu, 2021), as well as methodologies of analysis (Guercini, 2019), which add further elements of variety and complexity. Given such an articulated framework, it will come as no surprise that the debate may confront different outcomes depending on the approach taken.

Indeed, heuristics can be viewed negatively, as a procedure that avoids an analysis of all the elements deemed relevant, or positively as an otherwise unfeasible problem solving and as a path that through simplicity contains some forms of error (Geman, Bienenstock and Doursat, 1992). In this negative view, heuristics are the cause of systematic errors (Tversky and Kahneman, 1974), procedures that do not guarantee correct results, although they may provide certain benefits (Chow, 2015). Instead, in a positive view (Guercini and Lechner, 2021) heuristics are "fast and frugal" (Gigerenzer and Todd, 1999) in that they "employ a minimum of time, knowledge, and computation to make adaptive choices in real environments" (Gigerenzer and Todd, 1999, p. 14). For Simon (1957; 1990), humans rely on heuristics not only because of cognitive limitations (Miller, 1956), but also because of the "task environment". Rational models are inapplicable when some of the relevant information is unknown or must be estimated from small samples, a situation typical of the real environment as a "large world", quite different from "small worlds" inferred from axioms (Savage, 1954). The negative view finds expression in the "heuristics and biases" program, which associates the adoption of heuristics for making judgments with systematic errors (biases). Heuristics correspond to "shelf" rules, in that they can be activated when needed, defined as "representativeness", "availability" and "simulation", "anchoring and adjustment" (Tversky and Kahneman, 1974). This research program aims to obtain "a map of bounded rationality" by exploring the "systematic distortions" that separate what most people believe and the choices possible to a "rational" agent (Kahneman 2003, p. 1449). The heuristics for problem solving imitated to make early computers "smart" (Simon, 1963) were followed by heuristics subject to a negative view as a source of systematic errors, characterizing in this sense a new phase of the "psychology of preferences and decision-making" (Piattelli Palmarini, 2005, p. 3).

This view has also been influential in the literature related to corporate actors, starting with entrepreneurial ones (Manimala, 1992; Haley and Stumpf, 1989). Heuristics are studied as "intuitive statistics" naturally adopted but considered inferior to more complex rational methods for forming correct judgments.

Later other authors describe additional heuristic behaviors by defining them directly in terms of the errors associated with them. For example, additional heuristics are: (a) base level neglect, (b) conjunction error, and (c) attribute substitution (Piattelli Palmarini, 2005, p. 90). Recently heuristics have been examined in acquisition processes, emerging from the analysis of individual processes as a non-avoidable element in infrequent organizational processes (Vuori, Laamanen and Zollo, 2022).

In contrast, a positive view of the role of heuristics emerges from the "fast and frugal research program" proposed by Gigerenzer and colleagues (Gigerenzer and Todd, 1999). In this fast and frugal heuristics approach, heuristics are compared with other "more complex" models proving in many cases to be surprisingly accurate and thus effective, without using much information and computation. Besides simplicity and speed, another character is that of transparency, which is also a relevant aspect in the processes of communicating criteria for decisions (Katsikopoulos, Şimşek, Buckmann and Gigerenzer, 2020). Heuristic processes are situated in a perspective of "ecological rationality" proper to "homo heuristicus" that may be more realistic and effective than the "logical rationality" proper to "homo economicus" (Gigerenzer and Brighton, 2009; Musgrave, 1974).

How does this debate impact marketing studies? On a general level, the need for problem solving and uncertainty about market developments makes the use of heuristics widespread and is reported to characterize the concept of marketing itself (Hunt, 2002). In fact, it has been observed how the marketing concept that emerges in the middle of the last century (Keith, 1960), evolves to incorporate a set of heuristics of a prescriptive nature, which dictate to managers a marketing course of action with the goal of improving business performance (Merlo, Lukas and Whitwell, 2008, p. 197). The marketing concept itself

> is not a concept in the normal sense of the term. Rather, it is a philosophy of doing business based on a set of three normative decision rules: (1) firms should be customer oriented; (2) all marketing activities of the firm should be integrated; and (3) profit rather than sales should be the orientation of the firm. (Hunt, 2002, p. 146)

Thus, it is the very adoption of the marketing concept that is verifiable through a heuristic process and assumes its traits at the level of decision models. The marketing concept was seen by Felton (1959) as coordination of marketing activities to achieve the highest corporate profits in the long run, while McNamara sees it as "a philosophy of business management, based upon a company-wide acceptance of the need for customer orientation, profit orientation, and recognition of the important role of marketing in communicating the needs of the market to all major corporate departments" (McNamara, 1972, p. 51). Kohli and Jaworski (1990), recalling Kotler (1988), confirm this view by defining three pillars of the marketing concept, namely "(1) customer focus, (2) coordinated marketing, and (3) profitability" (Kohli and Jaworski, 1990, p. 3).

In fact, the marketing concept suggests a certain type of approach to corporate decision making, and is realized when certain rules are followed by firms, according to a "recipe" (Houston, 1986) that may suggest a form of rule-based decision making (Merlo, Lukas and Whitwell, 2008). This same approach sees in the marketing orientation literature (Narver and Slater, 1990) the suggestion that the market-oriented organization may be based on the "robustness and domain specificity of the market orientation heuristics" (Merlo, Lukas and Whitwell, 2008, p. 197). Kohli and Jaworksi (1990) recognize some of the first heuristics necessary for firms to become market-oriented, namely "generate market intelligence", "disseminate market intelligence", and "respond to market intelligence" (Kohli and Jaworski, 1990, p. 3). Merlo, Lukas and Whitwell (2008) conclude that the presence of heuristics in marketing depends on both the maturity of the discipline and its impact, to which follows an exportation of the marketing approach to fields other than its original ones, an exportation that occurs precisely through the dissemination of marketing heuristics (Merlo, Lukas and Whitwell, 2008, p. 198). Indeed, the marketing approach soon transcends the boundaries of the business sphere to include non-for-profit organizations (Kotler and Levy, 1969) and all organizations operating in the marketplace (Luck, 1969), and then to the contexts of politics or cultural heritage (McLean, 2012; O'Shaugnessy, 2001).

Other elements for reflection on decision-making models suggested by the adoption of the marketing concept are found in the "scope" of the marketing concept (Hunt, 1976), the nature of "business process" rather than "social process" (Kotler and Levy, 1969), the view of marketing as "art" rather than "science" (Brown, 1996; Buzzel, 1963; Taylor, 1965; Halbert, 1965). Note how the term "scope" again refers to the scope of marketing effectiveness seen as a set of heuristics, that is, as the domain in which marketing heuristics find widespread and effective use (Guercini, 2019). According to Kotler (2016), marketing can be regarded as the first true behavioral economics, the study of which started with economists interested not so much in theoretical aspects as in institutional aspects, namely the behavior of wholesalers, jobbers, agents, and retailers (Kotler, 2016).

Decisions based on heuristics are associated with bounded rationality (Simon, 1990) and adaptive or ecological rationality (Gigerenzer and Brighton, 2009), and as we have seen they have the character of decision rules (March, 1994). However, they also have other important attributes such as "simplicity" and "robustness" (Martignon and Schmitt, 1999) and "transparency" (Katsikopoulos, Şimşek, Buckmann and Gigerenzer, 2020, p. 26). Simplicity refers to the small number of data required and the simple way of processing them to arrive at the formation of a judgment or choice (Katsikopoulos, Şimşek, Buckmann and Gigerenzer, 2020, p. 32). Robustness consists in the fact that heuristics work in that they are able to extract relevant information from the data while avoiding noise (Martignon and Schmitt, 1999, p. 565), so being less sensitive to the error component of variance. Transparency occurs because of the fact that most actors can understand it, store it, execute it and teach it (Katsikopoulos, Şimşek, Buckmann and Gigerenzer, 2020, p. 26). In this sense, therefore, we can say that heuristics are "simple", "robust", "transparent" rules whose effectiveness depends on the context and can characterize the behavior and cognition of consumers and marketers.

2.2   RULE-BASED DECISION MAKING AND MARKETERS' IDENTITY IN MARKETING PROCESSES

In current parlance, "rational" is roughly the equivalent of "intelligent" or "successful" (March, 1994, p. 1). Managers and entrepreneurs are expected to be more rational than consumers in the activity related to their role, given the context and resources available to them. Rational theories of choice assume consequential, preference-based decision-making processes (Simon, 1990). They are consequential in the sense that action depends on anticipations of the future effects of current actions. Alternatives are interpreted in terms of expected consequences (Simon, 2000). They are preference-based in the sense that consequences are evaluated in terms of personal preferences. In this view of rationality, "alternatives are compared in terms of the extent to which their expected consequences are thought to serve the preferences of the decision maker. A rational procedure is one that pursues a logic of consequence" (March, 1994, p. 2). A similar logic is invoked for causation in the comparison with effectuation (Sarasvathy, 2001).

The logic of "consequences" implicit in the idea of rationality may be unworkable under conditions of uncertainty, in which such consequences are not calculable (no matter whether because of the characteristics of the problem or the limits of the decision maker's knowledge). Instead, the logic of "appropriateness" can be effective, since under it one acts from the consolidation of one's "identity" (March, 1994, p. 57). This means that the actors' decisions can be guided by their identity even before their preferences, in the sense that decision rules can be primarily a definition of what we want to be before what we want to achieve. When individuals and organizations realize their identities, they follow the rules or procedures that they consider appropriate to the situation in which they find themselves. In other words, we move from assuming as a fundamental question "What kind of situation is this?" to "What kind of person am I? Or what kind of organization is this?" to taking as the fundamental question "What does a person such as I, or an organization such as this, do in a situation such as this?" (March, 1994, p. 58). The process that follows this second question is not a random, arbitrary, or trivial process, but a systematic, reasoning, and sometimes very complicated process. If rational means thoughtful, we can find in this a form of rationality of an organizational and identity type. For this the logic of appropriateness is comparable to the logic of consequences. In this case, decision making is about establishing identities and matching rules to recognized situations (March, 1994).

Heuristics are in many cases the result of learning processes and through the maturation of experiences by decision makers (Levinthal, 2011). The concept of heuristics compares with that of routines (Nelson and Winter, 1982), which has had great fortune within the strategic management literature (Cohen, Burkhart, Dosi, Egidi, Marengo, Warglien and Winter 1996; Zollo, Reuer and Singh, 2002). Routines provide a very detailed and often almost automatic response to particular problems, consequently addressed without further grasping their problematic nature. Heuristics, on the other hand, provide a common structure for a more or less wide range of similar problems, but without offering much detail about the specific solutions to be adopted, and thus preserving the perceived problematic nature of the issue to be addressed. In fact, heuristics are simplified rules that suggest the appropriate use of limited information for decision-making (March 1994, 13), whereas routines are presented as a detailed system of rules and precise steps that can be applied consistently in different environments. Thus heuristics are not a type of routine but a distinct construct, differing in the amount of structure, range of problems, cognitive commitment, findability of results, and strategic importance of actions (Cohen, Burkhart, Dosi, Egidi, Marengo, Warglien and Winter, 1996).

Marketers deal less frequently with risk conditions than with uncertainty and risk conditions together (Mousavi and Gigerenzer, 2014, pp. 1671ff.). The issue of uncertainty is relevant because, unlike risk, it presupposes the impossibility of assessing alternatives and the probability of their occurrence (Knight, 1921). For March, uncertainty can be imagined to exist either because some processes are uncertain at their most fundamental levels or because decision makers' ignorance of the mechanisms that drive the process causes outcomes to appear uncertain (March, 1994, pp. 5–6). However, unlike Knight, for March risk seems to correspond to a situation specific to the general category of uncertainty, where the precise consequences are uncertain but their probabilities are known (March, 1994, p. 6). Under conditions of risk it can be assumed that the actor will seek the situation that can produce the best outcome, but under conditions of uncertainty this is not calculable, so the approach must change, which is what happens when the search for maximization is replaced by the search for satisficing (Artinger, Gigerenzer and Jacobs,

2022). March, again, then recalls the importance of the shift to the study of "limited (or bounded) rationality", since

> the decision rules used by real decision makers seem to differ from the ones imagined by decision theory. Instead of considering 'expected values' or 'risk', as those terms are used in decision theory, they invent other criteria. Instead of calculating the 'best possible' action, they search for an action that is 'good enough'. (March, 1994, pp. 8–9)

In studying the psychology of individual decision making corresponding to these conditions of bounded rationality (Simon, 2000), studies related to individual information use and problem solving are examined, evaluating some of the speculations developed in the context of such research. March focuses in particular on four (editing, decomposition, heuristics, and framing), among which heuristics correspond to situations in which "decision makers recognize patterns in the situations they face and apply rules of appropriate behavior to those situations" (March, 1994, p. 13).

Heuristics are also defined as relatively simple algorithms, the use of which is possible regardless of the often limited mathematical abilities people have (Fischbein, 1989). Heuristics are thus employed in a variety of contexts, as evidenced by an extensive literature produced by authors adhering to different approaches (Payne, Bettman, and Johnson, 1993; Kahneman, 2011). In some cases then, these rules turn out to be surprisingly effective, extremely widespread, and adapted to the conditions of the context, highlighting the traits of an "ecological rationality" (Artinger, Gigerenzer and Jacobs, 2022). More generally, knowledge of how people should make decisions cannot be studied without considering how people are able to make decisions (Mousavi and Gigerenzer, 2014, p. 1672). Heuristics are not to be adopted only if there are time constraints or processing costs, or lack of adequate computing capacity, but because of their superior effectiveness under given conditions of the task environment (Gigerenzer, 2019; Luan, Reb and Gigerenzer, 2019).

The use of heuristics in decision making is associated with certain preconditions such as: (a) an initial state of dissatisfaction; (b) a goal state that must be achieved; (c) the existence of path constraints; (d) the need for a solution; and (e) the need for a method of problem-solving and for finding solutions (Holyoak, 1990). The view on rule-based decision making is related to conditions such as: (1) the existence of particular constraints that do not allow the examination of all possible operational sequences; and (2) the search for a satisfactory solution instead of an optimal situation (Merlo, Lukas and Whitwell, 2008).

In fact, what matters more than the strength per se of decision-making models are the conditions of effectiveness (Guercini, 2019). For Merlo, Lukas and

Whitwell (2008, p. 199), an effective heuristic is one that provides a balance between complexity and ease of execution, has been empirically tested and refined over time, is easy to communicate and understand, and finally provides clear guidelines on its implementation, i.e., is relatively "simple" (Merlo, Lukas and Whitwell, 2008, p. 199). The effectiveness of heuristics depends on the context, and its change can make previously effective heuristics obsolete (Guercini and Lechner, 2021). For example, some goods-based models developed in a production-oriented economy may no longer be as relevant in a new context in which the provision of services rather than tangible goods is central to economic exchange (Vargo and Lusch, 2004). In a later article, Vargo and Lusch point out how value creation in this "service-dominant logic" can be better understood by reversing the logics in decision making where "the predominant reliance on heuristics rather than rational, calculative decision making" means that "rational thought might be best understood as a subcategory of heuristic thought, arguably a somewhat inefficient and often ineffective one" (Vargo and Lusch, 2014, pp. 239 and 246).

2.3 THE EVOLUTION OF THE THEME OF HEURISTICS IN THE MARKETING LITERATURE

The presence of heuristics within the marketing literature generally comes in the form of "recipes" for experience-based decisions, either to describe what is being done (description) or to give guidance on how best to operate (prescription).

As pointed out by Gummesson, "research in marketing is there to be used in real life; it is not an academic parlor game" (Gummesson, 2017, p. 16). The same scholar then urges not to avoid but instead to take note of complexity, pointing to the core of marketing and looking at how to deal with uncertainty with the tools available to market actors (checklists, heuristics, etc.) with a focus on decisions, actions and results (Gummesson, 2017).

Research on the topic of heuristics carried out in the marketing literature largely sees the assumption that heuristics may lead to biases, particularly in the study of consumption behavior (Bettman, Luce, and Payne, 1998). In any case, if heuristics are used, it should be done consciously, bearing in mind that their possible limitations are also to be explored (Piattelli-Palmarini, 2005).

Using heuristics according to a more conscious process allows one to appreciate the strengths and weaknesses of specific heuristics (Merlo, Lukas and Whitwell, 2008; p. 196). Judgments based on heuristics are primarily examined for the fact that they lead to errors (Dane and Pratt, 2007), but the biases associated with heuristics are only a part of the total error (Geman, Bienenstock and Doursat, 1992), as the growing focus on noise notes (Gigerenzer and

Brighton, 2009; Kahneman, Sibony and Sustein, 2021). This is especially true since heuristics do not aim for optimal outcomes, but are nonetheless capable of achieving a problem solving goal. Evaluating heuristic methods thus requires a subjective judgment of correctness (Merlo, Lukas and Whitwell, 2008, p. 196). But we might ask: Is there any possibility of making an ex ante prediction that can be evaluated as surely optimal? If it is agreeable that heuristics can fail to provide a solution at all, if in other words fallibility is an intrinsic connotation of a heuristic (Piattelli-Palmarini, 1994, p. 22), can it be said that there are models for forming judgments that are infallible? Artinger, Gigerenzer and Jacobs (2022) suggest conditions of ecological rationality, reviewing the literature on the topic of satisficing in economics, psychology, and management, distinguishing a research tradition that examines risk situations, in which satisficing is typically inferior to optimization strategies, from a research tradition that examines uncertainty situations, in which satisficing often emerges from empirical evidence and can be very effective (Artinger, Gigerenzer and Jacobs, 2022).

Marketing has offered a field of application to models and arguments about decision-making processes developed in strategy and entrepreneurship studies (Sull and Eisenhardt, 2015), particularly the field of international marketing and international business (Bingham and Eisenhardt, 2011; Guercini and Milanesi, 2020; 2022). The heuristics adopted in internationalization processes can be of various types (Bingham and Eisenhardt, 2011); they can result in already defined rules ("close heuristics"), or they can be "open heuristics", where the decision model is subject to adaptation in the presence of new experience data (Guercini and Freeman, 2023). In fact, in "close heuristics", the rules are already fully defined, so the marketer only has to apply them. In the case of "open heuristics", on the other hand, the rules are already present but are incomplete, or at any rate subject to being modified, integrated during application, to adapt them to a context of which the rule only later integrates some elements. Whether the heuristic falls into one or the other category may depend on either the actor, the problem, or the task environment. In bargaining processes, for example, some research (Guercini and Freeman, 2023) has highlighted the problems associated with manufacturers' use of certain heuristics in defining demands (the "open high heuristic"), where experimental studies showed as a result that "the effectiveness of signaling mechanisms depends not only on the economic characteristics of the bargaining situation, but also on shared individual and social contexts that influence how signals are transmitted and interpreted" (Srivastava, Chakravarti, and Rapoport, 2000, p. 163).

Other studies instead examine the construct of "spontaneity", defined as the ability to make decisions in the moment, associating it with generally superior performance in international marketing (Souchon, Hughes, Farrell, Nemkova, and Oliveira, 2016). Spontaneity "allows people to react to events as they unfold, or to be able to continue to move forward despite the unexpected" (Gesell, 2005, p. 4). Other approaches take a naturalistic decision-making (NDM) perspective, aiming to "to describe how people actually make decisions in real-world settings" (Klein, 2008, p. 456). The theme is not far from that of "knowledge in use" (La Rocca and Snehota, 2011) and appears connected to that of the use of heuristics in business networks (Guercini, La Rocca and Snehota, 2022).

The relationship between heuristics and experience is examined by Gilbert-Saad, McNaughton, and Siedlok (2021), since the use of heuristics has often been associated with the expert decision maker, highlighting three types of heuristics used by the inexperienced decision maker: the metacognitive heuristics; the heuristics representing the criteria; and then, the heuristics detailing the execution of a selected option (Gilbert-Saad, McNaughton and Siedlok, 2021, p. 1706).

The relevance of using heuristics in international business and marketing has received attention in its own right, highlighting how in the literature the decision areas in which heuristics are prevalent include typical strategic international marketing issues such as foreign market entry, post-entry international expansion, and foreign market selection (Guercini and Milanesi, 2020). The topic has been examined in the international marketing literature, where adaptive and incremental decision making has long been a focus of attention (Cavusgil and Godiwalla, 1982). More recently, several papers have dealt with individual heuristics such as those based on country of origin (Ommen, Heußler, Backhaus, Michaelis and Ahlert, 2010) or country of reference, in which behaviors prevalent among consumers in the country of origin are imitated (Chen, Wang, and Huang, 2020).

A less extensive part of the marketing literature then deals with data analysis heuristics used by academic researchers. For example, Li, Johnson, and Toubia (2016) ask about the number of questions it is appropriate to ask during surveys, as for each answer obtained to a question, data are obtained with respect to certain parameters of interest. Irwin and McClelland (2001) examine types of heuristics that involve data analysis through the simplest types of multiple regression analysis, but the authors point out how they can be considered misapplied in many other cases, when inappropriately generalized to all models of moderated multiple regression, a widespread case in marketing since moderated relationships are central to this disciplinary field, if one considers that, for example, the effect of promotion on sales does not depend only on the chosen market segment (Irwin and McClelland, 2001, pp. 100ff.).

2.4   HEURISTICS IN MARKETING THEORY AND MANAGEMENT

In theoretical marketing, Hunt (2002) distinguishes less sophisticated heuristics, which can be thought of as simple "rules of thumb" without significant empirical support, from heuristics defined as "grounded rules", for which there is a greater empirical basis. The role of empirical support in the formation of judgment rules is also highlighted by other authors (Pfeffer and Sutton, 2006). Hunt again saw the topic of heuristics in the area of philosophy of science, where they were examined in the context of the distinction between description and prescription (Hunt, 2002).

Management and marketing are in a mutual relationship of heuristics importing and exporting in the sense that certain times research on the topic in management has fed into marketing, at others it is research on the topic done in marketing that influences management (Merlo, Lukas and Whitwell, 2008). The strategic management literature has been permeable to the debate on the topic of heuristics that has matured in the field of psychology and cognitive sciences, in particular reproducing the comparison between, and on the one hand, an approach geared toward viewing heuristics as a source of error in entrepreneurial behavior (Manimala, 1992; Busenitz and Barney, 1997), on the other hand, a view of heuristics as effective solutions to complex problems (Davis, Eisenhardt and Bingham, 2009; Eisenhardt and Sull 2001; Åstebro and Elhedhli, 2006; Katsikopoulos and Gigerenzer, 2012).

Heuristics are interrelated; in fact, they often have to cope with problems that require the use of a coordinated set of other/additional problem-solving methods, including common sense and other heuristics (Guercini, La Rocca, Runfola, and Snehota, 2015). We could say, with an already valued literary image, that "no heuristic is an island" (Håkansson and Snehota, 2017). For example, in order to be market-oriented, an organization should adopt the heuristic of "customer focus", which, however, is related to others that concern, for example, the organization of internal resources (Merlo, Lukas and Whitwell, 2008, p. 199).

The topic of heuristics retains a relatively small presence in the marketing literature, but with a seeking progression of interest in recent years. In support of these very general considerations, we can bring the data available from the Scopus database. Selecting all products that present in the title, abstract or keywords simultaneously the words "marketing" and (Boolean) "heuristic", within the subject area "business, management and accounting", written in English, we found (on 12/30/2022) 448 products, published between 1962 and 2022, and in particular 33 in 2022, 27 in 2021, 25 in 2020, 16 in 2019, 18 in 2018. There are 119 products in the five-year period 2018–2022, 115 products

Table 2.1   *Evolution of research on the topic "heuristic" in the marketing literature*

Products with the following word(s) in the title, abstract or keywords / years	1962–2022	2003–2007	2008–2012	2013–2017	2018–2022
(a) "marketing" and "heuristic*"	448	45	86	115	119
(b) "marketing"	104,440	18,174	16,591	22,119	25,329
(a) / (b) %	0.43	0.25	0.52	0.52	0.47

Source: Author's elaboration on database Scopus, data extracted on December 30, 2022.

in the five-year period 2013–2017, 86 in the five-year period 2008–2012, 49 in the five-year period 2003–2007. The figure thus marks an increase over time, with a less rapid dynamic in recent years although more growing in the long term than that of publications with the word "marketing" in the same area and language, where on the same date (12/30/2022) we find 104,440 products published in the same years (between 1962 and 2022), of which 5,732 in 2022, 5,014 in 2021, 5,243 in 2020, 4,767 in 2019, 4,573 in 2018; on a broader horizon, there are a total of 25,329 products in the five-year period 2018–2022, 22,119 in 2013–2017, 16,591 in 2008–2012, 18,174 in 2003–2007 (see Table 2.1).

The literature on heuristics in marketing has different components. There are works that can propose heuristics without naming the term, and that see decision making, problem solving, and rules of thumb essentially defined over a long time span, either prior to the emergence of the marketing concept in the 1950s and 1960s, or contemporaneous with the emergence of the concept, or in the years immediately following. This literature is essentially developed by marketing experts who have either an academic background or are from the world of practitioners. A common trait is the valorization of experiences gained in the corporate field and of field experience (Keith, 1960), even when influenced by the attention given in the same years to the topic of bounded rationality and satisficing (Simon, 1990). Then, beginning in the 1970s and 1980s, there is a literature that proposes the extension to the topic of marketing of the implications of research on the topic of heuristics matured in applied psychology, which enhances research particularly in the field of consumption by highlighting systematic errors and associating heuristics with bias (Bettman, 1979; Bettman, Johnson and Payne, 1990; Huber and Klein, 1991). Part of this research involves multi-stage decision models to evaluate alternatives within the same category or to assess compatibility with products or services already in use (Aribarg and Foutz, 2009; Gilbride and Allenby, 2004).

This includes evaluating the consumer's decision-making pattern in relation to the decision context (Thaler, 1985). The form taken by the decision context assumes centrality and the heuristics with which the decision maker is endowed are activated or not depending on the choice context. From here emerges a further role, distinct from the marketer and consumer, which is the "choice architect", who "has the responsibility for organizing the context in which people make decisions" (Thaler and Sustein, 2008, p. 3). From the identification of this role emerges the concept of a "nudge", defined as "any aspect of choice architecture that alters people's behavior in a predictable way without forbidding any options or significantly changing their economic incentives", with some specifications, in that to count as a nudge "the intervention must be easy and cheap to avoid. Nudges are not mandates." For retail marketers, "putting the fruit at eye level counts as nudge. Banning junk food does not" (Thaler and Sustein, 2008, p. 6). The scope of Thaler and colleagues' contribution is broader than that of marketing, but it is interesting to note that some of Thaler's early writings start from the observation of consumption behavior and are published in some cases in marketing journals (Thaler, 1985). The possibilities of application naturally involve consumption processes with an approach to the problem that the authors themselves define as "libertarian paternalism" and that involves areas of potentially great interest to the community and still playing the role of heuristics in a positive way (see the case of eating habits proposed by Seabra, 2019). Another element of interest is the distinction between Econs and Humans, which is particularly interesting with respect to the marketing activities and decision-making processes of marketers. The Humans are homo sapiens and are represented as real humans who have limited memory and make systematic mistakes (Thaler and Sustain, 2008). The Econs, on the other hand, originates from the idea of homo economicus, or economic man, which corresponds to the decision maker model of economic theory, who does not make perfect predictions but unbiased predictions. This is not to say that Econ does not make errors, so much so that error is not only bias but also noise (Geman, Bienenstock and Doursat, 1992; Kahneman, Sibony and Sustein, 2021). The same concept of nudges, which is seen by Thaler primarily in relation to the public sector and sees government officials as potential choice architects, however, has a broader scope that certainly includes, as evidenced by many examples, the market context, identifying "private nudges", with the purpose of improving decisions since

> a nudge is any factor that significantly alters the behavior of Humans, even though it would be ignored by Econs. Econs respond primarily to incentives ... Humans respond to incentives too, but they are also influenced by nudges. By properly deploying both incentives and nudges, we can improve our ability to improve people's lives, and help solve many of society's major problems. And we can do so while still insisting on everyone's freedom to choose. (Thaler and Sustein, 2008, p. 8)

Among the errors associated with heuristics, "planning fallacy" is "the systematic tendency toward unrealistic optimism about the time it takes to complete projects", while "status quo bias" occurs when "people have a strong tendency to go along with the status quo or default option" important because first, "never underestimate the power of inertia" and second "power can be harnessed. If private companies or public officials think that one policy produces better outcomes, they can greatly influence the outcome by choosing it as the default" (Thaler and Sustein, 2008, pp. 7–8). Similar heuristics are examined by Frederick (2002) as automated choice heuristics, focusing on two automated choice heuristics that are precisely "choosing by liking heuristic" (choice based on an affective evaluation of immediate liking) and "choosing by default" (choosing the option that first comes to mind or is already stored in the choice system because, for example, it matches the previous purchase).

Thus, some pointers emerge for marketers: (1) to observe the heuristics adopted by other actors; (2) to be aware of the heuristics we tend to adopt and their conditions of effectiveness; but also (3) to assume the role of the choice architect who can influence the effects of the decision models adopted by other actors. The "status quo bias" is primarily a "status quo heuristic" to take note of in order to assume the role of choice architect, to shape the context of the formation of judgments and choices by other actors. Ultimately, with nudges we take note that people use heuristics whose activation depends on elements of the environments in which the marketer (think of a retailer) can become a choice architect.

2.5   HEURISTICS IN MARKETING ACADEMIC RESEARCH PROCESS

As pervasive as it is at different levels (theoretical, organizational, operational), the topic of heuristics and their mechanisms has been largely forgotten by marketing researchers (Merlo, Lukas and Whitwell, 2008, p. 200). The treatment of this topic has always been rather difficult, perhaps because it is too obvious or too vague (Perkins, 1981, p. 195). Recently, with reference to the topic of actors in business interaction and relationship building within networks, Lowe and Tapachai (2021) link the concept of heuristics to that of "habitus". Habitus is "the main intersection catalyst or chiasmus between structure and agency facilitating enacted, emergent properties of business relationships", so habitus "is identified as a translation vehicle" that "provides critical brokerage between actors' resource structures and activities. It is a key concept that helps us understand how structures and agentic behaviors are equally important and mutually constituting influences upon emergent properties of business interaction" (Lowe and Tapachai, 2021, p. 893). The notion of habitus suggests that interaction involves adaptive cognitive and behavioral influences that correspond in cultural context, suggesting a relationship between behavior and effectiveness in context similar to the adaptive nature of heuristics (Lowe and Tapachai, 2021, p. 899).

To pose the topic of heuristics in marketing is to examine an iceberg in which only a small tip corresponds to the studies in which the term "heuristic" finds use, where at the same time the margins of the submerged part of the iceberg are not always easily confined and distinguishable from the rest of the sea around them. However, the use of the term "heuristic" gives us an important perspective where the connotations, implications, diffusion, effectiveness and thus competitive accuracy of the decision-making models matter (Gigerenzer and Brighton, 2009). Many of the patterns and decision rules proposed by marketing can be seen as heuristic rules. One can consider the heuristics made available in the marketing literature by comparing them with the following proposed by Polya (1945): (1) if you can't solve a problem right away, try an indirect proof; (2) if you can't solve a problem, then if there is an easier problem you can solve: find it; (3) draw a diagram when trying to solve a problem.

Take as a marketing example, the decision between the alternatives of "penetration" and "skimming" in pricing for new products. Penetration pricing is a lower price applied when one wants to achieve high sales more quickly, while skimming pricing is a higher price adopted when one wants to achieve high margins on newly marketed products (Dean, 1976; Spann, Fischer, and Tellis, 2015). It is then indicated that starting from a skimming price it is easy to subsequently move to a penetration price, while starting from a penetration price it is more difficult for the market to subsequently accept a higher, skimming price (Dean, 1976). What has just been stated suggests heuristics for defining the price of the new product. If decisions are rule-based using a few cues, they are simple, fast and transparent recurring features of heuristics. Certainly the information used is essential, and the decision about what price to adopt in the new product launch may require the use of a lot of information. It is also true that the possibility of adopting a higher price after the product has been unveiled and has settled on a lower price may appear to be simply a logical, if not common-sense assessment, according to the rule that previously more expensive things are more likely to find a market even at a lower price than expected (Tellis, 1986), although this logic is being challenged by the development of dynamic pricing (Elmaghraby and Keskinocak, 2003).

In this book we take a view on heuristics as a possibility for marketers. Specifically, the main reason for our focus on the "fast and frugal heuristics approach" (Gigerenzer and Todd, 2012) lies in what we believe is its particular closeness and usefulness to the perspective of the business decision maker. This approach focuses on observing the ways in which decisions are formed in real-world contexts in which the allocation of time and information is limited and in the presence of an otherwise complex problem such as a prediction about the future or the definition of a necessary action in a limited time.

For effectiveness assessment, Gigerenzer proposes testing formalized heuristic models through comparison with alternative models (Gigerenzer and Gaissmaier, 2011). The translation of heuristics into formal models that can be tested represents in some respects the main scientific contribution proposed by Gigerenzer to the evolution of heuristics research. It takes an organic view of the heuristic process by recognizing three "building blocks" (Gigerenzer and Todd 1999): (a) "search rules", which indicate how to search for information in the form of "cues" (when faced with a problem, what information is sought?); (b) "stopping rules", which specify when to stop the search activity (when is information gathering stopped, or equivalently, what makes the information gathered deemed sufficient to formulate a decision?); (c) "decision rules", which specify how the final decision is achieved from the information collected (given information deemed sufficient for a decision, how is it translated into a judgment or choice, based on what algorithm?). For example, Simon's (1990) "satisficing heuristic" translated into "building blocks" involves the following steps: (a) identifying options (search rule); (b) stopping as soon as a certain option exceeds an aspiration level (stopping rule); (c) choosing the latter (decision rule).

Heuristics rely on little information by avoiding the so-called "overfitting" problem. Consider two random samples from a population of past events, for example, a company's customer list sorted by the turnover achieved with each customer in the last two years (2021 and 2022). The customer-turnover list for the first year (2021) can be seen as a data set to be analyzed to generate learning and build a model that explains the distribution of turnover across customers (learning set), while the second year (2022) can be seen as a data set on which to test the model built on the previous year's data (test set). A model "overfits" the learning set if there is an alternative model that is less accurate in representing the distribution that was the subject of the learning set, but is more accurate in the test set (Gigerenzer 2007, 246). Decision models that employ a large number of variables may be more accurate when it comes to representing known trends (learning set) that have occurred in the past under risky conditions (hindsight task), but intuitions based on simple "rule of thumb" may be more accurate than complex calculations when it comes to making predictions under uncertainty (foresight task – Gigerenzer, 2007, p. 84).

Heuristics are important and widespread in the behaviors of individual actors and in organizations, as this may have evolutionary explanations (Nelson and Winter, 1982). These reasons have been identified in the fact that heuristics are models of inference: (1) that refer to human core capacities; (2) that do not necessarily use all available information and process the information they have through simple computations; and (3) that are easy to understand, apply and explain (Katsikopoulos, 2011), promoting transparency (Katsikopoulos, Şimşek, Buckmann and Gigerenzer, 2020). In this way, heuristics can help solve problems faster and with less information and more accuracy than sophisticated analytical models (Gigerenzer and Gaissmaier, 2011). The scope in which this occurs represents the scope of heuristic rules (Guercini, 2019).

In economics, the use of heuristics violates the basic principles of choice models of economic rationality, whereby actors behave in a way that maximizes their expected utility (Artinger, Gigerenzer and Jacobs, 2022). It is well known how decision-making models adopted by people in the real world reveal considerable deviation from the expectations of economic rationality, including inconsistent preferences influenced by past experiences in the same context, violating the axioms of rationality models (Fawcett, Waller, Miller, Schwieterman, Hazen and Overstreet, 2014).

Naturalistic observation, however, leads one to see heuristics not only as models of decision-making associated with bias, but their actual performance is worthy of attention if it is true that evolution has selected decision makers who widely adopt heuristics. There are different perspectives on the degree of specificity that can characterize the tools that decision makers can use (Guercini, 2012). While best known fast and frugal approach heuristics have a wide scope and apply to very different situations as tools applicable to many different contexts, in the naturalistic decision making approach experience has been seen to underlie the learning of specific patterns that apply to particular contingencies characterized through elements that include many facets (Klein, 2017).

A comparison in this regard is proposed by dual system theory in information processing from which decision making also follows. The heuristic mode of decision making by marketers is described here as such as relying primarily on decision shortcuts, such as social consensus or currently held beliefs, activating a system (system 1) of a more impulsive type that corresponds to the heuristic information processing mode, or at the opposite to an approach based on weighing more elements, of a deliberate type and based on computational effort (system 2) that corresponds to the systematic information processing mode (Chaiken, 1980). In system 1, it has been argued that cognitive biases play an important role (Kahneman, 2011; Tversky and Kahneman, 1974). Chaiken (1987) envisions two different ways of processing information: the "systematic" way and the "heuristic" way. This "heuristic-systematic model" ranks as one of the most relevant within an overall dual-process perspective (Kahneman, 2011). In the model, "systematic processing" attempts to understand information through careful analysis and is accomplished when the actor has the motivation and skill to accomplish it, taking into account the content of the information and not just more superficial cues (Chaiken and Ledgerwood, 2012). Instead, "heuristic processing" is seen as relatively automatic and focused on salient and easily processed elements (or cues) that activate shortcuts through which individuals exert limited cognitive effort, processing information according to simplified patterns (Hernández-Ortega, Stanko, Rishika, Molina-Castillo and Franco, 2022, p. 1075). According to the heuristic-systematic model, individuals are more likely to engage in heuristic processing when they consider heuristic information sufficient for the decision they need to make and when they have low motivation to process the information (Chaiken, 1980).

This dual view has had an impact on marketing research as evidenced in the literature. This is the context of Cheema and Patrick's (2012) study, which fully adopts dual system theory to highlight how even the adoption of system 1, characterized by the use of heuristics, is strongly related to environmental conditions such as heat. The authors assume a view of heuristics as associated with bias, whereby in the presence of an environment characterized by heat, performance on complex tasks declines as an effect of increased reliance on system 1 (Cheema and Patrick, 2012, p. 992).

The relationship between social media and loyalty programs is examined by Hernández-Ortega, Stanko, Rishika, Molina-Castillo, and Franco (2022). The authors use the heuristic-systematic model to theorize and demonstrate the role of customer experience dimensions in brand-generated social media content in generating different responses to loyalty program and non-loyalty program adoption. Tan, Geng, Katsumata, and Xiong (2021) investigate the effects of advertisement systematic cues of different types with reference to firm and influencer, arguing that "findings demonstrate the co-occurrence of heuristic and systematic information processing in the social media advertising context" (Tan, Geng, Katsumatra, and Xiong, 2021, p. 1).

The comparison of heuristic and systematic processing also finds use in studies that examine how informational cues influence evaluations about credibility and information posted by YouTube Influencers (Xiao, Wang, and Chan-Olmsted, 2018), thus not limited to consumers. Indeed, there is a multiplicity of contributions in the marketing literature both on the side of heuristics in consumer behavior and on the side of individual and organizational marketers that are examined in the next chapter.

REFERENCES

Aribarg, A., & Foutz, N. Z. (2009). Category-based screening in choice of complementary products. *Journal of Marketing Research, 46*(4), 518–530.

Artinger, F., Petersen, M., Gigerenzer, G., & Weibler, J. (2015). Heuristics as adaptive decision strategies in management. *Journal of Organizational Behavior, 36*(S1), S33–S52.

Artinger, F. M., Gigerenzer, G., & Jacobs, P. (2022). Satisficing: Integrating two traditions. *Journal of Economic Literature, 60*(2), 598–635.

Åstebro, T., & Elhedhli, S. (2006). The effectiveness of simple decision heuristics: Forecasting commercial success for early-stage ventures. *Management Science, 52*(3), 395–409.

Atanasiu, R. (2021). The lifecycle of heuristics as managerial proverbs. *Management Decision, 59*(7), 1617–1641.

Bettman, J. R. (1979). *An information processing theory of consumer choice.* Addison-Wesley Publishing, Reading MA.

Bettman, J. R., Johnson, E. J., & Payne, J. W. (1990). A componential analysis of cognitive effort in choice. *Organizational Behavior and Human Decision Processes, 45*(1), 111–139.

Bettman, J. R., Luce, M. F., & Payne, J. W. (1998). Constructive consumer choice processes. *Journal of Consumer Research, 25*(3), 187–217.

Bingham, C. B., & Eisenhardt, K. M. (2011). Rational heuristics: the 'simple rules' that strategists learn from process experience. *Strategic Management Journal, 32*(13), 1437–1464.

Brown, S. (1996). Art or science?: Fifty years of marketing debate. *Journal of Marketing Management, 12*(4), 243–267.

Busenitz, L. W., & Barney, J. B. (1997). Differences between entrepreneurs and managers in large organizations: Biases and heuristics in strategic decision-making. *Journal of Business Venturing, 12*(1), 9–30.

Buzzell, R. D. (1963). Is marketing a science? *Harvard Business Review, 41*(1), 32–40.

Cavarretta, F. L. (2021). On the hard problem of selecting bundles of rules: a conceptual exploration of heuristic emergence processes. *Management Decision, 59*(7), 1598–1616.

Cavusgil, T. S., & Godiwalla, Y. M. (1982). Decision-making for international marketing: A comparative review. *Management Decision, 20*(4), 47–54.

Chaiken, S. (1980). Heuristic versus systematic information processing and the use of source versus message cues in persuasion. *Journal of Personality and Social Psychology, 39*(5), 752–766.

Chaiken, S. (1987). The heuristic model of persuasion. In Zanna, M. P., Olson, J. M., & Herman, C. P. (eds.) *Social influence: The Ontario Symposium.* Routledge, vol. 5, pp. 3–39.

Chaiken, S., & Ledgerwood, A. (2012). A theory of heuristic and systematic information processing. In van Lange P. A. M., Kruglanski A. W., & Higgins E. T. (eds.), *Handbook of theories of social psychology.* Thousand Oaks, CA: Sage, pp. 246–266.

Cheema, A., & Patrick, V. M. (2012). Influence of warm versus cool temperatures on consumer choice: A resource depletion account. *Journal of Marketing Research, 49*(6), 984–995.

Chen, T. T., Wang, S. J., & Huang, H. C. (2020). "Buy, buy most Americans buy": country of reference (COR) effects and consumer purchasing decisions. *International Marketing Review, 37*(3), 533–558.

Chow, S. J. (2015). Many meanings of 'heuristic'. *The British Journal for the Philosophy of Science, 66*(4), 977–1016.

Cohen, M. D., Burkhart, R., Dosi, G., Egidi, M., Marengo, L., Warglien, M., & Winter, S. (1996). Routines and other recurring action patterns of organizations: contemporary research issues. *Industrial and Corporate Change, 5*(3), 653–698.

Dane, E., & Pratt, M. G. (2007). Exploring intuition and its role in managerial decision making. *Academy of Management Review, 32*(1), 33–54.

Davis, J. P., Eisenhardt, K. M., & Bingham, C. B. (2009). Optimal structure, market dynamism, and the strategy of simple rules. *Administrative science quarterly, 54*(3), 413–452.

Dean, J. (1976). Pricing policies for new products. *Harvard Business Review, 54*(6), 141–153.

Eisenhardt, K. M., & Sull, D. N. (2001). *Strategy as simple rules.* Harvard Business Publications, 107–112.

Elmaghraby, W., & Keskinocak, P. (2003). Dynamic pricing in the presence of inventory considerations: Research overview, current practices, and future directions. *Management Science, 49*(10), 1287–1309.

Evans, J. S. B. (2009). How many dual-process theories do we need? One, two, or many?. In Evans, J. S. B. & Frankish (eds.) *In two minds: Dual processes and beyond.* Oxford University Press, Oxford, pp. 33–54.

Fawcett, S. E., Waller, M. A., Miller, J. W., Schwieterman, M. A., Hazen, B. T., & Overstreet, R. E. (2014). A trail guide to publishing success: tips on writing influential conceptual, qualitative, and survey research. *Journal of Business Logistics, 35*(1), 1–16.

Felton, A. P. (1959). Making the marketing concept work. *Harvard Business Review, 37*, 55–65.

Fischbein, E. (1989). Tacit models and mathematical reasoning. *For the Learning of Mathematics, 9*(2), 9–14.

Frederick, S. (2002). Automated choice heuristics. In Gilovich, T., Griffin, D., and Kahneman, D. (eds.) *Heuristics and biases: The psychology of intuitive judgement.* Cambridge University Press, Cambridge, pp. 548–558.

Geman, S., Bienenstock, E., & Doursat, R. (1992). Neural networks and the bias/variance dilemma. *Neural Computation, 4*(1), 1–58.

Gesell, I. (2005). Practiced spontaneity: Using improv theater skills to help teams master change. *The Journal for Quality and Participation, 28*(1), 4.

Gigerenzer, G. (2007). *Gut feelings: The intelligence of the unconscious.* Penguin, New York.

Gigerenzer, G., & Brighton, H. (2009). Homo heuristicus: Why biased minds make better inferences. *Topics in cognitive science, 1*(1), 107–143.

Gigerenzer, G., & Gaissmaier, W. (2011). Heuristic decision making. *Annual Review of Psychology, 62*, 451–482.

Gigerenzer, G., & Selten, R. (eds.). (2002). *Bounded rationality: The adaptive toolbox.* MIT Press, Cambridge, Mass.

Gigerenzer, G., & Todd, P. M. (1999). Fast and frugal heuristics: The adaptive toolbox. In Gigerenzer, G., Todd, P. M. (eds.), *Simple heuristics that make us smart.* Oxford University Press, Oxford, 3–34.

Gigerenzer, G. (2021). Axiomatic rationality and ecological rationality. *Synthese, 198*, 3547–3564.

Gilbert-Saad, A., McNaughton, R. B., & Siedlok, F. (2021). Inexperienced decision-makers' use of positive heuristics for marketing decisions. *Management Decision, 59*(7), 1706–1727.

Gilbride, T. J., & Allenby, G. M. (2004). A choice model with conjunctive, disjunctive, and compensatory screening rules. *Marketing Science, 23*(3), 391–406.

Green, K. C., & Armstrong, J. S. (2015). Simple versus complex forecasting: The evidence. *Journal of Business Research, 68*(8), 1678–1685.

Guercini, S., & Freeman, S. M. (2023). How international marketers make decisions: exploring approaches to learning and using heuristics. *International Marketing Review*, *40*(3), 429–451.

Guercini, S., & Lechner, C. (2021). New challenges for business actors and positive heuristics. *Management Decision*, *59*(7), 1585–1597.

Guercini, S., & Milanesi, M. (2020). Heuristics in international business: a systematic literature review and directions for future research. *Journal of International Management*, 26(4), 100782.

Guercini, S., & Milanesi, M. (2022). Foreign market entry decision-making and heuristics: a mapping of the literature and future avenues. *Management Research Review*, *45*(9), 1229–1246.

Guercini, S. (2012). New approaches to heuristic processes and entrepreneurial cognition of the market. *Journal of Research in Marketing and Entrepreneurship*, *14*(2), 199–213.

Guercini, S. (2019). Heuristics as tales from the field: the problem of scope. *Mind & Society*, *18*(2), 191–205.

Guercini, S., La Rocca, A., & Snehota, I. (2022). Decisions when interacting in customer-supplier relationships. *Industrial Marketing Management*, *105*, 380–387.

Guercini, S., La Rocca, A., Runfola, A., & Snehota, I. (2015). Heuristics in customer-supplier interaction. *Industrial Marketing Management*, *48*, 26–37.

Gummesson, E. (2017). From relationship marketing to total relationship marketing and beyond. *Journal of Services Marketing*. 31(1), 16–19.

Håkansson, H., & Snehota, I. (eds.). (2017). *No business is an island: Making sense of the interactive business world*. Emerald Group Publishing, Bingley, UK.

Halbert, M. (1965). *The meaning and sources of marketing theory*. McGraw-Hill, New York.

Haley, U. C., & Stumpf, S. A. (1989). Cognitive trails in strategic decision-making: linking theories of personalities and cognitions. *Journal of Management Studies*, *26*(5), 477–497.

Hatchuel, A. (2001). Towards design theory and expandable rationality: the unfinished program of Herbert Simon. *Journal of management and governance*, *5*(3/4), 260–273.

Hernández-Ortega, B. I., Stanko, M. A., Rishika, R., Molina-Castillo, F. J., & Franco, J. (2022). Brand-generated social media content and its differential impact on loyalty program members. *Journal of the Academy of Marketing Science*, *50*(5), 1071–1090.

Holyoak, K. J. (1990). 'Problem Solving'. In D. N. Osherson, D. N. and Smith, E. E. (eds.), *An Invitation to Cognitive Science: Thinking*. MIT Press, Cambridge, Mass, Vol. 3.

Houston, F. S. (1986). The marketing concept: what it is and what it is not. *Journal of Marketing*, *50*(2), 81–87.

Huber, J., & Klein, N. M. (1991). Adapting cutoffs to the choice environment: the effects of attribute correlation and reliability. *Journal of Consumer Research*, *18*(3), 346–357.

Hunt, S. D. (1976). The nature and scope of marketing. *Journal of Marketing*, *40*(3), 17–28.

Hunt, S. D. (2002). *Foundations of marketing theory: Toward a general theory of marketing*. ME Sharpe, New York.

Hutchinson, J. M., & Gigerenzer, G. (2005). Simple heuristics and rules of thumb: Where psychologists and behavioural biologists might meet. *Behavioural processes*, *69*(2), 97–124.

Irwin, J. R., & McClelland, G. H. (2001). Misleading heuristics and moderated multiple regression models. *Journal of Marketing Research, 38*, 100–109.

Kahneman, D. (2003). Maps of bounded rationality: Psychology for behavioral economics. *American Economic Review, 93*(5), 1449–1475.

Kahneman, D. (2011). *Thinking, fast and slow*. Penguin Books, London.

Kahneman, D., Sibony, O., & Sunstein, C. R. (2021). *Noise: a flaw in human judgment*. Hachette UK.

Katsikopoulos, K. V. (2011). Psychological heuristics for making inferences: Definition, performance, and the emerging theory and practice. *Decision analysis, 8*(1), 10–29.

Katsikopoulos, K. V., Şimşek, O., Buckmann, M., & Gigerenzer, G. (2020). *Classification in the wild. The science and art of transparent decision making*. MIT Press, Cambridge, Mass.

Katsikopoulos, K. V., & Gigerenzer, G. (2013). Behavioral operations management: A blind spot and a research program. *Journal of Supply Chain Management, 49*(1), 3–7.

Keith, R. J. (1960). The marketing revolution. *Journal of Marketing, 24*(3), 35–38.

Kelman, M. (2011). *The heuristics debate*. Oxford University Press, Oxford.

Klein, G. A. (1998). *Sources of power: How people make decisions*. MIT Press, Cambridge, Mass.

Klein, G. (2015). A naturalistic decision making perspective on studying intuitive decision making. *Journal of Applied Research in Memory and Cognition, 4*(3), 164–168.

Knight, F. H. (1921). *Risk, uncertainty and profit*. Houghton Mifflin.

Kohli, A. K., & Jaworski, B. J. (1990). Market orientation: the construct, research propositions, and managerial implications. *Journal of Marketing, 54*(2), 1–18.

Kotler, P. (1967). *Marketing Management. Analysis, Planning and Control*. 1st edn, Prince-Hall, Englewood Cliffs, NJ.

Kotler, P. (1988). *Marketing Management. Analysisi, Planning, Implementation and Control*. 6th edn, Prince-Hall, Englewood Cliffs, NJ.

Kotler, P. (2016). Why Behavioral Economics Is Really Marketing Science. *Evonomics*. https://evonomics.com/behavioraleconomics-neglect-marketing/.

Kotler, P., & Levy, S. J. (1969). Broadening the concept of marketing. *Journal of Marketing, 33*(1), 10–15.

La Rocca, A., & Snehota, I. (2011). Knowledge in use when actors interact in business relationships. *IMP Journal, 5*(2), 79–93.

Levinthal, D. A. (2011). A behavioral approach to strategy—what's the alternative? *Strategic Management Journal, 32*(13), 1517–1523.

Li, Y., Wall, D., Johnson, E., & Toubia, O. (2016). Cognitively Optimized Measurement of Preferences. *Advances in Consumer Research, 44*, 532–535.

Lowe, S., & Tapachai, N. (2021). Bourdieusian interaction: actors' habitus, agentic activities and field resources. *Journal of Business & Industrial Marketing, 36*(6), 893–904.

Luan, S., Reb, J., & Gigerenzer, G. (2019). Ecological rationality: Fast-and-frugal heuristics for managerial decision making under uncertainty. *Academy of Management Journal, 62*(6), 1735–1759.

Luck, D. J. (1969). Broadening the concept of marketing. Too far. *Journal of Marketing*, 53–55.

Manimala, M. J. (1992). Entrepreneurial heuristics: A comparison between high PI (pioneering-innovative) and low PI ventures. *Journal of Business Venturing, 7*(6), 477–504.

March, J. G. (1994). *Primer on decision making: How decisions happen.* Simon and Schuster, New York.

Martignon, L., & Schmitt, M. (1999). Simplicity and robustness of fast and frugal heuristics. *Minds and Machines, 9,* 565–593.

McLean, F. (2012). *Marketing the museum.* Routledge, Abingdon.

McNamara, C. P. (1972). The present status of the marketing concept. *Journal of Marketing, 36*(1), 50–57.

Merlo, O., Lukas, B. A., & Whitwell, G. J. (2008). Heuristics revisited: Implications for marketing research and practice. *Marketing Theory, 8*(2), 189–204.

Miller, G. A. (1956). The magical number seven, plus or minus two: Some limits on our capacity for processing information. *Psychological Review, 63*(2), 81.

Mousavi, S., & Gigerenzer, G. (2014). Risk, uncertainty, and heuristics. *Journal of Business Research, 67*(8), 1671–1678.

Moustakas, C. (1990). *Heuristic research: Design, methodology, and applications.* Sage Publications, Newbury Park.

Musgrave, A. (1974). Logical versus historical theories of confirmation. *The British Journal for the Philosophy of Science, 25*(1), 1–23.

Narver, J. C., & Slater, S. F. (1990). The effect of a market orientation on business profitability. *Journal of Marketing, 54*(4), 20–35.

Nelson, R. R., & Winter, S. (1982). *An evolutionary theory of economic change.* Harvard University Press, Cambridge, Mass.

Newell, A., & Simon, H. A. (1972). *Human problem solving.* Prentice-Hall, Englewood Cliffs, NJ.

O'Shaughnessy, N. (2001). The marketing of political marketing. *European Journal of Marketing, 35*(9/10), 1047–1057.

Ommen, N. O., Heußler, T., Backhaus, C., Michaelis, M., & Ahlert, D. (2010). The Impact of Country-of-Origin and Joy on Product Evaluation: A Comparison of Chinese and German Intimate Apparel. *Journal of Global Fashion Marketing, 1*(2), 89–99.

Payne, J. W., Bettman, J. R., & Johnson, E. J. (1993). *The adaptive decision maker.* Cambridge University Press, Cambridge, UK.

Perkins, D. N. (1981). *The mind's best work.* Harvard University Press, Cambridge, Mass.

Pfeffer, J., & Sutton, R. I. (2006). Evidence-based management. *Harvard Business Review, 84*(1), 62.

Piattelli Palmarini, M. (2005). *Psicologia ed economia delle scelte. Quattro lezioni al Collegio di Francia.* Codice edizioni, Torino.

Polya, G. (1945). *How to solve it: A new aspect of mathematical method.* Princeton University Press, NJ.

Sarasvathy, S. D. (2001). Causation and effectuation: Toward a theoretical shift from economic inevitability to entrepreneurial contingency. *Academy of Management Review, 26*(2), 243–263.

Savage, L. J. (1954). *The foundation of statistics.* 2nd edn, Dover, New York.

Seabra, E. (2019). Understanding Gender Identities and Food Preferences to Increase the Consumption of a Plant-Based Diet With Heuristics. In Puachunder, J. M. (ed.), *Intergenerational Governance and Leadership in the Corporate World: Emerging Research and Opportunities.* IGI Global, Pennsylvania, 30–38.

Simon, H. A. (1963). *The heuristic compiler.* Rand Corporation, Santa Monica.

Simon, H. A. (1973). The structure of ill structured problems. *Artificial Intelligence, 4*(3–4), 181–201.

Simon, H. A. (1978). Information-processing theory of human problem solving. *Handbook of learning and cognitive processes*, *5*, 271–295.

Simon, H. A. (1979). Rational decision making in business organizations. *The American Economic Review*, *69*(4), 493–513.

Simon, H. A. (1990). Invariants of human behavior. *Annual Review of Psychology*, *41*(1), 1–20.

Simon, H. A. (2000). Bounded rationality in social science: Today and tomorrow. *Mind & Society*, *1*, 25–39.

Souchon, A. L., Hughes, P., Farrell, A. M., Nemkova, E., & Oliveira, J. S. (2016). Spontaneity and international marketing performance. *International Marketing Review*.

Spann, M., Fischer, M., & Tellis, G. J. (2015). Skimming or penetration? Strategic dynamic pricing for new products. *Marketing Science*, *34*(2), 235–249.

Srivastava, J., Chakravarti, D., & Rapoport, A. (2000). Price and margin negotiations in marketing channels: An experimental study of sequential bargaining under one-sided uncertainty and opportunity cost of delay. *Marketing Science*, *19*(2), 163–184.

Sull, D., & Eisenhardt, K. M. (2015). *Simple rules: How to thrive in a complex world*. Houghton Mifflin Harcourt, Boston.

Tan, Y., Geng, S., Katsumata, S., & Xiong, X. (2021). The effects of ad heuristic and systematic cues on consumer brand awareness and purchase intention: Investigating the bias effect of heuristic information processing. *Journal of Retailing and Consumer Services*, *63*, 102696.

Taylor, W. J. (1965). "Is marketing a science?" revisited. *Journal of Marketing*, *29*(3), 49–53.

Tellis, G. J. (1986). Beyond the many faces of price: an integration of pricing strategies. *Journal of Marketing*, *50*(4), 146–160.

Thaler, R. (1985). Mental accounting and consumer choice. *Marketing Science*, *4*(3), 199–214.

Thaler, R. H., & Sunstein, C. R. (2008). *Nudge. Improving decisions about health, wealth, and happiness*. Penguin Books, London.

Todd, P. M., & Gigerenzer, G. E. (eds.) (2012). *Ecological rationality: Intelligence in the world*. Oxford University Press, Oxford, UK.

Tversky, A., & Kahneman, D. (1974). Judgment under Uncertainty: Heuristics and Biases: Biases in judgments reveal some heuristics of thinking under uncertainty. *Science*, *185*(4157), 1124–1131.

Vargo, S. L., & Lusch, R. F. (2004). Evolving to a new dominant logic for marketing. *Journal of Marketing*, *68*(1), 1–17.

Vargo, S. L., & Lusch, R. F. (2014). Inversions of service-dominant logic. *Marketing Theory*, *14*(3), 239–248.

Vuori, N., Laamanen, T., & Zollo, M. (2022). Capability Development in Infrequent Organizational Processes: Unveiling the Interplay of Heuristics and Causal Knowledge. *Journal of Management Studies*.

Xiao, M., Wang, R., & Chan-Olmsted, S. (2018). Factors affecting YouTube influencer marketing credibility: a heuristic-systematic model. *Journal of Media Business Studies*, *15*(3), 188–213.

Zollo, M., Reuer, J. J., & Singh, H. (2002). Interorganizational routines and performance in strategic alliances. *Organization Science*, *13*(6), 701–713.

3. Consumers' heuristics and marketer as choice architect

3.1 DECISION RULES AS COMPONENTS OF AN ADAPTIVE TOOLBOX FOR THE MARKETER

In this chapter we examine consumer heuristics as the object of study by marketers as potential choice architects of the consumption context. In the next chapter, however, we examine heuristics directly adopted by marketers.

Heuristics are relevant to marketers' decision-making processes as problem solving tools and learning objects (Titus, 2000). In particular, in the marketing environment, judgments made or otherwise formed by managers and entrepreneurs, but also by consumers, competitors and influencers, assume importance (Andersson, Aspenberg and Kjellberg, 2008; Mero, Vanninen and Keränen, 2023).

Managers' rationality is bounded given the complexity of the environment and the limitations of human information processes even for those who, like professional managers, have specific tools and skills (Nelson, 2008; Winter, 2000). Marketers often simplify decisions through the use of heuristics, starting with satisficing (Simon, 1955; 1990; Artinger, Gigerenzer, and Perke, 2022; Kienzler, 2018). As we saw in the previous chapter, the topic of heuristics has long been present in the marketing theory and consumer behavior literature, accompanied, however, by limited attention (Merlo, Lucas, and Whitwell, 2008). Marketers' heuristics, like those of other decision makers, are simple decision rules with little processing efforts (Goodrich, 2014). The use of heuristics is widespread in managerial decision making and is important for the competitive ability of firms in the relevant environment (Goll and Rasheed, 1997; Guercini, La Rocca, and Snehota, 2022; Merlo, Lucas, and Whitwell, 2008, p. 189).

Recent years have witnessed a debate that, albeit gradually, proposes a more nuanced view even in the specific terrain of academic marketing research, to which we give testimony in the next sections of the chapter. We started from the selection of the Scopus database described in the previous chapter (section 2.4), from which we derived articles that identify some kind of heuristic rule, often endowed with a specific name. The research papers that provided heuristics of greatest interest are given in the sections of this and the next chapter, and references are given in the bibliography.

The literature interested in heuristics referable to issues of relevance to marketing invests a research context that extends to other disciplines, such as management and psychology. This research now covers a rather wide time span, spread out over at least several decades, presenting itself heterogeneous in terms of topics, methodologies of analysis and study approaches. We present a set of heuristics to address marketing problems starting precisely from the literature focused on the topic of consumer behavior, which is essential for marketers' understanding of the market, including as potential architects of consumer choice (Thaler and Sustein, 2008).

Based on this literature, we can recognize at least two approaches that we will call "computational" or "cognitive", respectively. A first approach in fact sees the use of the term heuristics for decision models employed to obtain an approximate solution to a problem that is not possible or convenient to solve in terms of optimization (Lee and Kim, 1993). The solution is given by algorithms that can be formally processed but are referred to in this literature as heuristics because they do not consider all the elements necessary for optimization. According to this *computational approach* (Chow, 2015, p. 995), we speak of heuristics as being approximate solutions that are adopted as an alternative to an undefined or unachievable optimal solution because necessary elements are missing or because these elements are not acquirable and processable in a convenient way, at least with available resources (Lee and Kim, 1993). In this sense, the term heuristics finds use in a part of the literature on marketers' decisions that uses models that are difficult to manage in the absence of specific mathematical-statistical skills. These kinds of heuristics are present in many situations in which marketers have to make decisions, for example, when assessing customer heterogeneity in preferences or choice pattern (Kamakura, Kim, and Lee, 1996), or formulating the convenient numerosity of references for managing an assortment (Rooderkerk, van Heerde, and Bijmolt, 2013), or even estimating the effects of promotions through information "model-selection heuristics" (Kappe, Stadler Blank and DeSarbo, 2014). In all these cases, the data needed to evaluate a solution that decision makers can envision as optimal may be missing, so heuristics are used to address the problem. However, the lack of some of the data does not mean that little data is available. It is simply that the decision model offers a viable solution in a convenient way, however suboptimal (Lee and Kim, 1993). In this case, heuristics are not necessarily easy to compute and correspond to algorithms in themselves that are also complex and require the support of computer computation. They are therefore called heuristics even though they are solutions whose processing and management require specialized skills. In this literature heuristic models are treated like other decision models that have found application to marketing problems, such as Markov decision processes (MDPs) applied to valuation problems (Bitran and Mondschein, 1997; Memarpour, Hassannayebi, Miab, and Farjad, 2021), models for attribution in online advertising understood as an evaluation of the individual advertiser's contribution to the target's actions (Singal, Besbes, Desir, Goyal, and Iyengar, 2022), or even models applied to decisions for Internet shopping (Shi and Zhang, 2014). This type of approach is followed in some of the literature published in marketing journals (among others, Kamakura, Kim, and Lee, 1996; Rooderkerk, van Heerde, and Bijmolt, 2013; Sándor and Wedel, 2002; Krieger and Green, 1991), and partly in work related to marketing issues but published in management journals (e.g., Kappe, Stadler Blanck, DeSarbo, 2014; Lu and Posner, 1994; Moinzadeh, 1997; Ioannou, Kritikos, and Prastcos, 2003; Lee and Kim, 1993).

A second approach we present here qualifies the use of the term heuristics as rules for easily activated problem solving based on the cognition of decision makers even in the absence of specialized skills and on the basis of the most common memorization and computational abilities. In this case, the decision model not only seeks a shortcut from optimizing models (Lee and Kim, 1993), but is absolutely based on simple algorithms, so the heuristic solution is such as it is easy for the decision makers' cognition regardless of their specialized skills. According to this *cognitive approach* (Chow, 2015, p. 996), heuristics are not related to an approximate computational method as opposed to one that takes into account all theoretically relevant parameters as causes, but to the most congenial and easy computational and problem solving skills for marketers, even without advanced mathematical-statistical skills or without the support of computerized computational tools. In this case, heuristics are algorithms that can be solved through the widespread computational tools accessible to virtually all decision makers, be they consumers, managers, entrepreneurs or influencers, who are required to make judgments and choices. The literature proposes the concept of heuristics or simple rule with this meaning, which can be found in articles in business and industrial marketing journals (Jeon, 2022; Meneses, 2010; Otto, 2008; Saab and Botelho, 2020; Vanharanta and Easton, 2010; Guercini, La Rocca, Runfola, and Snehota, 2014; 2015; Guercini, La Rocca, and Snehota, 2022), international marketing (Chen, Wang, and Huang, 2020; Guercini and Freeman, 2023; Souchon, Huges, Farrell, Nemkova, and Oliveira, 2016), but also other management or entrepreneurship journals (Bingham and Eisenhardt, 2011; Eisenhardt and Zbaracki, 1992; Bingham, Eisenhardt, and Furr, 2007; Bennett and Vignali, 1996; Gilbert-Saad, McNaughton, and Siedlok, 2021; Guercini and Lechner, 2021).

These two approaches, the computational one and the cognitive one, highlight how the term heuristics is not associated with a single thinking-system, unlike what is perceived in dual system theory perspectives (Chaiken, 1980; Frankish, 2010; Kahneman, 2011). In fact, the term heuristics used in the computational key, corresponds to heuristics expressed in a formal language that do not seem adoptable in system 1 (thinking fast), but require the application of rules that, if followed, bring their effects, according to the contribution in system 2. In the cognitive approach, on the other hand, heuristics basically correspond to the meaning of heuristics adoptable in system 1 of the dual system approach. The dual system has been used in the consumer psychology perspective for its implications on the study of consumer behavior and consequently for marketing (Samson and Voyer, 2012). As much as sophisticated computational tools and expertise are not required, even simple rules can be modeled, because again, adopting the building blocks view of heuristics suggested by Gigerenzer (Gigerenzer and Todd, 1999), one recognizes: (1) information search activities; (2) stopping rules that suggest when the information found is sufficient; and finally (3) decision rules in the proper sense that allow one to convert that information into a decision (Brighton and Gigerenzer, 2009).

Another way of classifying adopted heuristics of relevance to marketers directly or indirectly through the study of consumer behavior is by domains of decision model application. Thus we find heuristics of consumers related to the role of brand recognition (Chrysochou, 2010), choice at the social group level (Yang, Zhao, Erdem, and Zhao, 2010), or previous shopping experiences for example with reference to prices (Gneezy, Gneezy, and Lauga, 2014). We also find marketers' heuristics related to evaluation of advertising investment (Goodrich, 2014), new product launch, pricing, and distribution choices (Yao and Oppewal, 2016).

Finally, a further way of classifying heuristics in the marketing literature concerns the role accorded to them, whether or not highlighting their positive or negative aspects. We will refer to the latter distinction in order to distinguish a view of heuristics as a source almost exclusively of biases or otherwise of errors and inaccurate evaluations (Mowen and Gaeth, 1992), from a view of heuristics that sees the characteristics of simplicity and speed but also of accuracy and transparency (Katsikopoulos, Şimşek, Buckmann and Gigerenzer, 2020).

3.2 THE LITERATURE ON CONSUMERS' HEURISTICS AS A SOURCE OF ERRORS

The earliest contributions on the role of heuristics in marketing are concentrated in the fields of consumer behavior, advertising budgeting, and product development. Consumers have been seen as the actors first associated with the use of heuristics, often in relation to the fact that such use produces bias and that based on this mode of judgment formation their behavior may be exposed to manipulation (Drolet, Luce, Simonson, 2009; Kivetz and Simonson, 2003). It is observed how consumers do not carry out extensive research and evaluation of alternatives and resort to simple shortcuts, such as the one whereby higher price, may correspond to higher quality (Bettman, Johnson, and Payne, 1991). Park and Lessig (1981) examine the impact of familiarity on consumer decisions, familiarity which is defined as "how much a person knows about the product" or "how much a person thinks s/he knows about the product" (Park and Lessig, 1981, p. 223), to which are associated differences in perceptual category breadth, usage of functional and nonfunctional product dimensions, decision time, and confidence, highlighting "decision biases and heuristics". Park and Lessig's article takes up the heuristics defined by Tversky and Kahneman (1974) and sees such a close connection between biases and heuristics that in the text of the article the second term (heuristics) always follows the first (biases), almost as an inevitably associated element.

Again with reference to the product, in this case not at the ideation stage but in the consumer's perception once it is launched in the market, Sevilla and Kahn (2014) identify a "completeness heuristic", according to which "people estimate an incompletely shaped product to be smaller and, therefore, prefer it less in general than a completely shaped one of equal size and weight" (Sevilla and Kahn, 2014, p. 57). The authors of this study also find that the smaller-sized estimates made on incompletely shaped products leads to increased quantities consumed for this type of product, showing that this "completeness heuristic" is in action even when incompletely shaped products are larger in primary size than the completely shaped ones with which they are compared (Sevila and Kahn, 2014, p. 66).

Consumers can adopt heuristics for both individual and group choices. Group decision-making heuristics (Yang, Zhao, Erdem, and Zhao, 2010), with reference to family groups in household settings, recognize three types of family decision-making strategies, which include the "Harsanyi decision heuristic" (Harsanyi, 1955), the "minimum decision heuristic" (MIN) and the "maximum decision heuristic" (MAX) (Atkinson, 1970).

An "observational heuristic" is studied by Simpson, Siguaw, and Cadogan (2008), who define it as the tendency of some consumers to use observation of the buying behavior of other unknown consumers as a purchase decision heuristic (Simpson, Siguaw, and Cadogan, 2008, p. 212). Consumer choices can also be influenced when the consumer is exposed to data about the stock price performance of the producing company's stock, as evidenced by a specific marketing literature that looks at stock market returns to events or announcements of events such as, for example, brand extensions or new product launches, viewing the heuristics adopted by consumers as a source of biases (Johnson and Tellis, 2005).

Ordabayeva and Chandon (2013) examine consumers' evaluation of packaging size and consider for this the "AddChange heuristic", whereby to calculate product package volume people add (rather than multiply) the percentage changes in height, width, and length, shown on the packaging, instead inferring size from their perceptions of package size, whereby perceptions are systematically biased by packaging features (Ordabayeva and Chandon, 2013, pp. 123, 124). Two other heuristic models are then considered in the same study, which are "surface area heuristic" and "contour heuristic". According to the contour heuristic, the perception of size is affected by the change in the perimeter of objects. Like the AddChange heuristic, the contour heuristic assumes an additive rather than a multiplicative process. Unlike the AddChange heuristic, however, the contour heuristic assumes that people compare the change in the reference contour. In contrast, "the surface area model suggests that perceived size is influenced by the surface area of objects and is therefore a quadratic function of height, width, and length. This is consistent with early research suggesting that volume perception may be sensitive to the surface area of objects" (Ordabayeva and Chandon, 2013, pp. 126 and 127).

Homer and Mukherjee (2018) examine the consumption of dietary supplements by comparing the perceived effectiveness of multi-ingredient versus single-ingredient products and finding a "more is better heuristic", whereby the product with more ingredients is perceived to be more effective, at least for small dosages (Homer and Mukherjee, 2018).

Mattila's (1998) study examines the propensity of consumers to rely on heuristic cues when asked to make satisfaction judgments in repeated purchase contexts. The study is experimental in nature and proposes as a result that a decision maker who processes information inefficiently may be subject to biased satisfaction judgments caused by their moods at the information encoding stage. Efficient information processors, on the other hand, tend to reduce the impact of mood in their post-purchase evaluations. In sum, motivation rather than information processing ability may be the key factor in a consumer's propensity to use heuristics during the post-purchase evaluation process (Mattila, 1998, p. 477).

Decision styles in relation to perceived risk are examined by Chang and Wu (2012) regarding purchase decisions in the online context, comparing systematic processing with heuristic processing (Chang and Wu, 2012, p. 381). Heuristics are defined as simple strategies to make decisions based on a single or a few cues, and specifically "when shoppers adopt heuristics strategy to make purchasing decisions, they will search some simple cues from their minds or the web site to be the basis of marketing decisions" (Chang and Wu, 2012, p. 382). The authors recognize the emotional value of heuristics as corresponding to shoppers' attitudes, but take a view that "these simple strategies always lead to biases" (Chang and Wu, 2012, p. 383). A study on the misunderstanding of consumers' use of credit cards showed that people with lower numerical competences tend to underestimate the payment required to settle a credit card debt in three years, while people with higher numerical competences tend to overestimate the payment, highlighting the role of a "principal-plus-adjustment heuristic" (Soll, Keeney, and Larrick, 2013, p. 67).

Referring instead to prices used in grocery distribution, a study by Yao and Oppewal (2016) highlights how unit price assumes importance for decisions when consumers are under time pressure. On the price-quality relationship, other experimental studies point to a "price-quality heuristic", already discussed in previous research (Nagle and Holden, 1995; Hanson and Putler, 1996), whereby consumers associate higher price with higher product quality, except that they then form judgments based on experience, resulting in a worse evaluation for the product with high price and low quality (Gneezy, Gneezy, and Lauga, 2014). This occurs in various contexts, for example from luxury products to hospitality services (Lee, 2013). The price-quality heuristic, or price-quality effect (PQE), also finds application in business-to-business markets, and not only in business-to-consumer markets, and just like consumers, organizations can also use price as a cue to infer quality or risk (Saab and Botelho, 2020). PQE is seen as a type of heuristic that occurs in different decision contexts. Heuristics that infer quality from the price level have been said to violate the basic principles of rational choice models (Hinterhuber, 2015). For PQE, in essence the role of price is not only to condition resource allocation, but there is a second one whereby "a higher price is usually taken as an indication of higher quality, even though the significance of such perceived correlation may vary across product categories" (Lee, 2013, p. 206).

The role of heuristics adopted by consumers for effective price communication of the services offered had already been examined by Gotlieb (1989), who highlighted their importance for the communications made regarding price by the marketer. Other work has seen the effect of strong discounting on the behavior of consumers who use heuristics in their decision-making processes (Jayakumar, 2016). In contrast, Kinnard, Capella, and Bonner (2013) examine the role of odd pricing in activating consumer heuristics with an underestimation effect. Also related to pricing, another heuristic referred to is the anchoring heuristic of the heuristics-and-biases research approach (Kumar and Pandey, 2017).

Goodrich (2014) explores the adoption of heuristics with reference to advertising, highlighting how humans show more attention to graphic stimuli, giving even practical guidance to advertisers about the placement of print advertisements based on their intended genre. In consumer-to-consumer communication in the electronic word of mouth, comments from other users can become recommendations that act as cues in activating heuristics decision making (Harris and Gupta, 2008). Peer recommendations are used by consumers as decision-making heuristic, and in some studies it appears that consumers prefer peer recommendations and editorial recommendations over other types of effort-reducing cues that might be available during an online search (Smith, Menon, and Sivakumar, 2005).

Chatterjee, Atav, Min, and Taylor (2014) examine the role of uncertainty avoidance in consumer decision making, reporting three studies in which participants choose between risk and certainty and referring to Prospect Theory to measure risk aversion. The results of the study show that consumers with higher uncertainty aversion anchor on the certainty loss and stay with their choice because they prefer the certainty of a small loss to the possibility of a larger loss, thus trying to convert uncertainty into a reliable form of risk (Mousavi and Gigerenzer, 2014). With reference to the traditional heuristics adopted by the consumer, uncertainty avoidance is proposed as a likely boundary condition (Chatterjee, Atav, Min, and Taylor, 2014, p. 357).

3.3   CONSUMERS' HEURISTICS AS SOURCE OF POSITIVE EFFECTS

As much as positive or negative aspects may be highlighted in the same research, the positive aspects of consumers' use of heuristics emerge particularly strongly in some of the literature. For example, Hausman (2000) associates the benefits of impulse buying with the use of heuristics, pointing out that the use of impulse buying allows for the containment of the information overload required to manage planned buying programs, and the use of heuristics can give affective/hedonistic benefits (Hausman, 2000, p. 406).

Building on a large body of literature that confirms that consumers use heuristic processes in forming judgments (among others, Bettman, Luce, and Payne, 1991; Hauser and Wernerfelt, 1990; Ariely, 2000), Yee, Dahan, Hauser, and Orlin (2007) examine noncompensatory decision processes and propose an exploration of new methods to study heuristic decision processes using "greedoid languages". The latter are languages developed to study conditions under which a greedy algorithm can solve optimization problems (Korte and Lovász, 1985). The paper then seeks to use greedoid methods to investigate consumer heuristic processes, where such methods provide a framework and theory to reduce the complexity of some problems (Yee, Dahan, Hauser, and Orlin, 2007, p. 540). Interestingly, the proposed language test suggests that a category of noncompensatory choice heuristics predict well (Yee, Dahan, Hauser, and Orlin, 2007, p. 546).

Heuristics are examined as mechanisms for risk reduction in pre-purchase evaluations and information seeking (Sheth and Venkatesan, 1968, p. 308). A study by Otterbring (2021) highlights how peer presence appears to increase consumers' reliance on heuristics and the accessibility of concepts linked to popularity, leading to congruent popular brand choices (Otterbring, 2021, p. 2).

Consumer behavior is also traced back to consumer choice of financial products (retail investors) who must choose between different funds in which to invest, where Morrin, Inman, Broniarczyk, Nenkov, and Reuter (2012) study the tendency of consumers to use the "1/n heuristic". This is a heuristic that has already been examined in other studies (Gigerenzer and Gaissmaier, 2011, pp. 470–471; Brighton and Gigerenzer, 2009, p. 130), where it is referred to as the "1/N rule", referring to research that highlights its effectiveness (DeMiguel, Garlappi, and Uppal, 2009), or where it has also been referred to as the "equality heuristic" (Messik, 1993). The authors decompose this heuristic into two dimensions underlying the variable "N" that represent in fact two different heuristics: (1) the tendency to invest in all available funds; (2) the tendency to spread the resources to be invested evenly among a set of selected funds. For financial product selection under the second option, fund size is examined as a parameter that can guide product selection (Morrin, Inman, Broniarczyk, Nenkov and Reuter, 2012).

Moser (2016) examines organic product consumption and related motivating beliefs with a simple decision-making heuristic as a predictor of organic buying. In this study, the first research question relates to the usefulness of heuristics for predicting organic buying decisions, while the second question examines the role of motivations and beliefs as cues that activate decision-making heuristics. Using a structural equation model, the study highlights the impact of heuristics and the beliefs that can activate them. Adopting a perspective mainly related to the fast and frugal heuristic approach, Moser highlights how heuristics are a special, practical decision-making process in which bounded rationality functions as practical rationality. Thus, heuristics make it easier to choose an object from a large set of alternatives, as

> heuristics exploit the available cues and objects of the environment ... it might be self-evident that the organic cue is used as the decision-making heuristic when deciding on organic product. However, this heuristic cue might only be transferred into behavior if further decisive factors are also considered. Consumers perceive especially availability and price as barriers to the purchase of organic products. (Moser, 2016, p. 553)

The excellent model fit and high percentage of variance explained in this research confirm the "buying organic heuristic" as a promising model for understanding purchase decisions in favor of organic products. Beliefs and heuristics were successfully integrated into the same framework. Indeed, "beliefs explained about 75 percent of the variance in the decision-making heuristic for organic products, the heuristics in turn predicted up to 20 percent of the variance in purchasing decisions in favor of organic products. These results confirm the hypothesis that beliefs are the underlying foundation on which heuristics are developed" (Moser, 2016, p. 557).

Other research about the use of heuristics by consumers appears descriptive of consumer behavior and prescriptive in defining the factors that marketers in the industry should take into account, adequately presenting the information on the basis of which consumers will make their decisions (Ariely, 2000).

The role of heuristics appears relevant in a comparison of sharing mechanisms for the success of a famous video game and mechanisms to promote primarily utilitarian products, highlighting how, with reference to consumers, "to learn about utilitarian products, they rely on simple cues and heuristics to process viral marketing messages about these products" (Schulze, Schöler, and Skiera, 2014, p. 1).

Anderson and Laverie (2022) examine the role of virtual reality content's innovativeness as a heuristic capable of signaling quality for "unbranded" real estate products. Here, elements perceived as innovative by the industry may not correspond to those perceived by consumers as the basis for defining a quality product, but the perceived innovativeness of the media may signal product quality to consumers for the offering and support purchase initiations (Anderson and Laverie, 2022, p. 1ff.).

O'Donnell and Evers (2019) see the contribution of consumer behavior research to help marketers in understanding how people think to express their preferences, looking at the specific case of willingness to pay (WTP). This study finds that choice preferences are determined by an "affect heuristic" (Zajonc, 1968), which is the preference for unknown characters to which the decision maker has been repeatedly exposed, exposure that increases positive evaluation and liking (O'Donnell and Evers, 2019, p. 1316). The same affect heuristic is referred to by some studies on the use of country of origin as cues for decisions based on heuristics, whereby the country of origin image provides a basis of easy requirements for processing information in the form of heuristics (Ommen, Heussler, Backhaus, Michaelis, and Ahlert, 2010).

Madrigal (2001) recognizes a heuristic process in social identity or identification and recalls how other research suggests that strong feelings toward an object can act as a heuristic that has a direct impact on consumer behavior. The internalization of a group's values, well-known norms, and goals through social identification has heuristic value in that it acts as a type of cognitive shortcut that "colors" judgment; the presence of a connection between a sponsor and the property can function as a heuristic signal in that it triggers behavioral intentions that are independent of an objective evaluation of the behavior (Madrigal, 2001, pp. 145, 150, 158).

The role of packaging in consumers' purchase decisions is recognized to be very important (Zhu, Chryssochoidis, and Zhou, 2019). Consumers may adopt different heuristics in their search information strategies, among which Zander and Hamm (2012) examine different information acquisition strategies making use of "lexicographic heuristic", "conjunctive heuristic", which respond well to conditions in which time is short, or others such as "elimination by aspects heuristic", "equal weight heuristic" and "majority of confirming heuristic", which require more time to decide on a product (Zander and Hamm, 2012, p. 312).

Marozzo, Raimondo, Miceli, and Scopelliti (2019) consider colors as one of the most important elements in packaging design and as heuristics in consumer evaluation processes. These authors adopt a concept of heuristics as simple rules or inferences that reduce the decision maker's effort in decision-making situations and are relevant to the low involvement of individuals who lack the willingness to engage in more extensive forms of processing, echoing Chaiken's approach (Chaiken, 1987). Colors act as heuristics to activate associations that consumers use to make inferences about products. Therefore, consumers tend to project the perceptual characteristics and meanings of colors in the natural state onto the product itself. This implies that seeing a food product in a color au naturel package leads consumers to believe that it is a natural product, and therefore more genuine and more authentic (Marozzo, Raimondo, Miceli, and Scopelliti, 2020, p. 916). Adopting the heuristic-systematic model, Kordrostami, Liu-Thompkins, and Rahmani (2022) consider that scarcity ceases to be a heuristic cue for consumers when it is incongruent with the presence of many reviews, which would suggest a large number of consumers who have accessed the product (Kordrostami, Liu-Thompkins, and Rahmani, 2022, p. 474).

Reviews in consumer-to-consumer marketplaces are examined by consumers through the heuristic-systematic model in the presence of possible manipulation by sellers, showing how the truthfulness of online review and seller responses may represent additional heuristics (Wang, Tariq, and Alvi, 2021). Wang, Shen, Song, and Phau (2020), with reference to the environmental issues of climate change and their impact on consumer evaluations and behavior propose that people with a wide psychological distance process information by adopting a systematic model instead of a heuristic model. The heuristic-systematic model is also examined by Hoek, Roling and Holdsworth to explore consumers' understanding of various ethical issues and a specific eco-label (Hoek, Roling, and Holdsworth, 2013).

A comparison of different models for estimating customer lifetime value in relation to each purchase occasion is proposed by Borle, Singh and Jain (2008). Specifically, the authors use a hierarchical Bayes approach to effect the estimation of customer lifetime value at each purchase occasion, and compare the performance of this model with other models used to estimate customer lifetime value at each purchase occasion. More specifically, these models for predicting the present value of future revenues from the customer include:

(1) an extended NBD-Pareto model; (2) the recency, frequency and monetary (RFM) value model; (3) two nested models from their proposed mode; and finally (4) a heuristic model that takes the average customer lifetime, the average interpurchase time, and the average dollar purchase amount observed in their estimation sample. As can be seen, a heuristic model is included among the competing models, and although the authors' proposed model appears to be the best-performing model, the heuristic model is no worse than other models in at least some of the purchase occasions (Borle, Sing and Jain, 2008, pp. 100ff.).

Also related to consumer buying processes, other studies show how the availability of large amounts of information, especially through the Internet, can overload the decision-making process and become a major issue for marketers as well, while attribute-based decision models may suffice to make good decisions (Fasolo, McClelland, and Todd, 2007). Broilo, Espartel, and Basso (2016) highlight how the increased volume of information available in the physical as well as online environment requires consumers who intend to purchase a product or service to choose, even before what to buy, which sources of information to consider and consult to form their judgments and choices. Through content analysis of material collected from qualitative interviews with consumers, the authors highlight for this the importance of heuristics in the form of socialized images relative to these sources (Broilo, Espartel, and Basso, 2016, pp. 193ff.).

Alba and Chattopadhyay (1985) examine the effects of a subset of competing brands, defined on the recall of other brands. All brands known to the consumer are defined as a "knowledge set", while a subset of this is referred to as a "retrieval set" and refers to the portion of the known brands that are recalled at a given point in time. The brands that the consumer will consider purchasing, or "consideration set", will necessarily be a subset of the knowledge set, but not necessarily a subset of the retrieval set. The authors specify that by "consideration set" they mean "to refer to the total set of brands a consumer would consider buying" (Alba and Chattopadhyay, 1985, p. 340).

Hauser (2014) sees the process of consumer product choice as beginning with the formation of a "consideration set" that selects a portion of products from those available that will be subject to subsequent screening and evaluation. In essence, the product choice process goes through a stage of forming a consideration set consisting of the products that are considered and among which will be the product(s) actually chosen, according to a "consider-then-choose" decision making process pattern (Payne, 1976). The definition of the consideration set can itself be the result of screening based on non-compensatory heuristics defined in relation to ethical aspects of the product or brand (Schamp, Heitmann, and Katzenstein, 2019). Consumers form the consideration set by resorting to a set of heuristics (Ariely, 2000).

Laroche, Kim, and Matsui (2003), through an empirical study of consumers' use of certain products (beer brands, fast food outlets), identify five heuristics which are: conjunctive; disjunctive; lexicographic; line additive; and geometric compensatory. These heuristics are seen as employed in the first stage of consideration set formation, where the conjunctive heuristic was found to be the most commonly used decision model in the empirical reference setting (Laroche, Kim, and Matsui, 2003).

With reference to the consideration set, Hauser's (2014) work is relevant to both the analysis of heuristics in consumer behavior and the analysis of marketers' decision models. In doing so, the author makes extensive use of the literature on the fast and frugal heuristics approach (Gigerenzer and Goldstein, 1996; Marewski, Gaissmeier, and Gigerenzer, 2010). In fact, consideration set formation becomes relevant for managerial decisions involving product development, marketing communications, etc., as the choices to be made depend on identifying and reacting to consumers' heuristics for consideration set formation, which represents a rational strategy from the consumer's perspective (Hauser, 2014, pp. 1689ff.). A large body of literature points out that consumers actually make use of these kinds of tools in decision-making processes (Brown and Wildt, 1992; Hauser and Wernerfelt, 1990; Paulssen and Bagozzi, 2005). Not only resorting to consideration-set training, but also the use of heuristics in such training is considered rational, and this is done both for reasons of efficiency (ratio of outcome to cost of the decision model) and for reasons of effectiveness (accuracy of the model's outcome), as evidenced by further literature (Bettman, Luce, and Payne, 1998; Brandstaetter, Gigerenzer and Hertwig, 2006; Gigerenzer and Goldstein, 1996; Tood and Gigerenzer, 2012).

The implications of Hauser's (2014) work are especially interesting for managerial decision making, as marketers must take into account consumers' use of heuristics for consideration-set formation. In this area, the author also outlines a possible type of integration between the use of new technologies and artificial intelligence to support managerial decision making. In fact, Hauser argues that the advancement of

> greedoid methods, Bayesian inference, machine-learning, incentive alignment, measurement formats, and unstructured direct elicitation make it feasible and cost-effective to understand, quantify, and simulate "what-if" scenarios for a variety of heuristics. These methods now apply to a broad set of managerial problems including applications in complex product categories with large numbers of product features and feature-levels. (Hauser, 2014, p. 1688)

The same author, along with others, has previously examined the use of cognitively simple decision rules in the formation of consideration sets by consumers, proposing two machine-learning methods for estimating simple rules for consideration-set formation. This paper considered "disjunctions-of-conjunctions

(DOC) decision rules that generalize well-studied decision models, such as disjunctive, conjunctive, lexicographic, and subset conjunctive rules" (Hauser, Toubia, Evgeniou, Befurt, and Dzyabura, 2010, p. 485).

The study by Bremer, Heitmann, and Schreiner (2017) starts from the view that the use of "screening heuristics" such as consideration set heuristics by consumers is a way to simplify decisions (Bettman, Luce, and Payne, 1998), especially given the increasing complexity of many consumer markets. This study, however, shows that the heuristics applied for consumer decisions are a much broader set and specifically include noncompensatory decision heuristics that infer judgments and take into account which can be used to improve choice predictions rather than using the hierarchical Bayesian technique (CBC-HB) (Bremer, Heitmann, and Schreiner, 2017, p. 532).

Konopka, Wright, Avis, and Feetham (2019) take contributions from several approaches, including dual process theory (Kahneman, 2011) and recognition heuristic (Gigerenzer and Goldstein, 1996) to view heuristic processing in brand choice. Also in the area of consumer response determinants to loyalty programs, Kivetz and Simonson (2003) examine the case where consumers involved in a loyalty program believe they have an effort advantage over others (idiosyncratic fit with the loyalty program) and "higher program requirements magnify this perception of advantage and can therefore increase the overall perceived value of the program" (Kivetz and Simonson, 2003, p.454), defining an "idiosyncratic fit heuristic" as a phenomenon that influences consumers' response to marketing programs and promotional offers and consists of the perceived relative advantage or fit with consumers' idiosyncratic preferences and conditions (Kivetz and Simonson, 2003).

3.4   MARKETERS' UNDERSTANDING OF THE HEURISTIC RULES USED BY CONSUMERS

In addition to research from which negative effects or positive effects emerge from the use of heuristics in consumer decision-making processes, a portion of the research describes the characteristics of the decision-making patterns adopted by consumers without highlighting any particular advantages or errors. Examining consumers in farmers' markets through an ethnographic survey, Garner (2022) identifies two dominant types of consumers, which he calls "hedonistic" and "utilitarian" consumers, respectively. The hedonistic consumer relies on heuristic cues for their decisions such as aesthetics or their relationship with the farmer, while the utilitarian consumer carefully analyzes marketing messages using central route cues and tends to be more aware of their purchase choices (Garner, 2022, pp. 66ff.).

In the research approach defined as Consumer Culture Theory (CCT), the distinction between structure and agent has been presented as aspects related to the study of social and cultural structures (the context) and social psychology perspectives and "strategies for the individuals in terms of satisfying desires, defining selves and constructing existence, respectively" (Askegaard and Linnet, 2011, pp. 386–387). It is seen as paradoxical that in this area "the legacy of CCT research has been working toward a predominantly agency-based view of the consumer, leading to a relative neglect of the structural foundations and limitations of the consumers' experiential universe" (Askegaard and Linnet, 2011, p. 386).

Recently, Higgins and O'Leary (2022) employ the term heuristics to explore the theme of social heroism in consumer research, employing the paradoxes of heroism as heuristics to explore the heroism of parent-carers and to see how this role can be tested. Through phenomenological interview, Ritch (2015) explores the fashion sustainability of current high street retailers' clothing brands in the UK, highlighting the confusion about "how sustainability applies to fashion and 'consumers' reliance on heuristics to guide sustainable preference, due to the lack of information and this implies that sustainable concepts are increasingly incorporated into everyday behaviors" (Ritch, 2015, p. 1162).

As we have seen, a part of marketing research on the topic of heuristics deals with the brand as a cue that activates certain heuristics of the consumer, simplifying their decision-making process. These kinds of heuristics can be taken into account by possible "choice architects", since consumers often base their choices on heuristics that simplify their choices, such as manufacturing brands (Chrysochou, 2010).

The view of the brand as a heuristic cue has long been present in the literature (Sheth and Venkatesan, 1968, p. 309) and has already been examined by Maheswaran, Mackie, and Chaiken (1992) within the framework of the heuristic-systematic model. The use of brand name as a cue for activating heuristics can be seen as a special case of recognition and likened to the use of individual words that can represent a cue in an effective heuristic decision model (see the case of the word "organic" studied by Vega-Zamora, Torres-Ruiz, Murgado-Armenteros, and Parras-Rosa, 2014).

The "brand name heuristic" is discussed by Gunasti and Ross (2010), who examine a taxonomy of alphanumeric brand names, based on the alignment between brand names and their connections to the product and its attributes. In this same study, it is acknowledged that consumers with a low need for cognition use a "the higher, the better heuristic" to select options labeled with alphanumeric brands, choosing the brand with the higher numeric portion, with a greater effect on consumer preferences predominantly for more technical products, even when consumers do not know the product category and the meaning of the attributes (Gunasti and Ross, 2010, pp. 1177ff.). When consumers obtain relevant information to define their behavior, the use of heuristics decreases; in this sense, heuristics can be used as a substitute for information (DelVecchio, 2001).

The implications of the role of heuristics given future digital communication and the role it may play in the consumer-retailer relationship is examined by Grewall, Herhausen, Ludwig, and Villaroel Ordenes (2022). Promotional selling per se has been examined as a stimulus/cue capable of activating heuristics in consumer decision processing (Ketron, Spears, and Dai, 2016), or heuristic algorithms devised with the stated intent of analyzing multiple variables jointly, e.g., "optimal pricing and advertising policies jointly for a new generation product in the presence of homogeneous forward-looking customers" (Najafi-Ghobadi, Bagherinejad, and Taleizadeh, 2022, p. 638), or heuristic policy that "decouples inventory replenishment, pricing, and component allocation decisions, in a coordinated way. The heuristic policy has a simple structure, and the control parameters of the heuristic policy can be obtained from tractable stochastic programs" (Oh, Sourirajan, and Ettl, 2014, p. 530).

Sela and Berger (2012) consider the numerosity of attributes taken by consumers to see how that numerosity affects the decision between different options. Attribute numerosity is generally seen as a heuristic cue for usefulness, so using a few cues to make decisions can be seen as limiting (Sela and Berger, 2012, p. 943). This study, however, also highlights how considering many attributes can produce bias, since the equitable increase in the amount of attributes throughout the choice set shifts choice toward hedonistic options, regardless of whether the attributes are hedonic, utilitarian, or mixed in nature. Consistent with this conceptualization, these effects are amplified when decision makers engage in heuristic processing and when priming makes utility salient (Sela and Berger, 2012, p. 942).

In summary, this chapter has proposed a literature review that addresses the topic of consumer heuristics by highlighting the variety of contributions to both fields of application and evaluation of the effects of using heuristics. Awareness and knowledge of the heuristics adopted by consumers is an essential component of marketers' understanding of the market. As such, consumer behavior and cognition is relevant to marketers' decision making. The consumer heuristics emerging from this literature review is not exhaustive but is based in every way on systematic work that starts, as we said in the introductory section of this chapter, on the work identified in section 2.4 of this volume. As a result of this review, a list of emerging heuristics is presented in Table 3.1.

It is important for marketers to know how consumers use heuristics in forming judgments and choices, not only in their purchasing behavior but also when they take on the role of influencers of other consumers. This knowledge of the consumer by marketers can result in an influencing capacity for the marketer. This influence can be seen both negatively for the manipulations made

Table 3.1   *A selection of consumer heuristics emerging from the literature*

Heuristic	Definition	Domain / scope	Approach
AddChange heuristic (Ordabayeva and Chandon, 2013)	To calculate product package volume adding, rather than multiply, the percentage changes in height, width, and length shown on the packaging	Evaluation and selection of consumer goods	Heuristics as a source of bias
Affect heuristic (Zajonc, 1968; O'Donnell and Evers, 2019)	Preference for unknown characters to which the decision maker has been repeatedly exposed, exposure that increases positive evaluation and liking	Evaluation and selection of consumer goods	Behavior description approach
Brand name heuristic (Gunasti and Ross, 2010)	To select options labeled with alphanumeric brands, choosing the brand with the higher numeric proportion	Evaluation and selection of consumer goods	Behavior description approach
Buying organic heuristic (Moser, 2016)	Consider the different alternatives and circumscribe the choice among organic products	Evaluation and selection of consumer goods	Heuristics as a source of positive effects
Colors' heuristic (Marozzo, Raimondo, Miceli, and Scopelliti, 2020)	Seeing a food product in a color au naturel package leads consumers to believe that it is a natural product, and therefore more genuine and more authentic	Evaluation and judgement on products and services	Behavior description approach
Completeness heuristic (Sevilla and Kahn, 2014)	People estimate an incompletely shaped product to be smaller and, therefore, prefer it less in general than a completely shaped on of equal size and weight	Evaluation and selection of consumer goods	Heuristic as a source of bias
Contour heuristic (Ordabayeva and Chandon, 2013)	The perception of size is based on the perimeter of the packaging of the product	Evaluation and selection of consumer goods	Heuristics as a source of bias
Equality heuristic (Messik, 1993)	Select all the available funds and spread the resources among them (similar to 1/N heuristic)	Retail market for financial products	Heuristics as a source of positive effects
Familiarity heuristic (Park and Lessig, 1981, among the others)	Preference based on how much a person thinks s/he knows about the product	Evaluation and selection of consumer goods	Heuristic as a source of bias

Heuristic	Definition	Domain / scope	Approach
More is better heuristic (Homer and Mukherjee, 2018)	Whereby the product with more ingredients is perceived to be more effective, at least for small dosages	Multi-ingredient versus single-ingredient products	Behavior description approach
Observational heuristic (Simpson, Siguaw, and Cadogan, 2008)	Observing of the buying behavior of other unknown consumers as base for purchase decision	Evaluation and selection of consumer goods	Behavior description approach
Price/quality heuristic (Nagle and Holden, 1995, among the others)	Higher price corresponds to higher quality, except that they then form judgements based on experience	Evaluation and selection of consumer goods	Behavior description approach
Scarcity heuristic (Kordrostami, Liu-Thompkins, and Rahmani, 2022)	Scarcity incongruence with the presence of many reviews, which would suggest a large number of consumers who have accessed the product	Evaluation and judgement of reviews and product success	Behavior description approach
Screening heuristic (Ariely, 2000; Hauser, 2014, Laroche, Kim and Matsui, 2003, among the others)	To select from many alternatives first form a consideration set. Several heuristic rules are available to form the set (conjunctive, disjunctive, lexicografic etc.)	Evaluation and selection of a very large set of consumer goods	Heuristics as a source of positive effects
Social identification heuristic (Madrigal, 2001)	The source of a message "colors" the judgment (for example, the presence of a connection between a sponsor and the property)	Evaluation and judgments on products and services	Behavior description approach
Surface area heuristic (Ordabayeva and Chandon, 2013)	The perception of the volume is based on the surface of the packaging	Evaluation and selection of consumer goods	Heuristics as a source of bias

Source: Author's elaboration.

in favor of the company and positively when exercised with the "libertarian paternalism" that Thaler and Sustein (2008, p. 5) discuss. Not surprisingly, the same authors mention that nudges are realizable in both the public and private sectors. In this sense, awareness of consumer heuristics can be the starting point for the marketer to assume the role of choice architect. With respect to the assumption of such a role, the marketer must in fact first develop an understanding of consumer heuristics, and second determine how this translates into their own choices and actions, depending on the goals and foreseeable effects for the actions taken (Thaler, 2018).

Even before assessing the possibilities of manipulation or the realization of environments conducive to the formation of desirable judgments and choices, marketers can help consumers learn heuristic rules where they are needed to contribute to their own ability to evaluate and choose. In this sense, training consumers means transferring information but also heuristics through communication processes that are often referable not only to knowledge of the basket of product attributes but before that to the characteristics of consumption contexts and the types of products and services that may be on offer. In other words, consumption heuristics can be relevant for marketers to set up processes for shaping consumption actors, as is the case, for example, in relation to the realization of conscious and sustainable consumption, where conscious consumer behaviors can be associated with the identification of critical factors on which to form judgments and choices (Johnson, Shu, Dellaert, Fox, Goldstein, Häubl, Larrick, Payne, Peters, Schkade, Wansink and Weber, 2012).

In conclusion, awareness of the heuristics of other market actors starting with consumers is an essential part of market context knowledge and assumes greater importance for marketers' strategic marketing (Varadarajan, 2010; Guercini, 2019).

REFERENCES

Alba, J. W., & Chattopadhyay, A. (1985). Effects of context and part-category cues on recall of competing brands. *Journal of Marketing Research, 22*(3), 340–349.

Anderson, K. C., & Laverie, D. A. (2022). In the consumers' eye: A mixed-method approach to understanding how VR-Content influences unbranded product quality perceptions. *Journal of Retailing and Consumer Services, 67*, 102977.

Andersson, P., Aspenberg, K., & Kjellberg, H. (2008). The configuration of actors in market practice. *Marketing Theory, 8*(1), 67–90.

Ariely, D. (2000). Controlling the information flow: Effects on consumers' decision making and preferences. *Journal of Consumer Research, 27*(2), 233–248.

Artinger, F. M., Gigerenzer, G., & Jacobs, P. (2022). Satisficing: Integrating two traditions. *Journal of Economic Literature, 60*(2), 598–635.

Askegaard, S., & Linnet, J. T. (2011). Towards an epistemology of consumer culture theory: Phenomenology and the context of context. *Marketing Theory, 11*(4), 381–404.

Atkinson, A. B. (1970). On the measurement of inequality. *Journal of Economic Theory, 2*(3), 244–263.

Bennett, R., & Vignali, C. (1996). Dancall Telecom A/S in the UK mobile telephone market. *Management Decision, 34*(8), 6–16.

Bettman, J. R., Johnson, E. J., & Payne, J. (1991). Consumer decision making. *Handbook of Consumer Behaviour*, 50–84.

Bettman, J. R., Luce, M. F., & Payne, J. W. (1998). Constructive consumer choice processes. *Journal of Consumer Research, 25*(3), 187–217.

Bingham, C. B., & Eisenhardt, K. M. (2011). Rational heuristics: the 'simple rules' that strategists learn from process experience. *Strategic Management Journal, 32*(13), 1437–1464.

Bingham, C. B., Eisenhardt, K. M., & Furr, N. R. (2007). What makes a process a capability? Heuristics, strategy, and effective capture of opportunities. *Strategic Entrepreneurship Journal, 1*(1–2), 27–47.

Bitran, G. R., & Mondschein, S. V. (1997). Periodic pricing of seasonal products in retailing. *Management Science, 43*(1), 64–79.

Borle, S., Singh, S. S., & Jain, D. C. (2008). Customer lifetime value measurement. *Management Science, 54*(1), 100–112.

Brandstätter, E., Gigerenzer, G., & Hertwig, R. (2006). The priority heuristic: making choices without trade-offs. *Psychological Review, 113*(2), 409–432.

Bremer, L., Heitmann, M., & Schreiner, T. F. (2017). When and how to infer heuristic consideration set rules of consumers. *International Journal of Research in Marketing, 34*(2), 516–535.

Broilo, P. L., Espartel, L. B., & Basso, K. (2016). Pre-purchase information search: too many sources to choose. *Journal of Research in Interactive Marketing. 10*(3), 193–211.

Brown, J. J., & Wildt, A. R. (1992). Consideration set measurement. *Journal of the Academy of Marketing Science, 20*, 235–243.

Chaiken, S. (1980). Heuristic versus systematic information processing and the use of source versus message cues in persuasion. *Journal of Personality and Social Psychology, 39*(5), 752–766.

Chaiken, S. (1987). The heuristic model of persuasion. In Zanna, M. P., Olson, J. M., & Herman, C. P. (eds.) *Social influence: the Ontario Symposium*, Routledge, Abingdon, Vol. 5, 3–39.

Chang, M. -L., & Wu, W. -Y. (2012). Revisiting perceived risk in the context of online shopping: An alternative perspective of decision-making styles. *Psychology and Marketing, 29*(5), 378–400.

Chatterjee, S., Atav, G., Min, J., & Taylor, D. (2014). Choosing the sure gain and the sure loss: Uncertainty avoidance and the reflection effect. *Journal of Consumer Marketing, 31*(5), 351–359.

Chen, T. T., Wang, S. J., & Huang, H. C. (2020). "Buy, buy most Americans buy": country of reference (COR) effects and consumer purchasing decisions. *International Marketing Review, 37*(3), 533–558.

Chow, S. J. (2015). Many meanings of 'heuristic'. *The British Journal for the Philosophy of Science, 66*(4), 977–1016.

Chrysochou, P. (2010). Food health branding: The role of marketing mix elements and public discourse in conveying a healthy brand image. *Journal of Marketing Communications, 16*(1–2), 69–85.

DelVecchio, D. (2001). Consumer perceptions of private label quality: the role of product category characteristics and consumer use of heuristics. *Journal of Retailing and Consumer Services, 8*(5), 239–249.

DeMiguel, V., Garlappi, L., & Uppal, R. (2009). Optimal versus naive diversification: How inefficient is the 1/N portfolio strategy? *The Review of Financial Studies, 22*(5), 1915–1953.

Drolet, A., Luce, M. F., & Simonson, I. (2009). When does choice reveal preference? Moderators of heuristic versus goal-based choice. *Journal of Consumer Research, 36*(1), 137–147.

Eisenhardt, K. M., & Zbaracki, M. J. (1992). Strategic decision making. *Strategic Management Journal, 13*(S2), 17–37.

Fasolo, B., McClelland, G. H., & Todd, P. M. (2007). Escaping the tyranny of choice: When fewer attributes make choice easier. *Marketing Theory, 7*(1), 13–26.

Frankish, K. (2010). Dual-process and dual-system theories of reasoning. *Philosophy Compass, 5*(10), 914–926.

Garner, B. (2022). An ethnographic analysis of consumer information processing and decision-making at farmers' markets. *Journal of Consumer Marketing, 39*(1), 66–77.

Gigerenzer, G., & Brighton, H. (2009). Homo heuristicus: Why biased minds make better inferences. *Topics in cognitive science*, *1*(1), 107–143.

Gigerenzer, G., & Gaissmaier, W. (2011). Heuristic decision making. *Annual Review of Psychology*, *62*, 451–482.

Gigerenzer, G., & Goldstein, D. G. (1996). Reasoning the fast and frugal way: models of bounded rationality. *Psychological Review*, *103*(4), 650–669.

Gigerenzer, G., & Todd, P. M. (1999). Fast and frugal heuristics: The adaptive toolbox. In Gigerenzer, G., Todd, P. M. (eds.), *Simple heuristics that make us smart*. Oxford University Press, Oxford, 3–23.

Gilbert-Saad, A., McNaughton, R. B., & Siedlok, F. (2021). Inexperienced decision-makers' use of positive heuristics for marketing decisions. *Management Decision*, *59*(7), 1706–1727.

Gneezy, A., Gneezy, U., & Lauga, D. O. (2014). A reference-dependent model of the price–quality heuristic. *Journal of Marketing Research*, *51*(2), 153–164.

Goll, I., & Rasheed, A. M. (1997). Rational decision-making and firm performance: the moderating role of the environment. *Strategic Management Journal*, *18*(7), 583–591.

Goodrich, K. (2014). The gender gap: Brain-processing differences between the sexes shape attitudes about online advertising. *Journal of Advertising Research*, *54*(1), 32–43.

Gotlieb, J. B. (1989). Developing more effective price communication in services marketing. *Journal of Services Marketing*, *3*(4), 25–35.

Grewal, D., Herhausen, D., Ludwig, S., & Ordenes, F. V. (2022). The future of digital communication research: Considering dynamics and multimodality. *Journal of Retailing*, *98*(2), 224–240.

Guercini, S. (2019). Heuristics as tales from the field: the problem of scope. *Mind & Society*, *18*(2), 191–205.

Guercini, S., & Freeman, S. M. (2023). How international marketers make decisions: exploring approaches to learning and using heuristics. *International Marketing Review*, *40*(3), 429–451.

Guercini, S., & Lechner, C. (2021). New challenges for business actors and positive heuristics. *Management Decision*, *59*(7), 1585–1597.

Guercini, S., La Rocca, A., Runfola, A., & Snehota, I. (2014). Interaction behaviors in business relationships and heuristics: Issues for management and research agenda. *Industrial Marketing Management*, *43*(6), 929–937.

Guercini, S., La Rocca, A., Runfola, A., & Snehota, I. (2015). Heuristics in customer-supplier interaction. *Industrial Marketing Management*, *48*, 26–37.

Guercini, S., La Rocca, A., & Snehota, I. (2022). Decisions when interacting in customer-supplier relationships. *Industrial Marketing Management*, *105*, 380–387.

Gunasti, K., & Ross Jr, W. T. (2010). How and when alphanumeric brand names affect consumer preferences. *Journal of Marketing Research*, *47*(6), 1177–1192.

Hanson, W. A., & Putler, D. S. (1996). Hits and misses: Herd behavior and online product popularity. *Marketing letters*, *7*, 297–305.

Harris, J., & Gupta, P. (2008). 'You should buy this one!' the influence of online recommendations on product attitudes and choice confidence. *International Journal of Electronic Marketing and Retailing*, *2*(2), 176–189.

Harsanyi, J. C. (1955). Cardinal welfare, individualistic ethics, and interpersonal comparisons of utility. *Journal of Political Economy*, *63*(4), 309–321.

Hauser, J. R. (2014). Consideration-set heuristics. *Journal of Business Research*, *67*(8), 1688–1699.

Hauser, J. R., Toubia, O., Evgeniou, T., Befurt, R., & Dzyabura, D. (2010). Disjunctions of conjunctions, cognitive simplicity, and consideration sets. *Journal of Marketing Research*, *47*(3), 485–496.

Hauser, J. R., & Wernerfelt, B. (1990). An evaluation cost model of consideration sets. *Journal of Consumer Research*, *16*(4), 393–408.

Hausman, A. (2000). A multi-method investigation of consumer motivations in impulse buying behavior. *Journal of Consumer Marketing*, *17*(5), 403–419.

Higgins, L., & O'Leary, K. (2022). 'Clap for "some" carers': Problematizing heroism and ableist tenets of heroic discourse through the experiences of parent-carers. *Marketing Theory*, *23*(1), 11–33.

Hinterhuber, A. (2015). Violations of rational choice principles in pricing decisions. *Industrial Marketing Management*, *47*, 65–74.

Hoek, J., Roling, N., & Holdsworth, D. (2013). Ethical claims and labelling: An analysis of consumers' beliefs and choice behaviours. *Journal of Marketing Management*, *29*(7–8), 772–792.

Homer, P. M., & Mukherjee, S. (2018). The impact of dietary supplement form and dosage on perceived efficacy. *Journal of Consumer Marketing*, *35*(2), 228–238.

Ioannou, G., Kritikos, M., & Prastacos, G. (2003). A problem generator-solver heuristic for vehicle routing with soft time windows. *Omega*, *31*(1), 41–53.

Jayakumar, T. (2016). Behavioral lessons from Flipkart's big-billion day sale. *Competitiveness Review*, *26*(4), 453–475.

Jeon, Y. (2022). Let me transfer you to our AI-based manager: Impact of manager-level job titles assigned to AI-based agents on marketing outcomes. *Journal of Business Research*, *145*, 892–904.

Johnson, J., & Tellis, G. J. (2005). Blowing bubbles: Heuristics and biases in the run-up of stock prices. *Journal of the Academy of Marketing Science*, *33*(4), 486–503.

Johnson, E. J., Shu, S. B., Dellaert, B. G., Fox, C., Goldstein, D. G., Häubl, G., Larrick, R. P., Payne, J. W., Peters, E., Schkade, D., Wansink, B., & Weber, E. U. (2012). Beyond nudges: Tools of a choice architecture. *Marketing letters*, *23*, 487–504.

Kahneman, D. (2011). *Thinking, fast and slow*. Penguin Books, London.

Kamakura, W. A., Kim, B. D., & Lee, J. (1996). Modeling preference and structural heterogeneity in consumer choice. *Marketing Science*, *15*(2), 152–172.

Kappe, E., Stadler Blank, A., & DeSarbo, W. S. (2018). A random coefficients mixture hidden Markov model for marketing research. *International Journal of Research in Marketing*, *35*(3), 415–431.

Katsikopoulos, K. V., Şimşek, O., Buckmann, M., & Gigerenzer, G. (2020). Classification in the wild. *The science and art of transparent decision making*. MIT Press, Cambridge, Mass.

Ketron, S., Spears, N., & Dai, B. (2016). Overcoming information overload in retail environments: Imagination and sales promotion in a wine context. *Journal of Retailing and Consumer Services*, *33*, 23–32.

Kienzler, M. (2018). Value-based pricing and cognitive biases: An overview for business markets. *Industrial Marketing Management*, *68*, 86–94.

Kinard, B. R., Capella, M. L., & Bonner, G. (2013). Odd pricing effects: an examination using adaptation-level theory. *Journal of Product & Brand Management*, *22*(1), 87–94.

Kivetz, R., & Simonson, I. (2003). The idiosyncratic fit heuristic: Effort advantage as a determinant of consumer response to loyalty programs. *Journal of Marketing Research*, *40*(4), 454–467.

Konopka, R., Wright, M. J., Avis, M., & Feetham, P. M. (2019). If you think about it more, do you want it more? the case of fairtrade. *European Journal of Marketing*, *53*(12), 2556–2581.

Kordrostami, E., Liu-Thompkins, Y., & Rahmani, V. (2022). Coordinating supply-related scarcity appeals with online reviews. *Marketing Letters*, *33*(3), 471–484.

Korte, B., & Lovasz, L. (1985). Basis graphs of greedoids and two-connectivity. In R. W. Cottle (ed.), *Mathematical Programming Essays in Honor of George B. Dantzig Part I*. North-Holland, Amsterdam, 158–165.

Krieger, A. M., & Green, P. E. (1991). Designing pareto optimal stimuli for multiattribute choice experiments. *Marketing Letters*, *2*(4), 337–348.

Kumar, S., & Pandey, M. (2017). The impact of psychological pricing strategy on consumers' buying behaviour: A qualitative study. *International Journal of Business and Systems Research*, *11*(1–2), 101–117.

Laroche, M., Kim, C., & Matsui, T. (2003). Which decision heuristics are used in consideration set formation? *Journal of Consumer Marketing*, *20*(3), 192–209.

Lee, F. S. J. (2013). Hospitality products and the consumer price-perceived quality heuristic: An empirical perspective. *Services Marketing Quarterly*, *34*(3), 205–214.

Lee, W. J., & Kim, D. (1993). Optimal and heuristic decision strategies for integrated production and marketing planning. *Decision Sciences*, *24*(6), 1203–1214.

Lu, L., & Posner, M. E. (1994). Approximation procedures for the one-warehouse multi-retailer system. *Management Science*, *40*(10), 1305–1316.

Madrigal, R. (2001). Social identity effects in a belief-attitude-intentions hierarchy: Implications for corporate sponsorship. *Psychology and Marketing*, *18*(2), 145–165.

Maheswaran, D., Mackie, D. M., & Chaiken, S. (1992). Brand name as a heuristic cue: The effects of task importance and expectancy confirmation on consumer judgments. *Journal of Consumer Psychology*, *1*(4), 317–336.

Marewski, J. N., Gaissmaier, W., & Gigerenzer, G. (2010). Good judgments do not require complex cognition. *Cognitive processing*, *11*, 103–121.

Marozzo, V., Raimondo, M. A., Miceli, G., & Scopelliti, I. (2020). Effects of au naturel packaging colors on willingness to pay for healthy food. *Psychology and Marketing*, *37*(7), 913–927.

Mattila, A. (1998). An examination of consumers' use of heuristic cues in making satisfaction judgments. *Psychology and Marketing*, *15*(5), 477–501.

Memarpour, M., Hassannayebi, E., Fattahi Miab, N., & Farjad, A. (2021). Dynamic allocation of promotional budgets based on maximizing customer equity. *Operational Research*, *21*(4), 2365–2389.

Meneses, G. D. (2010). Refuting fear in heuristics and in recycling promotion. *Journal of Business Research*, *63*(2), 104–110.

Merlo, O., Lukas, B. A., & Whitwell, G. J. (2008). Heuristics revisited: Implications for marketing research and practice. *Marketing Theory*, *8*(2), 189–204.

Mero, J., Vanninen, H., & Keränen, J. (2023). B2B influencer marketing: Conceptualization and four managerial strategies. *Industrial Marketing Management*, *108*, 79–93.

Messick, D. M. (1993). Equality as a decision heuristic. In Mellers, B. A. & Baron, J. (eds.), *Psychological perspectives on justice: Theory and applications*. Cambridge University Press, Cambridge, 11–31.

Moinzadeh, K. (1997). Replenishment and stocking policies for inventory systems with random deal offerings. *Management Science*, *43*(3), 334–342.

Morrin, M., Inman, J. J., Broniarczyk, S. M., Nenkov, G. Y., & Reuter, J. (2012). Investing for retirement: The moderating effect of fund assortment size on the 1/n heuristic. *Journal of Marketing Research, 49*(4), 537–550.

Moser, A. K. (2016). Buying organic – decision-making heuristics and empirical evidence from germany. *Journal of Consumer Marketing, 33*(7), 552–561.

Mousavi, S., & Gigerenzer, G. (2014). Risk, uncertainty, and heuristics. *Journal of Business Research, 67*(8), 1671–1678.

Mowen, J. C., & Gaeth, G. J. (1992). The evaluation stage in marketing decision making. *Journal of the Academy of Marketing Science, 20*(2), 177–187.

Nagle, T. T., & Holden, R. K. (1995). *The strategy and tactics of pricing.* Prentis Hall, Englewood Cliffs, NJ.

Najafi-Ghobadi, S., Bagherinejad, J., & Taleizadeh, A. A. (2022). Optimal marketing policy for managing new generation products in the presence of forward-looking customers by considering product diffusion. *Journal of Modelling in Management, 17*(2), 633–654.

Nelson, R. R. (2008). Bounded rationality, cognitive maps, and trial and error learning. *Journal of Economic Behavior & Organization, 67*(1), 78–89.

O'Donnell, M., & Evers, E. R. K. (2019). Preference reversals in willingness to pay and choice. *Journal of Consumer Research, 45*(6), 1315–1330.

Oh, S., Sourirajan, K., & Ettl, M. (2014). Joint pricing and production decisions in an assemble-to-order system. *Manufacturing and Service Operations Management, 16*(4), 529–543.

Ommen, N. O., Heußler, T., Backhaus, C., Michaelis, M., & Ahlert, D. (2010). The Impact of Country-of-Origin and Joy on Product Evaluation: A Comparison of Chinese and German Intimate Apparel. *Journal of Global Fashion Marketing, 1*(2), 89–99.

Ordabayeva, N., & Chandon, P. (2013). Predicting and managing consumers' package size impressions. *Journal of Marketing, 77*(5), 123–137.

Otterbring, T. (2021). Peer presence promotes popular choices: A "Spicy" field study on social influence and brand choice. *Journal of Retailing and Consumer Services, 61*, 102594.

Otto, P. (2008). A system dynamics model as a decision aid in evaluating and communicating complex market entry strategies. *Journal of Business Research, 61*(11), 1173–1181.

Park, C. W., & Lessig, V. P. (1981). Familiarity and its impact on consumer decision biases and heuristics. *Journal of consumer research, 8*(2), 223–230.

Paulssen, M., & Bagozzi, R. P. (2005). A self-regulatory model of consideration set formation. *Psychology & Marketing, 22*(10), 785–812.

Payne, J. W. (1976). Heuristic search processes in decision making. Advances in Consumer Research, 3, 321–327.

Ritch, E. L. (2015). Consumers interpreting sustainability: Moving beyond food to fashion. *International Journal of Retail and Distribution Management, 43*(12), 1162–1181.

Rooderkerk, R. P., van Heerde, H. J., & Bijmolt, T. H. A. (2013). Optimizing retail assortments. *Marketing Science, 32*(5), 699–715.

Saab, A. B., & Botelho, D. (2020). Are organizational buyers rational? using price heuristics in functional risk judgment. *Industrial Marketing Management, 85*, 141–151.

Samson, A., & Voyer, B. G. (2012). Two minds, three ways: Dual system and dual process models in consumer psychology. *AMS Review, 2*(2–4), 48–71.

Schulze, C., Schöler, L., & Skiera, B. (2014). Not all fun and games: Viral marketing for utilitarian products. *Journal of Marketing, 78*(1), 1–19.

Schamp, C., Heitmann, M., & Katzenstein, R. (2019). Consideration of ethical attributes along the consumer decision-making journey. *Journal of the Academy of Marketing Science, 47*(2), 328–348.

Sela, A., & Berger, J. (2012). How attribute quantity influences option choice. *Journal of Marketing Research, 49*(6), 942–953.

Sevilla, J., & Kahn, B. E. (2014). The completeness heuristic: Product shape completeness influences size perceptions, preference, and consumption. *Journal of Marketing Research, 51*(1), 57–68.

Sheth, J. N., & Venkatesan, M. (1968). Risk-reduction processes in repetitive consumer behavior. *Journal of Marketing Research, 5*(3), 307–310.

Shi, S. W., & Zhang, J. (2014). Usage experience with decision aids and evolution of online purchase behavior. *Marketing Science, 33*(6), 871–882.

Simon, H. A. (1955). A behavioral model of rational choice. *The Quarterly Journal of Economics*, 99–118.

Simon, H. A. (1990). Invariants of human behavior. *Annual Review of Psychology, 41*(1), 1–20.

Simpson, P. M., Siguaw, J. A., & Cadogan, J. W. (2008). Understanding the consumer propensity to observe. *European Journal of Marketing, 42*(1–2), 196–221.

Singal, R., Besbes, O., Desir, A., Goyal, V., & Iyengar, G. (2022). Shapley meets uniform: An axiomatic framework for attribution in online advertising. *Management Science, 68*(10), 7457–7479.

Smith, D., Menon, S., & Sivakumar, K. (2005). Online peer and editorial recommendations, trust, and choice in virtual markets. *Journal of Interactive Marketing, 19*(3), 15–37.

Soll, J. B., Keeney, R. L., & Larrick, R. P. (2013). Consumer misunderstanding of credit card use. *Journal of Public Policy and Marketing, 32*(1), 66–81.

Souchon, A. L., Hughes, P., Farrell, A. M., Nemkova, E., & Oliveira, J. S. (2016). Spontaneity and international marketing performance. *International Marketing Review, 33*(5), 671–690.

Thaler, R. H. (2018). Nudge, not sludge. *Science, 361*(6401), 431–431.

Thaler, R. H., & Sunstein, C. R. (2008). *Nudge. Improving decisions about health, wealth, and happiness*. Penguin Books, London.

Titus, P. A. (2000). Marketing and the creative problem-solving process. *Journal of Marketing Education, 22*(3), 225–235.

Todd, P. M., & Gigerenzer, G. E. (2012). *Ecological rationality: Intelligence in the world*. Oxford University Press, Oxford.

Tversky, A., & Kahneman, D. (1974). Judgment under Uncertainty: Heuristics and Biases: Biases in judgments reveal some heuristics of thinking under uncertainty. *Science, 185*(4157), 1124–1131.

Vanharanta, M., & Easton, G. (2010). Intuitive managerial thinking; the use of mental simulations in the industrial marketing context. *Industrial Marketing Management, 39*(3), 425–436.

Varadarajan, R. (2010). Strategic marketing and marketing strategy: domain, definition, fundamental issues and foundational premises. *Journal of the Academy of Marketing Science, 38*, 119–140.

Vega-Zamora, M., Torres-Ruiz, F. J., Murgado-Armenteros, E. M., & Parras-Rosa, M. (2014). Organic as a heuristic cue: What Spanish consumers mean by organic foods. *Psychology and Marketing, 31*(5), 349–359.

Wang, H., Shen, M., (Amy) Song, Y., & Phau, I. (2020). Do up-displayed eco-friendly products always perform better? the moderating role of psychological distance. *Journal of Business Research, 114*, 198–212.

Wang, Y., Tariq, S., & Alvi, T. H. (2021). How primary and supplementary reviews affect consumer decision making? Roles of psychological and managerial mechanisms. *Electronic Commerce Research and Applications, 46*, 101032.

Winter, S. G. (2000). The satisfyicing principle in capability learning. *Strategic management journal, 21*(10–11), 981–996.

Yang, S., Zhao, Y., Erdem, T., & Zhao, Y. (2010). Modeling the intrahousehold behavioral interaction. *Journal of Marketing Research, 47*(3), 470–484.

Yao, J., & Oppewal, H. (2016). Unit pricing matters more when consumers are under time pressure. *European Journal of Marketing, 50*(5–6), 1094–1114.

Yee, M., Dahan, E., Hauser, J. R., & Orlin, J. (2007). Greedoid-based noncompensatory inference. *Marketing Science, 26*(4), 532–549.

Zajonc, R. B. (1968). Attitudinal effects of mere exposure. *Journal of Personality and Social Psychology, 9*(2), 1–27.

Zander, K., & Hamm, U. (2012). Information search behaviour and its determinants: The case of ethical attributes of organic food. *International Journal of Consumer Studies, 36*(3), 307–316.

Zhu, G., Chryssochoidis, G., & Zhou, L. (2019). Do extra ingredients on the package lead to extra calorie estimates? *European Journal of Marketing, 53*(11), 2293–2321.

4. A set of rules for the marketers' adaptive toolbox

4.1   MARKETERS' HEURISTICS

After examining heuristics in consumer decision making in the previous chapter, the focus in this chapter shifts to marketers and their decision-making models. Marketers have different profiles, encompassing entrepreneurs, managers and their organizations. The content of the chapter is related in many ways to that of the previous chapter. For marketers, heuristics become relevant in at least two contexts: (1) the analysis of the formation of judgments and choices, and thus of the cognition and behavior of customers and other market actors; (2) the patterns followed in decision formation by managers and entrepreneurs. In essence, marketers refer to heuristics not only as architects of the choices of other actors, starting with consumers, but also and primarily as decision makers themselves. For marketers, heuristics can represent tools for problem solving to which they pay attention for aspects such as model effectiveness or legitimacy (Guercini, La Rocca, Runfola and Snehota, 2015). This is because heuristics can take on criticality, consequently being the subject of limited sharing with others within or outside the organization, either to maintain advantageous conditions derived from their use or to privilege the use of more complex and legitimized decision-making models in communication (Guercini, La Rocca, Runfola and Snehota, 2015).

Marketing is certainly one of the most prominent areas among the applications of heuristics studies, as the presence of simple models that in some cases predict more accurately than complex and sophisticated models is recognized (Brighton and Gigerenzer, 2015). The presence of applications to marketing in the writings of authors who specifically study heuristics have in some cases strong connections to general management, where there are works that have been influential in the study of the topic even outside of management (Barnard, 1938; Simon, 1979).

In many cases, research on marketers' decision making highlights the prevalence of heuristics in the behaviors of entrepreneurs and managers, without necessarily comparing them with alternative decision-making models. For example, Kordrostami, Liu-Thompkins, and Rahmani (2022) see supply-related scarcity appeal as a common marketing tactic that occurs when a firm limits the number of products available to the market (Ku, Kuo and Kuo, 2012). Similarly, He and Iorger (2005) examine the buying strategies of small buyers in online e-marketplaces, identifying buyer coalition formation and bundle search strategies. Their proposed mechanism includes a heuristic bundle search algorithm and distributed coalitions, a mechanism that is tested by them through simulation.

The finding of the prevalence of heuristics in marketers' decision making appears to be reinforced by the identification of very general heuristics that find use in many domains. Examples of this are some recurring rules in decision making related to firm-market relationships, among which are the following: (1) multipliers; (2) thresholds; and (3) calends (Guercini, 2019).

"Multipliers" are an often important element in solving many problems, from pricing (mark-up) to forecasting sales from partial data. For example, in the textile industry (Guercini and Runfola, 2021) it has been found that the event of attending trade fairs/exhibitions is not only an opportunity to contact customers and observe competitors, but also an essential basis for estimating the budget (sales forecast) for the season/year, calculated by applying a multiplier (usually between 10 and 15) to the amount of orders obtained at the trade fairs (one or more) attended (Guercini, 2019).

The multiplier heuristic finds application of the "mark-up" for pricing. Business decision makers define the selling price by applying, precisely, a multiplier, the mark-up (e.g., multiplying the purchasing price by 1.2 or 2.5 to get the selling price, depending on the type of product and distribution format) to the purchase price, to define the price to be displayed for sale to the end customer.

We can describe the "building blocks" of the following multiplicative heuristics (Gigerenzer and Brighton, 2009): (a) a search rule, which indicates to search for input data (e.g., orders collected at a reference fair, or the purchase price of a product); (b) a stop rule, whereby the search stops when input data (data on orders collected, price paid to the supplier per unit of product) has been acquired; (c) a decision rule, which consists of applying the multiplier to the input data, which may vary depending on the decision context. Here the scope problem emerges at two levels: at the scope level of the rule as a whole (the tasks in which to use the multiplication operation); at the scope level of the factor used at the block level (for example, the numerical value of the multiplier).

"Multipliers" can be found in the literature whenever the topic of mark-up is identified (Akçay, Natarajan and Xu, 2010; Arcelus and Srinivasa, 1987; Shafahi and Haghani, 2014; Takano, Ishii and Muraki, 2014), as well as when discussing methods for decision-making (Cotterill and Putsis, 2001; Greenbank, 1999; Vilcassim and Chintagunta, 1995). In the field of advertising, heuristics have been considered in defining the advertising budget, which consists of a multiplier (percentage) of expected sales (Lilien, Silk, Choffray and Rao, 1976; Zufryden, 1989). This also includes work that examines optimization heuristics, using the term in the sense of an algorithm capable of achieving this result in the context of using software that processes a computer-based, interactive marketing model (Basu and Batra, 1988). Also in relation to advertising budget choices, other studies highlight the relationship between brand size in terms of sales and the share of the budget to be allocated to advertising, pointing to a contrary to the sale proportion or "compensatory parity heuristics", according to which "large (small) brands should invest in advertising proportionally less (more) than small (large) brands" (Naik, Prasad and Sethi, 2008, p. 129).

The "threshold" heuristic emerges when a judgment or choice depends on the outcome of whether a certain predetermined or otherwise definable threshold is reached based on the judgment or choice. The threshold can be found primarily as a satisfactory level (Artinger, Gigerenzer and Jacobs, 2022), but also in other heuristics. For example, in a survey of a group of textile firms (Guercini and Runfola, 2021), a rule emerged that was applied to sales in individual foreign markets and adopted by firms with a low country risk appetite, indicating that exports to a single foreign country should be kept within a certain threshold of total sales (e.g., within 10 percent). This rule was justified by the need to contain country risk by distributing it among several countries, and was considered so important that the founder of one of the companies studied had passed it on to his children as an important indication for the future of the company, and the children had adhered to it in their years of management (Guercini and Freeman, 2023).

Threshold heuristics have the following "building blocks" (Gigerenzer and Brighton, 2009): (a) a search rule, which indicates to search for input data (e.g., the current level of sales in a country compared to total sales); (b) a stop rule, which indicates to stop when input data have been acquired (percentage compared to total sales, or absolute value); and (c) a decision rule, whereby the threshold is applied to the input data and can vary depending on the decision context. The scope problem arises for threshold heuristics at two levels: the scope of the rule as a whole (the application of a threshold); the scope of the factor used at the block level (e.g., the numerical value of the threshold).

"Thresholds" are present in other cases (Bhaskaran, Ramachandran and Semple, 2010; Deshpande, Cohen and Donohue, 2003), e.g., whenever a watershed level is defined, at which judgment changes and a change in behavior is expected.

Heuristics of "calends" emerge when applying certain dates/days identified in a calendar, which define the time at which a judgment and/or choice should be defined, from some input data referable to these dates. For example, from the research on textile companies already mentioned (Guercini and Runfola, 2021) emerged the case of a company engaged in the purchase of expensive raw materials produced in distant countries and in certain seasons of the year (such as cashmere for the production of luxury garments). This company had identified certain weeks or calends in which to observe commodity price trends in order to form an estimate of price trends over the coming year (for example, certain days in April, when shearing is concentrated in China and Central Asia). The decision for these types of enterprises is very delicate because making the mistake of buying means either running out of raw material to process during the year, or paying additional costs that can eliminate profit margins considering the impact of raw material costs on the price of sales. These dates (or calends) were kept confidential by entrepreneurs, even if they were known in the industry, because their knowledge was still considered a competitive factor, and the heuristics of calends applied by one company might differ slightly from those applied by another company.

In the pre-industrial world, calends allowed for forecasting with few means and in a transparent way, so observing the weather at certain times of the year allowed for estimates of the season or harvest. Again, the "building blocks" of calends heuristics were those already identified for the heuristics previously described (Gigerenzer and Brighton, 2009): (a) a search rule, which in this case consists of acquiring an input data on a specific day (e.g., the price level of a specific commodity on some specific days of the year, either given directly or calculated indirectly); (b) a stopping rule, whereby to stop when the input data has been acquired (e.g., the absolute value and/or price trends on those days); and (c) a decision rule, whereby the judgment or choice is made based on the input data, which may vary depending on the decision context.

The problem of the scope of the calends again arises at two levels: scope of the rule as a whole; and scope of the factor used at the block level (e.g., which days to indicate or the method for identifying them; units of time other than days).

In summary, what we call "calends" are rules based on identifying the appropriate time at which to engage in behavior, such as gathering information and making a judgment or choice (Jagannathan, Marakani, Takehara and Wang, 2012; Useem, 2006); they can be related to literature dealing with issues such as seasonality in new product launches (Bruce, Daly and Kahn, 2007; Radas and Shugan, 1998) and planning or promoting at the right time in a season or cycle (Borle, Singh and Jain, 2008; Rajagopalan and Swaminathan, 2001).

The temporal dimension that characterizes calends can also be found in other types of heuristics. For example, making the customer wait is examined as a heuristic that, although it may carry negative evaluation risks, can also be associated with a perception of higher product quality and value (Giebelhausen, Robinson, and Cronin, 2021). Not only is this a heuristic for the marketer, but its operation is grounded in the fact that expectation can be a cue that can stimulate heuristics about the customer's perception of the accessibility and exclusivity of the product, so the adoption of such a heuristic is a way for the marketer to assume a role as an architect of customer choice.

Relevant heuristics for marketers are not only those adoptable directly for their own decisions, but also those adopted by other market actors (such as competitors, customers, influencers), which may be other managers and entrepreneurs within their organizations, or consumers. As we saw in the previous chapter, there is a large literature on heuristics adopted by consumers that examines how these have relevance to the formation of judgments and choices. Knowledge of these heuristics is relevant to marketers' judgments and choices, including activities that may be relevant to the choice context of other actors, according to the logic inherent in the choice architect (Thaler and Sustein, 2008).

Read, Dew, Sarasvathy, Song, and Wiltbank (2009) question the marketing approach segued by entrepreneurs and managers with little entrepreneurial expertise, showing that there is a significant difference in the heuristics employed by the two types of marketers. Specifically, actors who are experienced entrepreneurs tend to use effectual or nonpredictive logic to deal with market uncertainty and help build new markets, following an "effectuation heuristic" or "heuristics advocated by an effectual logic", where "effectuation is an inversion of predictive rationality" (Read, Dew, Sarasvathy, Song, and Wiltbank, 2009, p. 2).

Among the ways to analyze the heuristics adopted by marketers, one of the most relevant is to start from the specifics of the marketing domain in which they are employed. The next sections examine some of the most relevant issues in the literature under review, from which several heuristics emerge that contribute to the adaptive toolbox of the marketers.

4.2   HEURISTICS IN CUSTOMER/SUPPLIER CLASSIFICATION, SELECTION AND TARGETING

Gigerenzer and Gaissmaier (2011) examine the role of some heuristics for customer classification. In particular, the proposed theme is that of distinguishing customers who are likely to buy again in a given time frame (active customers) from those who are not (inactive customers). Companies have a large customer database containing the amount, type, and date of each customer's previous purchases. Based on this information, managers may need to predict which customers will be active in the future. Gigerenzer and Gaissmeier (2011) write that "statistically sophisticated academics might opt for a Bayesian analysis, regression analysis, or some other optimizing strategy to predict the probability that a customer with a given purchase history is active at some future time. Researchers in business share this vision, and the state-of-the-art approach is the Pareto/NBD model ..." (Gigerenzer and Gaissmeier, 2011, p. 455) citing the negative binomial distribution (Schmittlein and Peterson, 1994). However, citing the work of Wübben and Wangenheim (2008), Gigerenzer and Gaissmaier report that expert managers use "a simple recency-of-last-purchase rule" that essentially corresponds to the "hiatus heuristic" defined as follows: "if a customer has not purchased within a certain number of months (the hiatus), the customer is classified as inactive; otherwise, the customer is classified as active" (Gigerenzer and Gaissmaier, 2011, p. 455). In fact, in their article published in the *Journal of Marketing*, Wübben and Wangenheim (2008) propose the study of a "hiatus heuristic" as an intuitive rule based on a limited body of information, but one that is frequently resorted to (Parikh 1994). In specific industries (apparel distribution, airlines, digital music distribution), the effectiveness of the "hiatus heuristic" is compared with that of statistically more sophisticated rules employed in customer database analysis software and based on more information and processing capacity, and it is verified that the rule heuristic is more accurate than such rules (particularly the Pareto NBD model) in predicting the characteristic of "active customer" or "inactive customer" (Wübben and Wangenheim 2008). This investigation suggests that heuristics may be more effective than decision-making models that take into account a larger number of parameters, an aspect that is also known as "less is more effect" (Goldstein and Gigerenzer, 1999) and is present in management where it is considered effective to recognize and focus on a few relevant aspects (Etzioni, 2001).

The use of heuristics to evaluate a list of suppliers or customers and arrive at a short list of a few alternatives also emerges from studies conducted in business-to-business markets (Wu, Little, and Low, 2016). Some research is available that challenges the view of heuristics as a source of biases based on emerging evidence from the study of decision-making models adopted by banking institutions in customer management. In general, in marketing as in other areas of management, heuristics can translate the concept of competitive priorities into managerial parameters, thus enabling the incorporation of relevant factors into the process of forming judgments and choices (for the case of manufacturing process design, see Sheu and Krajewski, 1996).

As much as some research shows how business actor behavior can be analogous to consumer behavior when conditions of information access and data processing capabilities are substantially similar (Dugar and Chamola, 2021), the business actor is the subject of specific analyses with different premises and outcomes. Research conducted by Bauer, Schmitt, Morwitz and Winer (2013) examines how sales managers in retail banking perform some typical customer management prediction tasks. The growing importance of customer management to both practitioners and academics requires addressing a knowledge gap about how managers actually make decisions on this topic. To address this gap, the study by Bauer and colleagues uses a specific tool to track the customer management process and it emerges that the majority of managers take an adaptive approach and that some managers use fast and frugal heuristics, based on their own experience. This way of decision making does not impact the accuracy of the predictions, and the use of fast and frugal heuristics is associated with proportionally greater use of data/cues with high predictive quality and such that result in significant improvement in accuracy (Bauer, Schmitt, Morwitz and Winer, 2013, pp. 436ff.). Another research conducted on how customer management decisions are made carried out on some leading Nordic retail banks indicates how the use of managerial heuristics is surprisingly widespread and, contrary to what might be suggested by previous research (counterintuitively), that decision making based on heuristics such as rules of thumb can frequently outweigh the weight of measures such as customer lifetime value in customer management decisions (Persson and Ryals, 2014). This study, after highlighting on a descriptive level how widespread the use of heuristics is in the area of customer management for the services offered by these banks, takes on a normative level an open stance about the outcome of the use of these decision models, partly because they have been adopted by successful banks, but that it then becomes important for both managers and academics to understand the conditions under which heuristic decision making can be more successful than and analytical approach (Persson and Ryals, 2014, pp. 1725ff.).

Decision making by financial system actors had been addressed by Gwin (1985) for financial institution branching decisions. These decisions were assumed to be similar to those made for retail site location decisions, being made through an assessment of potential locations at the micro level. The strengths and weaknesses of this type of assessment process are that of careful examination through exploration, as it can be quite costly. Gwin proposed for this a "macro heuristic" that would allow an initial selection phase to be done, which is also important in reducing the cost of decision making, in such a way as to focus the micro-type analysis on a less extensive subset of alternatives than the one initially examined, resulting in reduced costs. Such a process could be important especially when there were very expensive alternatives to evaluate, for example located in other states (Gwin, 1985, pp. 259 ff.).

Gahler and Hruschka (2023) compare 11 heuristic pricing rules that do not require knowledge of the price response function, identifying certain features that are associated with the best performing heuristics. To these are added general optimization methods, which include "meta-heuristics," compared to traditional optimization models, and especially in choices related to customers for starting a new store (Hurley, Mouthinho and Witt, 1998).

The use of heuristics in retailers' assortment selection, and thus in the shopping trip destination decision, is examined by Chernev (2008), who examines a marketing-relevant consumer decision strategy referred to as the "quantity-matching heuristic". Chernev examines consumer strategies, but these can easily suggest heuristics that can be adopted by distributors, particularly retailers, who consequently adopt their own heuristics to encourage choices favorable to them by consumers (following a "choice architect" logic). According to this heuristic, assortment will be preferred as much as the number of available options matches the number of items to be purchased. In other words, the quantity-matching heuristic is one whereby consumers decide on a shopping trip when they find a match between the size of an assortment and the number of to-be-purchased items puts consumers in a position to simplify the selection process and eliminate the need for cost-benefit evaluations of individual choice alternatives (Chernev, 2008, p. 173). Rooderkerk, Heerde, and Bijmolt (2013) study the problem of the retailer who intends to find the assortment that maximizes the category profit. To do this they develop a method involving the proposed "new very large neighborhood search (VLNS) heuristics" (Rooderkerk, Heerde, and Bijmolt, 2013, p. 712). Lim, Rodrigues, and Zhang (2004) examine heuristic models for efficient shelf-space allocation by retailers, comparing different types of tools (comprising different heuristic algorithms such as the one developed by Yang, 2001) with a metaheuristic approach to space allocation. Not only can heuristics characterize consumers' decisions regarding assortment, but a study by Ülkümen, Chakravarti, and Morwitz (2010) suggests that it is consumers' exposure to different types of categories or assortments in a context of which consumers have had experience (context 1) that contributes to a mind-set that changes how consumers process information in a new decision context not unrelated to the previous one (context 2). This study examines the "susceptibility to heuristics" between the effects on decisions in one context and the other, so if in context 1 the consumer had been exposed to broad categories, in dealing with context 2 we will have the "use of few, salient contextual cues influences reliance on heuristics", while if in context 1 the consumer had been exposed to narrow categories, in addressing context 2 we will have the "use of both salient and nonsalient cues influences reliance on heuristics" (Ülkümen, Chakravarti, and Morwitz, 2010, p. 661).

Hartmann, Nair, and Narayanan (2011) in their research on decision models used for targeting, propose a quasi-experimental approach to discuss "how regression discontinuity designs arise naturally in settings where firms target marketing activity at consumers" illustrating "how this aspect may be exploited for econometric inference of causal effects of marketing effort" (Hartmann, Nair and Narayanan, 2011, pp. 1079 and 1096). The authors propose to incorporate the use of heuristics in the formulation of such models, and thus to overcome the view of rules of thumb and heuristics prevalent in marketing efforts, whereby "heuristics had previously been thought of as a 'nuisance' issue that had to be dealt with an estimation by researchers of as evidence of inefficient marketing decision making by firms" (Hartmann, Nair and Narayanan, 2011, p. 1096). Hartmann and colleagues therefore propose using heuristics in targeting models adopted by marketers "by facilitating identification and are also useful to firms as they enable credible measurement of the return on investment on their marketing spend ... even if firms are unable to implement the individual-level policies that can be suggested by individual-level models" (Hartmann, Nair, and Narayanan, 2011, pp. 1095–1096).

The use of simple heuristics in forecasting for customer prioritization is examined by Huang (2012) comparing "simple heuristics" versus "more complicated models". The author demonstrates the usefulness of some forecasting heuristics, in the context of a study that answers the "why" and "when" questions about the empirical characteristics of a specific forecasting context for customer prioritization. Through simulations, it emerges that: (1) one is not usually able to identify the future "top-X% of customer in a customer base accurately, even if we know the exact data generation process" (Huang, 2012, p. 497); (2) tested through simulation it emerges how a simple heuristic can perform as well as a probabilistic model even; (3) the relative performance of the model and heuristics must be considered when testing the data. In essence, "the heuristic works because the minimal information it relies upon is relatively robust and relevant in a random world" (Huang, 2012, p. 497). Forecasting had been associated with other types of heuristics, such as the "adaptive extended exponential smoothing methodology" (AEES), which corresponded to a type of heuristic that "allows the model additional smoothing constant adaptability to improve forecasting accuracy", and that "when empirically tested ..., the heuristic AEES approach generally provided improved or comparable accuracy" (Metzer and Gomes, 1994, p. 372).

Knott, Hayes, and Neslin (2002) propose a next-product-to-buy (NPTB) model to improve the efficacy of cross-selling programs, where the NPTB model is a forecasting equation that can be used to predict which product is most likely to be next purchased by a particular customer. To prove the effectiveness of the proposed model, the authors compare it with models they describe as heuristic, evidently seeing the former as a non-heuristic model in that it lacks the character of simplicity, seeing heuristics as tools that can be easily activated without special processing effort on the part of the decision maker. The article thus speaks of "demographics heuristic" referring to a certain income threshold, above which the marketer (in the example a banking institution interested in placing financial products as loans) selects the customer as a potential target (Knott, Hayes, and Neslin, 2002, p. 65). The article is interesting because it highlights how certain segmentation variables can be seen as cues for marketers' decision making in segmentation and target selection. Other studies employ heuristic algorithms to forecast supply and demand and predict whether or not there appears to be a shortage in the market in the next year (Lin, Wang, Lo, Hsu, and Wang, 2006).

Liu and Wang (2010) propose using "80:20 heuristics" to identify the salient factors underlying the formulation of a marketing strategy. The use of heuristic algorithm is proposed in "treatment" problems, that is, "delivering the optimal product of service recommendation to the right customer", where typically "there are multiple products available to promote, and often there is a budget or quantity constraint due to limited resources. The situation can be described in an optimization problem formulation in which there is an objective and a set of constraints" (Lo and Pachamanova, 2015, pp. 79–80). To approach this problem, "uplift" or "true lift" modeling methods are examined to find customers whose decisions will be positively influenced by marketing interaction (Radcliffe and Surry, 1999).

4.3 MARKETERS' HEURISTICS FOR BUSINESS RELATIONSHIPS

In a business-to-business context, specifically examining a distribution network, Wang, Gu and Dong (2013) study the effects of a punishment event by going beyond dyadic view of punishment to see how it changes the attitudes and behaviors of other actors in the network. From a social learning perspective, the authors examine the "fairness heuristic" in this area, considering both a direct deterrence mechanism and a trust-building process in relation to the fairness judgement of the punishment (Wang, Gu, and Dong, 2013, p. 628). Applying equitable sanctions to the behavior of various actors within a distribution network has not only direct deterrence effects, but also effects at the indirect level by producing the generation of greater trust. The fairness heuristic is linked to the issue of trust-building (Lind, Kulik, Ambrose, and Park, 1993), whereby people are apparently sensitive to (un)farness in their relationship with others, using procedural justice judgments whose effects are mediated by the decision to accept or reject the directives of an authority. People may not be able to explore the causes of punishment, whereas they may form fairness judgments on the basis of social comparisons (Adams, 1963). The perception of fairness thus becomes an important element in determining the trust of other actors in the distribution network (Wang, Gu, and Dong, 2013, p. 630).

Of a different type, on the other hand, appears the "Chi-square-based heuristic statistical procedure", which on the basis of one study turns out to be superior to the regression method for setting prices to be offered in tenders with the aim of increasing both sales turnover and profits (Ravichandran, 2011).

Staying with customer-supplier relationships in a business-to-business market, a research gap is found in this area about the decision-making process behind the choices and about how the related decisions are reached (Guercini, La Rocca, Runfola and Snehota, 2014; 2015; Gummesson, 2014). In industrial marketing and purchasing research, it has been suggested that interactive situations with high customer-supplier involvement require decisions that reflect an "adaptive", rather than an "axiomatic" conception of rationality, calling for greater integration of industrial marketing research with research in the field of applied psychology (Guercini, La Rocca and Snehota, 2022).

The business marketing literature has dealt with the topic of heuristics with reference to specific issues, such as pricing policies (Saab and Botelho, 2022; Hinterhuber, 2015; Monroe, Rikala and Somervuori, 2015), negotiations in sales processes (Guercini, La Rocca, Runfola and Snehota, 2015), and more generally interaction processes in business networks (Guercini, La Rocca, and Snehota, 2022).

In managing business-to-business relationships between buyer and seller, viewed as temporary organizations, Ghazimatin, Mooi, and Heide (2021) speak of a "discriminating alignment heuristic" for relationship management involving governance mechanisms and multiple attributes.

Vanharanta and Easton (2010) examine the "recognition-primed decision (RPD) model" (Klein, 1989) presenting empirical evidence on how mental simulation is used in an industrial network context. This approach appears to be related to the Naturalistic Decision Making approach, which takes a view of intuition and the role of experience for decision making that is distinct from and in some respects at odds with the fast and frugal approach, and so with the heuristics and biases approach (Klein, 2017), both presented in the first chapter. The RPD model attempts to explain how proficient decision makers can often make good decisions without analytically comparing all the strengths and weaknesses of various options. The cognitive processes described by the RPD model are preferred in the presence of experienced participants, pressure by time constraints, and dynamic context. In particular, the RPD model is related to the notion of "mental simulation as one cognitive process that experts use under particular circumstances" (Vanharanta and Easton, 2010, p. 426). Experienced managers seem to use prior knowledge and experience, even in ways that are not conscious and through intuition understood as the "ability to translate experience into action" (Vanharanta and Easton, 2010, p. 426; Klein, 2004). The RPD model is an explicit description of recognition-based decision strategies, that can be compared with the "recognition heuristic" (Goldstein and Gigerenzer, 2002; Marewski, Gaissmaier, Schooler, Goldstein, and Gigerenzer, 2010) which is associated with familiarity (hence "familiarity heuristic") and defined in these terms: "if one of two alternatives is recognized and the other is not, then infer that the recognized alternative has the higher value with respect to the criterion" (Gigerenzer and Gaissmaier, 2011, p. 460).

4.4 MARKETERS' HEURISTICS IN ADVERTISING AND COMMUNICATION

Robustness is one of the features associated with decision-making models based on simple heuristics. Rubel and Naik (2017) examine this feature with reference to models for managing advertising resources. Their study identifies a countervailing effect in that "advertising effectiveness increases and the carryover effect decreases as robustness increases", furthermore, a "profit-volatility trade-off, similar to the returns-risk trade-off in finance, emerges, whereby the volatility of profit stream decreases at the expense of reduced total profit as robustness increases", furthermore, the study proves that "unlike for-profit companies, managers of nonprofit organizations should optimally allocate budgets opposite the advertising-to-sales ratio heuristic; that is advertise more (less) when sales are low (high)" (Rubel and Naik, 2017, p. 453).

Part of the research links the study of marketers' heuristics to studies of the biases associated with this decision-making model. The relationship between heuristics used for budget allocation decisions from data on previous spending on advertising and sales outcomes are examined by Hutchinson, Alba, and Eisenstein (2010), with research that focuses on different types of heuristics as sources of biases. Specifically, the authors begin with an assessment of the use of numerical data as a basis for many decisions by marketing managers. In the experimental model adopted by these authors, the decision maker receives historical data about different resource variables (e.g., spending on different types of advertising) and outcome data (e.g., sales over time) and must evaluate how to allocate budget among different activities to maximize future results. In this approach, the decision maker assumes causality between type of allocation and type of outcome. Several classes of heuristics are identified: (1) "difference-based heuristics", which compare adjacent changes in expenditures with changes in sales; (2) "trend-based heuristics", which compare overall trends in expenditures with sales; (3) "exemplar-based heuristics", which emulate the allocation pattern and observations with the highest sales (Hutchinson and Alba, 1997; Hutchinson, Alba, and Eisenstein, 2010, p. 628). Hutchinson, Alba, and Eisenstein (2010) arrive at the following results: biases exist that are strong enough to lead to seriously suboptimal decisions; graphical data displays, real-world experience, or explicit training do not reduce observed biases; the observed biases are well explained by a relatively small set of natural heuristics that managers use when making data-based allocation decisions (Hutchinson, Alba, and Eisenstein, 2010, p. 627). "Exemplar-based heuristics" are the most frequently used and are responsible for most of the biases, while the least used are "trend-based heuristics"; "difference-based heuristics" are the ones that generate the most extreme allocation solutions (Hutchinson, Alba and Eisenstein, 2010, pp. 638 ff.).

Kumar and Salo (2018) examine the problem of low click-through rates in digital advertising and "visual heuristics", or "visual preference heuristics" (Townsend and Kahn, 2014), which can be adopted by marketers to improve the performance of digital communication for example through email marketing. The "visual preference heuristic" suggests that consumers prefer information in visual form over verbal information for the presentation of, for example, a product, as images produce greater perceptions of variety than text (Townsend and Kahn, 2014, p. 994). Spatial perceptions as an area of research in marketing had already been related to the use of heuristics by consumers, who make distance judgments when deciding, for example, which store to visit or which street to take (Raghubir and Krishna, 1996), for example, speaking of "high as a volume heuristic", or "elongation heuristic" (Raghubir and Krishna, 1999). Kumar and Salo (2018) point out that

> design of email newsletters that consider e-mail characteristics should also include psychological aspects of human attention and visual heuristics into the design considerations ... the empirical evidence suggests that links placed in the left region are more likely to drive click-through rate than those placed in the right region of an email newsletter with links placed in the top-left region having the highest impact. We explain this phenomenon through information processing concepts drawn from cognitive psychology and visual heuristics. (Kumar and Salo, 2018, p. 537 and p. 546)

Communication can also be about emotion in the face of issues such as recycling behavior, where Meneses (2010) compares fear of environmental disasters with positive emotions of a contribution to environmental protection in both "environmental heuristics" and in promotional practice and environmental campaigns, recognizing that a focus only on fears is not fully justified. Ozuem, Howell, and Lancaster (2022) see the issue of integrated marketing communication (IMC) in a decentralized organizational structure and adopt a perspective of fast-and-frugal heuristics. In particular, these authors see heuristics as relevant to this theme in that they can be managed as a tool to achieve decision making in a coherent way, translating into simple rules to ensure the goals of IMC (Ozuem, Howell, and Lancaster, 2022, p. 275).

Hugh, Dolan, Harrigan, and Gray (2022) examine influencer marketing and identify heuristics that are adopted by actors who interact, particularly brands, with influencers to evaluate their effectiveness, highlighting how judgments can be based on heuristics grounded in a few cues, specifically examining indicators of popularity and attractiveness (Hugh, Dolan, Harrigan, and Gray,

2022, p. 3485ff.). The role of the influencer is the subject of the study by Rohde and Mau (2021) who identify a set of "social influence heuristics" aimed at capturing the relationship with the most interesting influencers. Seven of these heuristics are presented and discussed, comprising the "reciprocity heuristic", the "social proof heuristic", the "consistency heuristic", the "scarcity heuristic", the "linking heuristic", the "authority heuristic", and the "unity heuristic" (Rohde and Mau, 2021, pp. 2713 ff.). These heuristics have connections with more general rules or employed in other contexts, for example: the social proof heuristic is adopted because for most people, the positive comments from others about a product or influencer have an effect on the perception about that object (Cialdini and Goldstein, 2004; Reinikainen, Munnukka, Maity and Luoma-Aho, 2020); the reciprocity heuristic is as "tit-for-tat heuristic", which suggests to cooperate first and then imitate the other actor's last behavior (Axelrod, 1984; Cialdini and Goldstein, 2004; Gigerenzer and Brighton, 2009, p. 131).

Cornelissen (2003) considers the heuristic value of using metaphors for marketing actors, looking at categories such as the corporate identity metaphor and relationship marketing metaphor as examples, which can in this sense also be placed side by side with the metaphor that is surely also branding and the branding process. For example, the author recognizes as heuristics the need for "consistency and coherence in corporate communications and behavior", as far as "classifying/representing and distinguishing the organization" (Cornelissen, 2003, p. 215).

Still on the subject of branding, Scarpaci, Coupley, and Reed's (2018) study examines the "icon myth transfer effect" as a heuristic for cultural branding, in that the communication of national artists and cultural myths represent empirical insights for national cultural identity and generate top-of-mind, positive brand associations whose production can guide brand management. In essence, an "icon myths heuristic" is proposed for understanding and describing brands and as a pathway to cultural branding through an "icon myth transfer effect" (Scarpaci, Coupey, and Reed, 2018, p. 322).

The use of brand as a heuristic that can reduce risk in purchase decisions in business-to-business markets is examined in an article by Brown, Zablah, Bellenger, and Johnston (2011). Specifically, through in-depth interviews with managers, brands are viewed as risk-reducing heuristics, whereby the influence of brands in decision making grows as a function of risk. This hypothesis is confirmed through a survey-based study involving members of purchasing centers, from which it appears that the risk-brand sensitivity relationship is moderated by the intensity of competition, so the relationship is stronger when competition is low (Brown, Zablah, Bellenger, and Johnston, 2011, p. 195).

4.5   HEURISTICS IN INNOVATION SCREENING AND NEW PRODUCT SELECTION FOR THE MARKET

The topic of heuristics in marketing also passes through that of new product definition and launch. In this area, the term heuristics itself has been associated with creative methods, in line with the meaning of the term's Greek origin. Contributions on the role of heuristic methods for creativity can be found in this area (Knox, 1990). The new product theme, however, also has more specific applications in the field of marketing. West, Acar, and Caruana (2020) start from the observation that there is limited knowledge about how marketing managers make decisions about the selection of innovation projects to invest in. Initial screening of these projects, and subsequent decisions, are critical to the success of marketing efforts. The paper seeks to address two critical questions. The first concerns the identification of the specific types of decision making, and in particular, specific heuristics and intuitions used in innovation screening decisions. To address this first issue, the authors identify some specific decision-maker profiles about how individual managers make decisions. The second critical question concerns the connection between different marketing manager profiles and performance. Based on data collected on a sample of senior managers, it appears that when heuristics are used alone, or together with intuition, managers make decisions that are just as accurate as when they rely on analytical decision making. Decision making based on heuristics, however, is significantly faster, which is particularly important for decision making at the front-end of innovation (West, Acar, and Caruana, 2020, p. 1520).

Also at the product innovation front-end, viewed from a marketing perspective, Jensen, Hienerth, and Lettl (2014) examine user-generated ideas in the case of firm-hosted online communities, where "user-generated designs and user-designers can be used to help a focal producer firm to reduce its workload in the selection phase by predicting which user-generated designs it would most likely perceive as commercially attractive" (p. 75). The presence of thousands of proposals from the user community is addressed in the paper, the aim of which is "to provide the next step by developing a heuristic for filtering commercially attractive ideas that are generated in online user communities" (Jensen, Hienerth, and Lettl, 2014, p. 76). The authors propose three heuristics: (1) "too simple and excessively complex designs are most likely not promising in terms of commercial attractiveness"; (2) "designs that receive positive feedback from the peer community may likely be candidates for commercially attractive designs"; (3) "designs that are developed either by users who focus on very few designs or by extremely engaged user-designers are likely to be promising" (Jensen, Hienerth, and Lettl, 2014, p. 90).

In the field of new product development, heuristics have been adopted in relation to the need to respond to time pressures to, for example, get to market before competitors (Asch and Smith-Daniels, 1999), or the use of data to support new product design (Kohli and Krishnamurti, 1987). In new product decision support, Petrick and Echols (2004) propose a holistic heuristic approach that goes beyond financial criteria and includes aspects of techno-logical trajectory.

The marketing literature has long dealt with the problem of product design optimization by considering what are product line decisions (Green and Krieger, 1985; 1992; Kohli and Sukumar, 1990) and identified heuristics in this area to solve the buyer's problem, such as the "greedy heuristic" (Kuehn and Hamburger, 1963), the "interchange heuristic" applied to the location decision problems (Manne, 1964), and the "lagrangian relaxation heuristic" (Everett, 1963), some of which have been the subject of a number of applica-tions (Choi and Desarbò, 1993).

Heuristics for new-product marketing decisions can become part of a solu-tion to a more complex problem. This is true, for example, for new product choices or for pricing the entire range of products on sale. The sale promotion itself has been examined as a stimulus/cue capable of activating heuristics in consumer decision processing (Ketron, Spears, and Dai, 2016), or heuristic algorithms developed with the stated intent of analyzing multiple variables jointly, e.g., "optimal pricing and advertising policies jointly for a new gen-eration product in the presence of homogeneous forward-looking customers" (Najafi-Ghobadi, Bagherinejad, and Taleizadeh, 2022, p. 638), or heuristic policy that "decouples inventory replenishment, pricing, and component allocation decisions, in a coordinated way. The heuristic policy has a simple structure, and the control parameters of the heuristic policy can be obtained from tractable stochastic programs" (Oh, Sourirajan, and Ettl, 2014, p. 530).

An example of heuristic algorithms in this field can be the "heuristic search algorithms" adopted to explore the design space to make the design of new models highly efficient (Sándor and Wedel, 2002). In the case of a new com-mercial product, Rhim and Cooper (2005) design a heuristic algorithm based on genetic algorithms to generate and ultimately converge on a stable set and where the initial population is generated by a probabilistic add/drop heuristic that is a variant of conventional add/drop heuristics for facility-location prob-lems (adding or dropping the site).

As we have seen in this chapter and the previous one, the topic of heuristics is used with different meanings for consumer and marketers' decisions. The name heuristics in some cases is used as a decision model that can be tested and compared with other alternatives. In other cases it rather represents a label

Table 4.1   A selection of marketers' heuristics emerging from the literature

Heuristic	Definition	Domain / scope	Approach
Advertising-to-sales ratio heuristic (Rubel and Naik, 2017)	Define the advertising budget as a proportion of sales – emergent alternative heuristic: advertise more (less) when sales are low (high)	Managing advertising in nonprofit organizations	Heuristics as a source of bias (alternative heuristic)
Authority heuristic (Rohde and Mau, 2021; Thomas and Johnson, 2017)	Give heed to those whose authority you perceive to be high, derived from official credentials or perceived high status	Behavior in social media and dealing with influencers	Behavior description approach
Brand as risk-reducing heuristic (Brown, Zablah, Bellenger, and Johnston, 2011)	Brand plays a greater role the greater the buyer's perception of risk (and/or uncertainty)	Branding in business-to-business markets	Positive heuristics for choice architects
Calends heuristic (Guercini, 2019)	The definition of judgment and/or choice is made by identifying some identifiable dates or days in a calendar or from inputs referable to those dates	Forecast on consumption of raw materials at harvest time, fashion trends, etc.	Heuristics as a source of positive effects
Compensatory parity heuristic (Naik, Prasad and Sethi, 2008)	The share of the budget invested in advertising should be proportionately larger (small) for smaller (large) brands	Budget setting in brand-level advertising	Heuristics as a source of positive effects
Consistency heuristic (Rohde and Mau, 2021, Cialdini and Goldstein, 2004)	Define your previous behavior or attitude and behave consistently with it (or behave with the consideration that so will the clients)	Behavior in social media and dealing with influencers	Behavior description approach
Demographics heuristic (Knott, Hayes and Neslin, 2002)	It refers to a certain income (age) threshold above (below) which the customer becomes a potential target (specific case of threshold)	Market segmentation and target definition	Heuristics as a source of positive effects
Difference-based heuristics (Hutchinson, Alba and Eisenstein, 2010)	Define the change in advertising spending with the change in sales data (different models)	Defining the advertising budget	Heuristics as a source of bias
Exemplar-based heuristics (Hutchinson, Alba and Eisenstein, 2010)	It replicates the pattern of spending on advertising that yielded the highest sales (different models)	Defining the advertising budget	Heuristics as a source of bias

Heuristic	Definition	Domain / scope	Approach
Fairness heuristic (Wang, Gu and Dong, 2013)	Applies fair penalties in a distribution network (even when not convenient at the time) to build trust among actors	Generation of trust in distribution networks	Heuristics as a source of positive effects
Liking heuristic (Rohde and Mau, 2021; Cialdini and Goldstein, 2004, among the others)	People liked (by physical attractiveness, familiarity, similarity, etc.) are more persuasive and induce more favorable and behaviors	Behavior in social media and dealing with influencers	Behavior description approach
Mark-up heuristic (Arcelus and Srinivasan, 1987; Takano, Ishii and Muraki, 2014, among the others)	Price is defined by multiplying the cost by a coefficient (specific case of multiplier). Markup means both the procedure (applying a markup) and the coefficient	Defining the price from the cost (usually purchase cost, direct cost)	Behavior description approach
Multiplier heuristic (Guercini, 2019)	Applying a multiplier to the input data as an experience-based solution to a problem of setting a budget post, price, advertising investment quota, etc.	Setting prices, advertising investments, sales forecasts, among others	Heuristics as a source of positive effects
Quantity-matching heuristic (Chernev, 2008)	Define the assortment in such a way that the number of available options corresponds to the number of items that results in what customers buy together	Assortment definition by distributors and particularly retailers	Positive heuristics for choice architects
Recency of last purchase heuristic (Wübben and Wangenheim, 2008)	A customer is classified as inactive if they have not made any purchases within a certain number of months (special case of hiatus)	Classification of customers as "active" or "inactive"	Heuristics as a source of positive effects
Reciprocity heuristic (Rohde and Mau, 2021; Cialdini and Goldstein, 2004)	Keeping in mind that most human beings feel the need to reciprocate a precious gift with something similar (specific case of tit-for-tat)	Behavior in social media and dealing with influencers	Behavior description approach
Scarcity heuristic (Rohde and Mau, 2021; Koch and Benlian, 2015)	To make a product or brand perceived as valuable make it scarce (deliberate shortening)	Behavior in social media and dealing with influencers	Behavior description approach
Social proof heuristic (Rohde and Mau, 2021, Cialdini and Goldstein, 2004 and others)	Most people mimic what they perceive about others' cognition, emotions, and behaviors (specific case of imitation)	Behavior in social media and dealing with influencers	Behavior description approach

Heuristic	Definition	Domain / scope	Approach
Threshold heuristic (Guercini, 2019)	The attainment by a given parameter of a predetermined or otherwise defined threshold is the basis for making a judgment or choice (satisficing as special case)	Levels of costs/ revenues of certain origin or nature, levels of customer satisfaction, etc.	Heuristics as a source of positive effects
Trend-based heuristics (Hutchinson, Alba and Eisenstein, 2010)	Define the change in advertising spending by considering overall spending trends versus sales trends (different models)	Defining the advertising budget	Heuristics as a source of bias
Unity heuristic (Rohde and Mau, 2021)	Most people are more likely to be persuaded by those who are considered "in" by others in their same group (e.g., of consumers).	Behavior in social media and dealing with influencers	Behavior description approach
Visual preference heuristic (Townsend and Kahn, 2014)	In the online environment, consumer information in visual form improves communication performance over verbal form	Managing digital advertising and performance indicators	Heuristics as source of positive effects

Source: Author's elaboration.

that is used to describe a decision model that cannot be clearly modeled, and in still others to a decision model that corresponds to a simplified but not necessarily simple model. In Table 4.1 we report some of the heuristic decision models in the literature discussed in this chapter that can be seen as relevant to the marketer, as adopted by them directly or by consumers and otherwise relevant to their adaptive toolbox.

REFERENCES

Adams, J. S. (1963). Towards an understanding of inequity. *The Journal of Abnormal and Social Psychology*, *67*(5), 422.

Akçay, Y., Natarajan, H. P., & Xu, S. H. (2010). Joint dynamic pricing of multiple perishable products under consumer choice. *Management Science*, *56*(8), 1345–1361.

Arcelus, F. J., & Srinivasan, G. (1987). Inventory policies under various optimizing criteria and variable markup rates. *Management Science*, *33*(6), 756–762.

Artinger, F. M., Gigerenzer, G., & Jacobs, P. (2022). Satisficing: Integrating two traditions. *Journal of Economic Literature*, *60*(2), 598–635.

Ash, R., & Smith-Daniels, D. E. (1999). The effects of learning, forgetting, and relearning on decision rule performance in multiproject scheduling. *Decision Sciences*, *30*(1), 47–82.

Axelrod, R. (1984). *The Evolution of Cooperation*. Basic Books, New York.

Barnard, C. I. (1938). *The functions of the executive*. Harvard University Press, Cambridge, Mass.

Basu, A. K., & Batra, R. (1988). Adsplit: A multi-brand advertising budget allocation model. *Journal of Advertising*, *17*(2), 44–51.

Bauer, J. C., Schmitt, P., Morwitz, V. G., & Winer, R. S. (2013). Managerial decision making in customer management: Adaptive, fast and frugal? *Journal of the Academy of Marketing Science, 41*(4), 436–455.

Bhaskaran, S., Ramachandran, K., & Semple, J. (2010). A dynamic inventory model with the right of refusal. *Management Science, 56*(12), 2265–2281.

Borle, S., Singh, S. S., & Jain, D. C. (2008). Customer lifetime value measurement. *Management Science, 54*(1), 100–112.

Brighton, H., & Gigerenzer, G. (2015). The bias bias. *Journal of Business Research, 68*(8), 1772–1784.

Brown, B. P., Zablah, A. R., Bellenger, D. N., & Johnston, W. J. (2011). When do B2B brands influence the decision making of organizational buyers? an examination of the relationship between purchase risk and brand sensitivity. *International Journal of Research in Marketing, 28*(3), 194–204.

Bruce, M., Daly, L., & Kahn, K. B. (2007). Delineating design factors that influence the global product launch process. *Journal of Product Innovation Management, 24*(5), 456–470.

Chernev, A. (2008). The role of purchase quantity in assortment choice: The quantity-matching heuristic. *Journal of Marketing Research, 45*(2), 171–181.

Choi, S. C., & Desarbo, W. S. (1993). Game theoretic derivations of competitive strategies in conjoint analysis. *Marketing Letters, 4*(4), 337–348.

Cialdini, R. B., & Goldstein, N. J. (2004). Social influence: Compliance and conformity. *Annual Review of Psychology, 55*, 591–621.

Cornelissen, J. P. (2003). Metaphor as a method in the domain of marketing. *Psychology and Marketing, 20*(3), 209–225.

Cotterill, R. W., & Putsis Jr, W. P. (2001). Do models of vertical strategic interaction for national and store brands meet the market test? *Journal of Retailing, 77*(1), 83–109.

Deshpande, V., Cohen, M. A., & Donohue, K. (2003). A threshold inventory rationing policy for service-differentiated demand classes. *Management Science, 49*(6), 683–703.

Dugar, A., & Chamola, P. (2021). Retailers with traits of consumer: Exploring the existence and antecedents of brand loyalty in small unorganized retailers. *Journal of Retailing and Consumer Services, 62*, 102635.

Etzioni, A. (2001). Humble decision making. *Harvard Business Review on Decision Making (Harvard Business School Press: Boston, MA, 2001)*, 45–57.

Everett III, H. (1963). Generalized Lagrange multiplier method for solving problems of optimum allocation of resources. *Operations Research, 11*(3), 399–417.

Gahler, D., & Hruschka, H. (2023). Heuristic pricing rules not requiring knowledge of the price response function. *Review of Managerial Science, 17*, 2325–2347.

Ghazimatin, E., Mooi, E. A., & Heide, J. B. (2021). Mobilizing the temporary organization: The governance roles of selection and pricing. *Journal of Marketing, 85*(4), 85–104.

Giebelhausen, M. D., Robinson, S. G., & Cronin Jr., J. J. (2011). Worth waiting for: Increasing satisfaction by making consumers wait. *Journal of the Academy of Marketing Science, 39*(6), 889–905.

Gigerenzer, G., & Brighton, H. (2009). Homo heuristicus: why biased minds make better inferences, *Topics in Cognitive Science*, Vol. 1, pp. 107–43.

Goldstein, D. G., & Gigerenzer, G. (1999). The recognition heuristic: How ignorance makes us smart. In *Simple heuristics that make us smart*. Oxford University Press, Oxford, pp. 37–58.

Goldstein, D. G., & Gigerenzer, G. (2002). Models of ecological rationality: the recognition heuristic. *Psychological review, 109*(1), 75–90.

Gigerenzer, G., & Gaissmaier, W. (2011). Heuristic decision making. *Annual Review of Psychology, 62*, 451–482.

Green, P. E., & Krieger, A. M. (1985). Models and heuristics for product line selection. *Marketing Science, 4*(1), 1–19.

Green, P. E., & Krieger, A. M. (1992). An application of a product positioning model to pharmaceutical products. *Marketing Science, 11*(2), 117–132.

Greenbank, P. (1999). The pricing decision in the micro-business: a study of accountants, builders and printers. *International Small Business Journal, 17*(3), 60–73.

Guercini, S. (2019). Heuristics as tales from the field: the problem of scope. *Mind & Society, 18*(2), 191–205.

Guercini, S., & Freeman, S. M. (2023). How international marketers make decisions: exploring approaches to learning and using heuristics. *International Marketing Review, 40*(3), 429–451.

Guercini, S., & Runfola, A. (2021). Heuristics in decision-making by exporting textiles SMEs. *Journal of Global Fashion Marketing, 12*(1), 1–15.

Guercini, S., La Rocca, A., & Snehota, I. (2022). Decisions when interacting in customer-supplier relationships. *Industrial Marketing Management, 105*, 380–387.

Guercini, S., La Rocca, A., Runfola, A., & Snehota, I. (2014). Interaction behaviors in business relationships and heuristics: Issues for management and research agenda. *Industrial Marketing Management, 43*(6), 929–937.

Guercini, S., La Rocca, A., Runfola, A., & Snehota, I. (2015). Heuristics in customer-supplier interaction. *Industrial Marketing Management, 48*, 26–37.

Gummesson, E. (2014). The theory/practice gap in B2B marketing: Reflections and search for solutions. *Journal of Business and Industrial Marketing, 29*, 619–625.

Gwin, J. M. (1985). Financial institution branching decisions: A macro-heuristic. *Journal of the Academy of Marketing Science, 13*(1–2), 259–270.

Hartmann, W., Nair, H. S., & Narayanan, S. (2011). Identifying causal marketing mix effects using a regression discontinuity design. *Marketing Science, 30*(6), 1079–1097.

He, L., & Ioerger, T. R. (2005). Combining bundle search with buyer coalition formation in electronic markets: A distributed approach through explicit negotiation. *Electronic Commerce Research and Applications, 4*(4), 329–344.

Hinterhuber, A. (2015). Violations of rational choice principles in pricing decisions. *Industrial Marketing Management, 47*, 65–74.

Huang, C. (2012). To model, or not to model: Forecasting for customer prioritization. *International Journal of Forecasting, 28*(2), 497–506.

Hugh, D. C., Dolan, R., Harrigan, P., & Gray, H. (2022). Influencer marketing effectiveness: The mechanisms that matter. *European Journal of Marketing, 56*(12), 3485–3515.

Hurley, S., Moutinho, L., & Witt, S. F. (1998). Genetic algorithms for tourism marketing. *Annals of Tourism Research, 25*(2), 498–514.

Hutchinson, J. W., Alba, J. W., & Eisenstein, E. M. (2010). Heuristics and biases in data-based decision making: Effects of experience, training, and graphical data displays. *Journal of Marketing Research, 47*(4), 627–642.

Hutchinson, J., & Alba, J. W. (1997). Heuristics and biases in the "eyeballing" of data: The effects of context on intuitive correlation assessment. *Journal of Experimental Psychology: Learning, Memory, and Cognition, 23*(3), 591–621.

Jagannathan, R., Marakani, S., Takehara, H., & Wang, Y. (2012). Calendar cycles, infrequent decisions, and the cross section of stock returns. *Management Science, 58*(3), 507–522.

Jensen, M. B., Hienerth, C., & Lettl, C. (2014). Forecasting the commercial attractiveness of user-generated designs using online data: An empirical study within the LEGO user community. *Journal of Product Innovation Management, 31*(S1), 75–93.

Ketron, S., Spears, N., & Dai, B. (2016). Overcoming information overload in retail environments: Imagination and sales promotion in a wine context. *Journal of Retailing and Consumer Services, 33*, 23–32.

Klein, G. (1989). Recognition-primed decisions. In Rouse, W. B. (ed.), *Advances in man–machine system research 5*. JAI PressKlein, Greenwich: CT, 47−92.

Klein, G. (2015). A naturalistic decision making perspective on studying intuitive decision making. *Journal of Applied Research in Memory and Cognition, 4*(3), 164–168.

Knott, A., Hayes, A., & Neslin, S. A. (2002). Next-product-to-buy models for cross-selling applications. *Journal of Interactive Marketing, 16*(3), 59–75.

Knox, S. (1990). Creativity in marketing management—A unified approach. *Journal of Marketing Management, 5*(3), 245–257.

Koch, O. F., & Benlian, A. (2015). Promotional tactics for online viral marketing campaigns: how scarcity and personalization affect seed stage referrals. *Journal of Interactive Marketing, 32*(1), 37–52.

Kohli, R., & Krishnamurti, R. (1987). Heuristic approach to product design. *Management Science, 33*(12), 1523–1533.

Kohli, R., & Sukumar, R. (1990). Heuristics for product-line design using conjoint analysis. *Management Science, 36*(12), 1464–1478.

Kordrostami, E., Liu-Thompkins, Y., & Rahmani, V. (2022). Coordinating supply-related scarcity appeals with online reviews. *Marketing Letters, 33*(3), 471–484.

Ku, H. H., Kuo, C. C., & Kuo, T. W. (2012). The effect of scarcity on the purchase intentions of prevention and promotion motivated consumers. *Psychology & Marketing, 29*(8), 541–548.

Kuehn, A. A., & Hamburger, M. J. (1963). A heuristic program for locating warehouses. *Management Science, 9*(4), 643–666.

Kumar, A., & Salo, J. (2018). Effects of link placements in email newsletters on their click-through rate. *Journal of Marketing Communications, 24*(5), 535–548.

Lilien, G. L., Silk, A. J., Choffray, J. M., & Rao, M. (1976). Industrial Advertising Effects and Budgeting Practices: What is known about the effects of industrial advertising? And how does this information affect budget decisions? *Journal of Marketing, 40*(1), 16–24.

Lim, A., Rodrigues, B., & Zhang, X. (2004). Metaheuristics with local search techniques for retail shelf-space optimization. *Management Science, 50*(1), 117–131.

Lin, J. T., Wang, F. K., Lo, S. L., Hsu, W. T., & Wang, Y. T. (2006). Analysis of the supply and demand in the TFT–LCD market. *Technological Forecasting and Social Change, 73*(4), 422–435.

Lind, E. A., Kulik, C. T., Ambrose, M., & de Vera Park, M. V. (1993). Individual and corporate dispute resolution: Using procedural fairness as a decision heuristic. *Administrative Science Quarterly, 38*, 224–251.

Liu, C. H., & Wang, C. C. (2010). Formulating service business strategies with integrative services model from customer and provider perspectives. *European Journal of Marketing, 44*(9/10), 1500–1527.

Lo, V. S. Y., & Pachamanova, D. A. (2015). From predictive uplift modeling to prescriptive uplift analytics: A practical approach to treatment optimization while accounting for estimation risk. *Journal of Marketing Analytics, 3*(2), 79–95.

Loock, M., & Hinnen, G. (2015). Heuristics in organizations: A review and a research agenda. *Journal of Business Research, 68*(9), 2027–2036.

Manne, A. S. (1964). Plant location under economies-of-scale—decentralization and computation. *Management Science, 11*(2), 213–235.

Marewski, J. N., Gaissmaier, W., Schooler, L. J., Goldstein, D. G., & Gigerenzer, G. (2010). From recognition to decisions: Extending and testing recognition-based models for multialternative inference. *Psychonomic Bulletin & Review, 17*, 287–309.

Meneses, G. D. (2010). Refuting fear in heuristics and in recycling promotion. *Journal of Business Research, 63*(2), 104–110.

Mentzer, J. T., & Gomes, R. (1994). Further extensions of adaptive extended exponential smoothing and comparison with the M-competition. *Journal of the Academy of Marketing Science, 22*(4), 372–382.

Monroe, K. B., Rikala, V. M., & Somervuori, O. (2015). Examining the application of behavioral price research in business-to-business markets. *Industrial Marketing Management, 47*, 17–25.

Naik, P. A., Prasad, A., & Sethi, S. P. (2008). Building brand awareness in dynamic oligopoly markets. *Management Science, 54*(1), 129–138.

Najafi-Ghobadi, S., Bagherinejad, J., & Taleizadeh, A. A. (2022). Optimal marketing policy for managing new generation products in the presence of forward-looking customers by considering product diffusion. *Journal of Modelling in Management, 17*(2), 633–654.

Oh, S., Sourirajan, K., & Ettl, M. (2014). Joint pricing and production decisions in an assemble-to-order system. *Manufacturing and Service Operations Management, 16*(4), 529–543.

Ozuem, W., Howell, K., & Lancaster, G. (2022). Exploring the relationship between integrated marketing communications and decentralised organisational structure: A heuristics perspective. *Qualitative Market Research, 25*(2), 272–292.

Parikh, J. (1994). *Intuition: The New Frontier of Management*. Blackwell Business, Oxford, UK.

Persson, A., & Ryals, L. (2014). Making customer relationship decisions: Analytics v rules of thumb. *Journal of Business Research, 67*(8), 1725–1732.

Petrick, I. J., & Echols, A. E. (2004). Technology roadmapping in review: A tool for making sustainable new product development decisions. *Technological Forecasting and Social Change, 71*(1–2), 81–100.

Radas, S., & Shugan, S. M. (1998). Seasonal marketing and timing new product introductions. *Journal of Marketing Research, 35*(3), 296–315.

Radcliffe, N. J. and Surry, P.D. (1999) *Differential response analysis: Modeling true response by isolating the effect of a single action*. Proceedings of Credit Scoring and Credit Control VI, Credit Research Centre, University of Edinburgh Management School.

Raghubir, P., & Krishna, A. (1996). As the crow flies: Bias in consumers' map-based distance judgments. *Journal of Consumer Research, 23*(1), 26–39.

Raghubir, P., & Krishna, A. (1999). Vital dimensions in volume perception: Can the eye fool the stomach? *Journal of Marketing Research, 36*(3), 313–326.

Rajagopalan, S., & Swaminathan, J. M. (2001). A coordinated production planning model with capacity expansion and inventory management. *Management Science, 47*(11), 1562–1580.

Ravichandran, J. (2011). A chi-square-based heuristic statistical procedure for approximating bid price in a competitive marketplace: A case study. *Journal of Business and Industrial Marketing, 27*(1), 69–76.

Read, S., Dew, N., Sarasvathy, S. D., Song, M., & Wiltbank, R. (2009). Marketing under uncertainty: The logic of an effectual approach. *Journal of Marketing, 73*(3), 1–18.

Reinikainen, H., Munnukka, J., Maity, D., & Luoma-Aho, V. (2020). 'You really are a great big sister'–parasocial relationships, credibility, and the moderating role of audience comments in influencer marketing. *Journal of Marketing Management, 36*(3–4), 279–298.

Rhim, H., & Cooper, L. G. (2005). Assessing potential threats to incumbent brands: New product positioning under price competition in a multisegmented market. *International Journal of Research in Marketing, 22*(2), 159–182.

Rohde, P., & Mau, G. (2021). "It's selling like hotcakes": Deconstructing social media influencer marketing in long-form video content on youtube via social influence heuristics. *European Journal of Marketing, 55*(10), 2700–2734.

Rooderkerk, R. P., van Heerde, H. J., & Bijmolt, T. H. A. (2013). Optimizing retail assortments. *Marketing Science, 32*(5), 699–715.

Rubel, O., & Naik, P. A. (2017). Robust dynamic estimation. *Marketing Science, 36*(3), 453–467.

Saab, A. B., & Botelho, D. (2020). Are organizational buyers rational? using price heuristics in functional risk judgment. *Industrial Marketing Management, 85*, 141–151.

Sándor, Z., & Wedel, M. (2002). Profile construction in experimental choice designs for mixed logit models. *Marketing Science, 21*(4), 455–475.

Scarpaci, J. L., Coupey, E., & Reed, S. D. (2018). Artists as cultural icons: The icon myth transfer effect as a heuristic for cultural branding. *Journal of Product and Brand Management, 27*(3), 320–333.

Schmittlein, D. C., & Peterson, R. A. (1994). Customer base analysis: An industrial purchase process application. *Marketing Science, 13*(1), 41–67.

Shafahi, A., & Haghani, A. (2014). Modeling contractors' project selection and markup decisions influenced by eminence. *International Journal of Project Management, 32*(8), 1481–1493.

Sheu, C., & Krajewski, L. J. (1996). A heuristic for formulating within-plant manufacturing focus. *International Journal of Production Research, 34*(11), 3165–3185.

Simon, H. A. (1979). Rational decision making in business organizations. *The American Economic Review, 69*(4), 493–513.

Takano, Y., Ishii, N., & Muraki, M. (2014). A sequential competitive bidding strategy considering inaccurate cost estimates. *Omega, 42*(1), 132–140.

Thaler, R. H., & Sunstein, C.R. (2008). *Nudge. Improving decisions about health, wealth, and happiness.* Penguin Books, London.

Thomas, T., & Johnson, J. (2017). The impact of celebrity expertise on advertising effectiveness: The mediating role of celebrity brand fit. *Vision, 21*(4), 367–374.

Townsend, C., & Kahn, B. E. (2014). The "visual preference heuristic": The influence of visual versus verbal depiction on assortment processing, perceived variety, and choice overload. *Journal of Consumer Research, 40*(5), 993–1015.

Ülkümen, G., Chakravarti, A., & Morwitz, V. G. (2010). Categories create mind-sets: The effect of exposure to broad versus narrow categorizations on subsequent, unrelated decisions. *Journal of Marketing Research, 47*(4), 659–671.

Useem, M. (2006). How well-run boards make decisions. *Harvard Business Review, 84*(11), 130–136, 138, 158.

Van Maanen, J. (2011). *Tales of the field: On writing ethnography.* University of Chicago Press, Chicago.

Vanharanta, M., & Easton, G. (2010). Intuitive managerial thinking; the use of mental simulations in the industrial marketing context. *Industrial Marketing Management, 39*(3), 425–436.

Vilcassim, N. J., & Chintagunta, P. K. (1995). Investigating retailer product category pricing from household scanner panel data. *Journal of Retailing, 71*(2), 103–128.

Wang, D. T., Gu, F. F., & Dong, M. C. (2013). Observer effects of punishment in a distribution network. *Journal of Marketing Research, 50*(5), 627–643.

West, D. C., Acar, O. A., & Caruana, A. (2020). Choosing among alternative new product development projects: The role of heuristics. *Psychology and Marketing, 37*(11), 1511–1524.

Wu, A. Y. H., Little, V. J., & Low, B. (2016). Inbound open innovation for pharmaceutical markets: a case study of an anti-diabetic drug in-licensing decision. *Journal of Business and Industrial Marketing, 31*(2), 205–218.

Wübben, M., & Wangenheim, F. V. (2008). Instant customer base analysis: Managerial heuristics often "get it right". *Journal of Marketing, 72*(3), 82–93.

Yang, M. H. (2001). An efficient algorithm to allocate shelf space. *European Journal of Operational Research, 131*(1), 107–118.

Zufryden, F. S. (1989). How much should be spent for advertising a brand. An application of a pc-based approach for advertising planning. *Journal of Advertising Research, 29*(2), 24–34.

5. Marketing automation emergence and evolution

5.1 REVISITING THE CONCEPT OF MARKETING AND THE TREND OF AUTOMATION

This chapter develops the idea that the application of new technological systems and the resulting automation of marketing decision-making systems lead to further evolution of the focus of marketing processes. In a famous article published in 1960 in the *Journal of Marketing*, Robert J. Keith, then Vice President of Pillsbury, a large grain company later merged into General Mills, draws an analogy between the scientific revolution led by Kepler and Galileo and the changing issues at the center of attention of corporate management. From this analogy, Keith speaks of a "marketing revolution" and identifies several "eras" that from a "production-oriented" stage, saw the enterprise evolve in a "sales oriented" and then "marketing oriented" direction, eventually landing toward a "marketing control" orientation (Keith, 1960).

Although the idea of marketing revolution evoked by Keith has been first mythologized and then questioned (Jones and Richardson, 2007), his formulation retains the merit of proposing a path in which to place different orientations to marketing in an evolutionary vision. This evolution may take place at different times in different firms and industries, so that different eras may be co-present even in the same sector and with actors with differentiated competitive capacity. The idea that marketing affirms its role in an evolutionary path is in the broader context of the affirmation of the "new marketing concept" emerging from the literature of the 1960s and 1970s (Bell and Emory, 1971). This concept can also be seen in its dimension as a hinge between the production system and society, where consumers do not simply buy what they need, but on the contrary, are endowed with discretionary purchasing power and are interested in a differentiated supply (Kotler, 1989). The implications of the presence of consumer disposable income for discretionary spending qualify the middle-class concept, with relevant antecedents and consequences for societal characteristics and strategic marketing (Cavusgil and Guercini, 2014).

The success of the idea of "the marketing revolution" and the new marketing concept in it (Houston, 1986) corresponds to its widespread presence in marketing textbooks since the original edition of *Marketing Management* by Philip Kotler (1967). The evolutionary steps identified by Keith have been confirmed over the years with variations and additions, as in the case of the addition of customer and service orientation (Eiglier and Langeard, 1987; Vargo and Lusch, 2008).

In this chapter, we propose a vision of marketing that can be defined as "automated oriented". This new orientation has its antecedents in the spread of new technologies in marketing processes and its diffusion to the mass of businesses and consumers, revolutionizing the technologies on which marketing is based (Wood, 2015). The spread of these new technological solutions and their effective use has characterized the last decade in particular. We are talking about the use of mobile devices such as tablets and smartphones, the effective presence of wi-fi connections, and the spread of new software and applications. These dynamics have been the subject of increasing adoption and use, transforming the marketing environment and creating new models of commerce, promotion and sales, new types of advertising and marketing research, to the creation of digital versions of existing services and completely new services (Wood, 2015). These new technologies for marketing leverage digitization without being limited to it (think of neuromarketing, for example).

The impact of new technologies on marketing is recognized by the same proponents of the traditional marketing paradigm (Kotler, Kartajaya and Setiawan, 2016). In recent decades however, marketing activity itself, across different markets (including industrial and service markets) has increasingly been characterized by the use of new technologies for marketing activity. These new technologies for marketing first created a number of topics seen as additional, qualified under the label of web marketing and then digital marketing. Later these processes saw the rise of several specialized topics, such as Search Engine Marketing and Search Engine Optimization, Social Media Marketing, E-mail Marketing, Online marketing research, including Marketing listening. However, there is a need to frame these different techniques and application tools in an overall model that fosters an integrated view of them, similar to what happened in the 1950s and 1960s for the new tools and theoretical advances that had matured up to then (Kotler, Kartajaya and Setiawan, 2016).

The relevance of the new technological base and its impact on marketing activities has been enormous and is still in the making, without questioning the ideas behind the marketing concept, rather enhancing them and proposing a direct connection between analysis and response to the needs and desires expressed by customers (Wood, 2015). While confirming the assumptions of the marketing model developed in past decades (centrality of customer needs and desires, segmentation targeting and positioning of the company, policy making regarding operational levers), in the new context we make use of new technological systems and instrumentation (search engines, social media, research systems and automation of marketing actions) (Kotler, Kartajaya and Setiawan, 2016).

This new technological environment changes not only the modes of consumption, but also the conditions in which business actors operate (Van Bruggen and Wierenga, 2010). These actors are united with consumers by the challenge represented by the use of new instrumentation and the need to adapt to an environment in which their task changes. Our focus is on the side of the enterprise and thus the marketers (managerial and entrepreneurial), but many challenges are not only of the enterprise but also affect the consumer (Wierenga, 2002).

These trends have been qualified by various keywords: data driven marketing; algorithm-based marketing; artificial intelligence-based marketing, etc. Out of all of them, the most important phenomenon in our opinion is the relationship between technological and human components in marketing processes, well represented by the concept of marketing automation (Little, 2001).

Marketing automation is connected to other processes of automation affecting the production system on the one hand, the consumption system on the other, and society more generally. Just as mass production developed in relation to the emergence of a society of mass consumption and thus to mass marketing processes (Kotler, 1989), so automation is a paradigm that tends to assert itself in today's marketing concerning the ongoing automation in production processes and in the consumption environment, but more generally in society. In particular, marketing automation, given the complex nature of marketing activities, comes to significantly affect marketing processes in companies due to the emergence of the system of algorithms (instructions) capable of replacing marketers in many activities, regardless of whether these were previously classified in the sphere of strategic marketing (such as segmentation and targeting) or operational marketing (such as promotion or pricing).

We, therefore, examine the topic of marketing automation not only as a particular tool available to marketers, but more broadly as a possible new era for marketing with which marketers must contend. In fact, automation has been examined for a long time especially in the field of manufacturing, where people were being replaced by machines, generating great efficiency and productivity, along with fears about social consequences (Frey and Osborne, 2013). According to recent evidence, automation based on the introduction of artificial intelligence operates no differently from earlier stages of the automation process (Kaplan, 2017). In particular, rather than directly replacing marketers, it reduces the number of marketers needed by increasing the productivity of those who remain operational and changing the skills required of them (Frey and Osborne, 2017). In a highly tertiarized society, a large proportion of such job opportunities are provided by sectors such as marketing and related fields (advertising, market research, but even more so retail distribution), so an automation of marketing processes potentially leads to the replacement of many workers.

The threats of automation are compounded by those associated with artificial intelligence, starting with the disturbing one related to the so-called ominous "singularity" (Bostrom, 2014; Tegmark, 2017), or more simply the controversial aspects related to the impact of the emergence of a new society (Kaplan, 2017; Müller and Bostrom, 2016; Lazzeretti, Nannelli, Innocenti and Oliva, 2023). At this stage, however, we do not assume a perspective related to the study of society as a whole, but the approach we take is one that stands alongside marketers, whose perspective we thus assume, that is, the people in their organizations who form judgments, make choices, and engage in behaviors in the context of marketing automation.

In short, these new technologies have the characteristic of representing a change in the marketing environment and the tools available to marketers to cope with it. Automation affects the very role of marketers as these technologies present such characteristics that they can change their role to the point of replacement. The action of the machines generated by these technologies, adopting the imitation game proposed by Turing (1950), leads them to be in some cases an effective substitute for the human actor in tasks that involved thinking skills and intelligence, taking automation out of production and introducing it into marketing offices, often in the form of software or services delivered remotely with effects perceptible by other market actors, competitors, influencers and customers (Guercini, 2020; 2023).

In continuity with the idea of the evolution of the marketing concept, this automation, understood as the interface between technology and the activities of marketers, can thus define a new core element on which companies must focus.

5.2 THE EMERGENCE AND EVOLUTION OF MARKETING AUTOMATION

In an article more than two decades ago, Bucklin, Lehmann and Little (1998) recalled how marketing science research had been oriented toward "the development of tools and methods that help managers understand their markets and make decisions", but that now marketing was facing a change. The last decades of the twentieth century had been "the age of marketing decision support", but now it was predicted that "the next two decades will usher in the era of marketing decision automation. In other words the decisions we can support today are prime candidates to be decisions we can automate tomorrow" (Bucklin, Lechmann and Little, 1998, p. 235). This quote reminds us that the advent of automated marketing has as a prerequisite a long phase of upgrading information gathering and processing technologies (Benbasat, Goldstein and Mead, 1987; Van Bruggen, Smidts and Wierenga, 2001; Van Bruggen and Wierenga, 2010).

The automation process also affects marketing activities today and, as we have mentioned, is the focus of growing interest in the literature. Marketing automation is a specific and very important case of management automation. It is defined as automatic support for marketing decisions in the digital task environment (Little, 2001; Heimbach, Kostyra and Hinz, 2015). The central idea of marketing automation is the use of models to cope with the large amount of data produced automatically to react adaptively to customer, competitor, and influencer behavior, produce effective proposals and identify preferences (Bucklin, Lattin, Ansari, Bell, Coupey, Gupta, Little, Mela, Montgomery, and Steckel, 2002). Marketing automation is a "segment of information systems dedicated to management of marketing and sales" and "makes more efficient, automates, and measures all marketing and sales activities, at the same time, combining them with an individual customer, and their effect" (Benhaouer, 2018, p. 3).

In marketing, automation does not intervene suddenly and is a long-term trend that does not come with the most advanced solutions proposed by artificial intelligence today (Alpaydin, 2016; Kelleher, 2019). For this to come to fruition, it is necessary for technology to provide alternatives to traditional marketing processes, and for a criterion to be identified on the basis of which to choose to replace the human actor with forms of artificial intelligence. Decisions in automated marketing are based on models (made by machines) instead of the capabilities of marketers (made by people) (Wertenbroch, 2021). The process of automation in the marketing function has several motivations, most notably an improvement in efficiency, an improvement in the quality of decision making, and finally a development possibility for micromarketing and mass customization (Kotler, 1989). In fact, there is in the first place an opportunity to improve productivity by using models to make decisions more quickly and with less managerial labor cost. A second factor pushing for an adoption of automation is the fact that model-based decisions can be better, providing greater returns on investment (Walsh, 2019). A third factor is then related to the demand for mass customization of marketing activities, which by its nature requires the management of huge streams of data that are difficult to manage through a system mediated by manager intervention (Bucklin, Lhemann and Little, 1998). Perhaps even more relevant to remark the pervasiveness of the automation paradigm, it affects not only the processes put in place by companies that can equip themselves with automation systems to develop their marketing activities, but also affects the consumption process and consumer behavior, to the point that automation "is transforming many consumption domains, including everyday activities such as cooking or driving, as well as recreational activities like fishing or cycling" (Leung, Paolacci and Puntoni, 2018, p. 818). In addition to being pervasive, the automation paradigm turns out to be potentially dominant. In fact, contributing to its formation is the widespread idea of greater efficiency and effectiveness of the automation process entrusted to computer systems. The latter are capable of processing ever larger databases in ever faster times and with a processing capacity incomparably greater than that possible to people in such a short time, enshrining a superiority of automated processes over those based on the cognition and behavior of human actors. This superiority finds support in a view of human behavior itself that can be highly biased (Tversky and Kahneman, 1974) and as such manipulable.

Different perspectives have been highlighted with respect to the role of marketing automation and its adoption by businesses. In a logic close to or at least oriented toward the perspective of marketing effects on society and consumer marketing, questions are raised as to whether automated marketing can pose as utopia or dystopia (Wertenbroch, 2021). From a perspective of business adoption of marketing automation systems, the prevalence of effecting rather than causing approaches in choices even by large firms has been highlighted (Mero, Tarkiainen, and Tobon, 2020).

Automated marketing therefore reduces human intervention but at the same time increases personalization for the customer. In this sense, automation accomplishes with less personal presence along with more personalization. In marketing automation, marked personalization is indeed realized, but not through personal interaction (Grönroos, 1994). Personalization is accomplished by an automated system that processes data, resulting in the transposition of what is done between buyer and supplier in business markets but with a different path. The central idea is using models to cope with the large amount of data automatically produced by the digitalization of the business environment, enabling reacting adaptively to customer, competitor, and influencer behavior, producing effective proposals, and identifying preferences (Bucklin, Lattin, Ansari, Bell, Coupey, Gupta, Little, Mela, Montgomery, and Steckel, 2002). The heart of marketing automation is the automatic customization of marketing-decision support that "promises enhanced productivity, better decision-making, higher returns on marketing investments, and increased customer satisfaction and loyalty" (Heimbach, Kostyra and Hinz, 2015, p. 129).

The abundance of data available allows making decisions for marketing activities in an automatic form, starting from parameters set with specific software and algorithms. These algorithms use the data inputs to produce predictions and behaviors, sometimes almost in real time with respect to the production of data (for example, analytical data from social media or search engines to activate promotions to specific online customers). This support is important to respond to the speed with which market data is produced and used by marketers in the digital task environment (Hirt and Willmott, 2014).

In consulting, for example, "marketing automation class systems are a natural response to real needs of contemporary marketing. Their most important capability is an ability to connect an individual customer with a series of activities which she or he underwent, and their effect" (Benhauer, 2018).

Motivations for marketing automation have emerged for several decades now. The automation of the processes of analysis, evaluation, and choice, up to and including that of many operational actions, is a topical issue for marketing as a whole and one that is central to realizing "marketing automation" (Świeczak, 2013). Marketing automation can be seen as part of the more general phenomenon of automation, a trend affecting management processes concerning the technical process, particularly in manufacturing processes but now and in future also affecting marketing processes even in the conduct of the internet of things, both at the level of data collection and processing for decision making and decision making using forms of artificial intelligence (Upadhyay and Chitnis, 2022; Walsh, 2019).

Automation is a paradigm that has theoretical relevance for a much broader context than marketing, and whose characters it is useful to recall in order to frame the topic of marketing automation in more accomplished terms (Bagshow, 2015; Mero, Tarkiainen and Tobon, 2020). Automation is defined as "the use of machines and computers to do work that was previously done by people" (Oxford Advanced Learners' Dictionary) and "the use of machines and computers that can operate without needing human control" (Cambridge Dictionary), specifying that at the same time automation meant the loss of many factory jobs and that business process automation provides consistent, measurable and repeatable services at lower costs. The term is mainly used in English since the 1940s and later in connection with the development of cybernetics and systems theory, where the word "automation" is the result of an irregular formation from "automatic + action". Automation consists specifically of the use of technical means and procedures, nowadays especially electronic ones, which are aimed at ensuring an unfolding of processes in which human intervention is reduced or eliminated. The definitions thus emphasize the fact of reducing human intervention, not necessarily eliminating it, but certainly reducing it. Automation is thus the employment of a set of technical means and procedures which, by appropriately acting on particular contrivances or devices, ensure the automatic performance of a given process, the automatic operation of an industrial plant, a public service, etc. (Bright, 1958; Bainbridge, 1982; Silverman, 1996).

Automation can be seen as the technical and applied aspect of cybernetics and systems theory and concerns the use of complex and refined machines and procedures capable of regulating their own operation and of controlling by means of sensitive organs the quality of the work produced, particularly with reference to production cycles governed by process computers (Wiener, 1948). Automation has long been presented in the field of organizational models, with particular reference to technical variability, so it cannot be said to be a new theme from this point of view (Head, 1960). More than 60 years ago, Bright (1958) defined it as the most advanced mode of technique for the degree of mechanization. In this view, automation translates into continuous mechanization techniques and machine activities that are integrated with each other, employing forms of automatic regulation on individual machines and on the system as a whole, such that critical parameters are measured, optimal modes of operation are evaluated, and the whole system is regulated according to cybernetic principles (Wiener, 1948). While earlier forms of mechanization see human-machine systems, in automation we see machine-machine systems in action whereby the operation of the machine is regulated by another machine integrally (Cumming and Blitzer, 2010). Automation originally occurs on physical transformation operations (Bright for example sees the case of electric lamp manufacturing), but initially it extended to data and information processing, from that produced in the same processes, for what were then called electronic data processing systems (Goeldner, 1962). The automation to which we refer to today in some respects corresponds to the same principles, but is produced in a profoundly changed and more complex technological context in which machines are seen to take on decision-making tasks from data processing.

The distinction between "automation" and "automatization" sees the latter as a tendency toward the total replacement of human labor by automatisms, and does not coincide in its characteristics with the aspects that connote automation, including paradoxes and counterintuitive aspects in its effects (Bainbridge, 1982). Instead, automation is a long-term trend for business and management, and the relationship between automation and management includes both the management of automation and the automation of management (Walsh, 2019). From reading many definitions, the central concept of automation is to "replace" humans with machines. However, this is not necessarily done directly, as machines may not replace occupations entirely, but generate human labor efficiencies, higher productivity, and consequently the need for different managerial work focused on other and new tasks or performed by fewer people. Moreover, "replace/replica", also understood in this sense, can be seen in two ways: a "replacement" is a solution that is comparable and similar in functionality to the current item; a substitution is a solution that replaces the current item (Guercini, 2020; Walsh, 2019).

The antecedents of automation include both the availability of an "alternative" to the present arrangement and the application of a "criterion" to determine the replacement choice (Guercini, 2022). The alternative comes from technological development that provides machines capable of performing operations that replace human action. The criterion is the one used for judgment and choice by decision makers implementing substitution, which for example may be based on a preference or necessity criterion (Figure 5.1).

Consequences of automation include: a degree of achievement of results/ objectives (effectiveness); a degree of effort required to achieve certain results/ objectives (efficiency); and the impact on human activity, in terms of adaptation (Byrne and Parasuraman, 1996) with the possibility that it may result in disengagement, may involve empowerment (Silverman, 1966), or may paradoxically maintain old problems (Bainbridge, 1982).

Source: Author's elaboration.

Figure 5.1   The process of adoption by marketing automation solutions

5.3   AUTOMATION IN SPECIFIC MARKETING PROCESSES

Automation can affect several specific marketing processes such as: monitoring contact behavior on the internet; generating contact segmentation; managing email marketing for recommendations and promotion, customer relationships, and contact management; and processing analytics, reports, and advanced functionalities.

The use of "marketing automation" applies particularly to the activities of analysis, evaluation, and choice, and marketing automation signals the possibility of applying models with machines acting in integration or substitution of the managerial component. About 20 years ago Little (2001) proposed a framework for marketing automation that examined five levels of system operation comprising: (1) data inputs; (2) real time decision rules; (3) updates of the decision rules; (4) feedback to site management; and (5) strategy choice. In this area, development areas were identified for the study of marketing automation, including: (1) control system optimization tools; (2) database design for marketing automation; (3) recommendation engines; and (4) customer acquisition marketing (Little, 2001).

Marketing automation is examined from different perspectives in both consumer marketing and business-to-business marketing. Development in business-to-business marketing has recently been very rapid, as evidenced by the many works that have emerged in the literature (Järvinen and Taiminen, 2016; Mero, Leinonen, Makkonen, and Karjaluoto, 2022), to the point that some authors have described it, with a focus on sales, as one of the most talked about concepts in marketing at the moment, especially in the B2B domain (Järvinen and Taiminen, 2016). Automated marketing can operate within the "funnel" that leads from generating contacts to completing sales activities. The theme of converting contacts with customers, underlying the idea of the funnel, has been present in marketing for a long time and has origins going back a long way (Colicev, Kumar and O'Connor, 2019). The funnel theme is common to the online and offline buying process (Paschen, Wilson and Ferreira, 2020), as well as other business processes such as innovation (Rogers, 1995).

The digitization of marketing seems to be fostering a greater connection between business and consumer marketing. Online players, such as Alibaba, integrate presence in both business and consumer markets into their business model (Anwar, 2017).

The downstream integration of companies operating in business markets is evident in sectors traceable to luxury fashion, in which in order to meet the needs of their business customers and to have advantage points over competitors, business-to-business actors develop initiatives directed at ensuring the sustainability of the processes carried out by suppliers (Hoejmose, Brammer, and Millington, 2012).

In addition to social media, other areas in which a progressive use of the same automation tools can be observed are those of the digital store, supply chain integration, and the supplier relationship as a determinant of sustainable brand attributes.

The emergence in recent years of automation in supply chain management highlights connections between consumer marketing and business marketing in relation to the green supply chain (Hoejmose, Brammer, and Millington, 2012). As different as the distinction between marketing content is from the distinction between competitive domains, the diversity of marketing practices adopted are an important element of competitive processes. Marketing automation applies to marketing processes comprising of (among others): demand analysis; forecasting and planning; consumer behavior analysis and network listening; personalized communication and promotion; social media and engagement; yielding and pricing (Hoejmose, Brammer, and Millington, 2012).

Implementing marketing automation requires evaluating and answering several problems, choosing which decisions to automate, and assessing the impact of automation in relationships with customers, competitors, and influencers. Marketing automation typically comes to the enterprise in the form of a choice to adopt new software or systems (Van Bruggen and Wierenga, 2010). This adoption has as its antecedent the choice of the system that will then develop the processes of supporting managers' tasks and replacing them in decision-making processes through forms of automation, until the system is upgraded, replaced, or decommissioned. These systems fit into a context in which other trends are present: (1) the spread of "algorithm based" business models; (2) the realization of forms of segmentation and targeting entrusted to the use of large databases; (3) a system of marketing research through data recounting and listening in the network; (4) personalized forms of communication, such as those related to programmatic advertising; (5) automation of operational marketing processes, such as in price negotiation; (6) integration of collected data with corporate customer databases for promotional initiatives; (7) new forms of customer contact and interface (gaming, metaverse, chat bots).

The automation of marketing processes can be an essential component of the integration of artificial intelligence into business processes, even for firms without algorithm-based business models (Ritter and Pedersen, 2020; Guercini, 2023). In the case of social media use, there is a growing component in the literature that highlights the specificities of business marketing versus consumer marketing (Iankova, Davies, Archer-Brown, Marder and Yau, 2019). In particular, differences are identified in the relationship between the importance of social media and its perceived effectiveness, where business-to-business firms see social media use attributing less effectiveness overall, identifying it as less important for customer relationships (Iankova, Davies, Archer-Brown, Marder and Yau, 2019, p. 177). Despite this, the business-to-business context is one in which there were the first users of software to support customer profiling for personalization of offerings (Lamont, 2015; Järvinen and Taiminen, 2016). These are software whose use is often partial to its potential, since the features that can be activated require expertise, as well as time and infrastructure, to be usefully integrated. In fact, it appears that companies even in this area begin by automating things they have already done with previously present tools, only to make incremental advances later (Lee and Bradlow, 2011).

Introducing marketing automation and the impact on marketers' decision making implies the introduction of automation solutions achieved through the adoption of new software with strong individual and organizational commitment. Paradoxically, automation not only does not involve disengagement, but the marketer is required to acquire new competencies, defined as knowledge applied to a task, to interface with the system (Van Bruggen and Wierenga, 2010).

Automation, with the greater role given to machine capabilities, may be accompanied by a new vision of what are the "superior" ways of doing marketing, those that enable more accurate predictions or those that are more effective in results, defining a new emerging dominant approach. The ideas underlying this approach may be summarized as follows: (1) judgments and choices based on larger databases are superior to those based on using less extensive databases; (2) machines through artificial intelligence are able to process larger sets of data; (3) people's judgments and behaviors based mainly on heuristics are biased. These are assumptions supported by contributors that highlight bias (Kahneman, 2011), while constrating with research findings that show the effectiveness that can accompany human rule-based decision making (Gigerenzer, 2022).

Marketing automation finds particular impetus from innovations in artificial intelligence, offering solutions that can give organizations the ability to continue using it in innovative ways (De Rowe, 2016). Expressed in simple terms, marketing automation

> is a technology that allows companies to streamline marketing processes, better organize marketing tasks, fully automate marketing strategies and precisely measure their effectiveness, leading to increased return on marketing investment ... the goal of the marketing automation system is to automate repetitive marketing tasks. Company-generated content can be provided to prospects by a range of media including e-mail, social networks, specially designed landing pages or webinars. Messages reach prospects at an appropriate stage of the purchasing cycle. (Świeczak, 2013, p. 5)

In this area, marketing automation capabilities include: (1) maintaining databases of current and potential clients, with their respective e-mails and other contacts; (2) monitoring and analyzing customer behavior on mobile applications and certain websites; (3) segmenting prospects according to key variables captured in their online browsing; (4) monitoring e-mail processes; (5) identifying and managing contacts and visits in a business-to-business environment; and (6) more generally automated management of marketing activities. Automated marketing activities offer systems with even broader possibilities, for example in managing different communication channels (Porter and Heppelman, 2015).

Definitions that emerge later highlight other additional aspects. For example, marketing automation is identified by some directly with the use of software to automate marketing processes such as segmentation, integration of consumer data, and campaign management, identifying marketing automation as an integral component of CRM (Wood, 2015). In another recent definition, it emerges as "marketing automation involves a software platform that can be used to deliver content based on specific rules set by users (Oracle, 2016). The objective is to attract, build and maintain trust with current and prospective customers by automatically personalizing relevant and useful content to meet their specific needs" (Järvinen and Taiminen, 2016, p. 165).

5.4 MARKETING AUTOMATION AND ARTIFICIAL INTELLIGENCE

Over the past few years, we have witnessed a major change in the way marketing is done in companies. This change is connected to a large extent to new technologies and the role assumed by the digital environment as a context in which to carry out marketing activities. One impetus for change in this area is the spread of forms of artificial intelligence (Huang and Rust, 2021), which has overlaps but is conceptually distinct from the process of automation. Automated marketing can enhance the integration of artificial intelligence into the overall marketing process (Cui and Curry, 2005). Automated marketing is at a distinct but integrated level with artificial intelligence, and it has been defined as automated marketing decision support. Marketing decision support (Van Bruggen and Wierenga, 2010) can improve the productivity of strategic actors (Bucklin, Lehmann, and Little, 1998) by freeing them from the constraints between emerging data and required actions (see Figure 5.2).

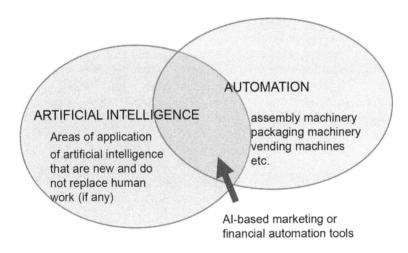

Source: Author's elaboration.

Figure 5.2   *Marketing decision support*

This section merely examines the distinction between automation and artificial intelligence, deferring a more in-depth look at the topic of artificial intelligence in marketing processes to the following sixth chapter. In artificial intelligence, the need to formulate decision models can be met by the machine by identifying the solution based on predetermined requirements, even in the most layered and complex forms. The model under which automation is achieved can be structured based on data analysis by the machine itself, and this model can also evolve through learning on regression or classification models (machine learning) and this evolution can be based on large, neural network models capable of making accurate data-driven decisions (deep learning) (Kelleher, 2019). In this way, automated marketing goes beyond a smart CRM to mark a new era evolution of the concept of marketing, in which the technological dimension is not just a supporting element, but an element whose characteristics can intermediate and shape a certain type of relationship between business and market in a digitization context (Brock and Von Wangenheim, 2019).

Artificial intelligence in strategic marketing is embodied in what some authors have recently called "predictive machines" (Agrawal, Gans and Goldfarb, 2018). These are tools for carrying out prediction and planning activities, a particularly complex area around which there has been a debate about rules for forecasting (Armstrong, Green and Graefe, 2015). Artificial intelligence applied to marketing processes uses algorithms to interact with customers, improving market understanding and developing processes that influence market actors (customers, opinion leaders, influencers, competitors). In the experience of marketers, the availability of big data has long underpinned automated marketing decisions based on parameters set by appropriate software. Algorithms use incoming data to produce predictions and actions directly, sometimes almost in real time. This support has become an opportunity as well as a necessity in the new digital environment, partly because of its increasing adoption by competitors. Indeed, when data are available and timely decisions are not made, competitors will have the upper hand (Paschen et al., 2020).

Artificial Intelligence can extend the field of marketing automation to complex processes of a strategic nature. As much as automation systems were conceivable even earlier, it is with the beginning of the 2000s that we see the setting up and exploitation of systems to monitor the behavior of those who frequent the Internet. It is in this area that marketing automation systems originated (Świeczak, 2013), capable of tracking the behavior of e-mail recipients at a given site. The information obtained makes it possible to identify the needs and provide a response in time and with a level of personalization that can only be dealt with by automated systems.

In recent years this process has been made even more evident by high impact events, such as the 2020 pandemic crisis and the geopolitical events that have occurred in the intervening years. It is not simply a matter of learning how to use digital marketing tools and systems, but of rethinking the entire marketing activity. In this area, a special space has the issue of changing the way decisions are made in the face of the automation phenomenon that characterizes marketing activities. Markets, especially large and global ones, have been characterized by the adoption of new technological solutions by companies. Automation is found when customer segmentation, customer targeting, communication and promotional initiatives, product offerings, and pricing, to name a few examples, are reliant on automated systems. This is a wide-ranging phenomenon, which is not limited to the adoption of artificial intelligence systems, but has in its diffusion the most obvious and important elements.

Indeed, automation involves not only a technological solution, but also a different organizational model on the business side, which is also relevant to the way marketers make decisions. Marketing automation has thus become one of the most popular subjects in the marketing world in recent years (Mero, Leinonen, Makkonen, and Karjaluoto, 2022). It is a phenomenon that has also absorbed significant investment from companies, which have sought in this way to adapt their marketing by hiring software products and systems in order to approach the marketing environment by adapting to its change and achieving greater effectiveness and efficiency (Morgan, Jayachandran, Hulland, Kumar, Katsikeas, and Somosi, 2022).

The concept of marketing automation has been around for some time, proposing a novel idea that may consist of a kind of coexistence of communication and sales activities (Little, 2001). Marketing automation also corresponds to the exploitation of great analytical potentialities and a real increase in the possibility of generating added value through them. The introduction of marketing automation has an impact not only on the marketing function, but on the entire business, since everything a marketing automation system provides, including the unique knowledge of a customer, is also a critical marketing value for any modern enterprise (Świeczak, 2013).

Marketing automation can be associated with several aspects of marketing. One very important element is the connection with communication (Heimbach, Kostyra and Hinz, 2015). Indeed, marketing automation has been seen concerning the evolution of marketing toward a new reality in which communication based on the mass distribution of a universal message, is superseded by personalized and fully automated customer contact. In this case, marketing automation is a concept centered on the merging of the marketing and sales departments to produce the best result. Another way to view marketing automation is to see it as systems that can improve marketing's contribution to the company's bottom line. Marketing automation means greater analytical capabilities, which as such is an asset, and thus growth in the equity dimension of the enterprise and generation of added value from customer knowledge that can integrate with all organizational processes (Wierenga, 2002).

For Bucklin, Lehmann, and Little (1998), marketing automation emerges when the use of data collection and processing technologies move from providing support for marketing decision making, to a stage of automating marketing decisions, whereby "decisions we can support today are prime candidates to be decisions we can automate tomorrow" (Bucklin, Lehmann, and Little, 1998, p. 235). Automated marketing finds its raison d'être in certain features of particular interest to business management. Specifically, marketing automation: (1) offers productivity advantages, as the use of models allows marketing processes to be managed while achieving better results in terms of less time and cost; (2) is associated with model-based decisions that can offer superior preemptions to decisions made by managers, due to the ability to use a better quality database with more powerful acquisition and elaboration processes; and (3) offers the ability to provide real-time decisions (Morgan, Jayachandran, Hulland, Kumar, Katsikeas, and Somosi, 2022).

Still in the realm of advisory services and business operations, marketing automation can be conceptualized as a technological tool and a set of tactics that enables companies to nurture prospects with relevant and highly personalized content that helps convert prospects into actual customers and turns them into satisfied customers (Hubspot, 2022).

Marketing automation can be seen as a process that tends to enhance marketing strategies through the use of software that automates processes, whereby certain repeated activities such as managing email campaigns, social media, and other online actions can be accomplished by a machine and freeing up marketing people for the time that would have been spent doing these activities manually and, most importantly, by having a greater influence on user decisions along the user lifecycle (Van Bruggen and Wierenga, 2010). In particular, some definitions focus on a view in which marketing automation is a tool of the development of each of the people taking part in the program (Oracle, 2016).

Biegel (2009), recalls the Winterberry Group definition, for which marketing automation can be defined as

> the utilization of marketing technology solutions to automate marketing processes including (though not limited to) planning, budgeting, segmentation, database management, analytics, creative execution, asset management, campaign execution, lead management and reporting. These marketing technologies are a combination of software, networks and hardware that allow the inputs, processing and outputs of marketing and business information and content. (Biegel, 2009, p. 2003)

Marketing automation has since been conceptualized as closely related to a category of software that optimizes, automates and measures marketing activities and flows to enable companies to improve in their efficiency and increase revenue faster (Miller, 2013).

The integration of artificial intelligence with marketing automation includes many hands-on activities and emerges more from practice than from an a priori model. For example, while in the simplest form, marketing automation means sending targeted e-mails for upselling activities and offers relevant to the needs of clients in a given organization, with artificial intelligence automation is intended to replace or augment the capabilities of managers, where "automation enables managers to easily track market structure evolution by sampling review over time" (Lee and Bradlow, 2011, p. 888).

5.5   HUMAN DECISION MAKING IN MARKETING AUTOMATION

The adoption of artificial intelligence applied to marketing processes, whether business-to-business or business-to-consumer, suggests in perspective a different distinction, which is that between markets in which actors make use of automated tools (automated marketing) and markets in which actors make use exclusively or almost exclusively of contact between human actors (human marketing). This second distinction may cut across industrial and consumer markets, in the sense that in both the former and the latter we can have, alongside contexts in which forms of contact based on the use of artificial intelligence and forms of automated decision-making are employed, others in which decision making remains the essential preserve of the human actor.

It can be assumed that in all areas where decisions must be based on the use of data, and where the greater the importance of processing a large amount of data in a short time, the greater the potential role of artificial intelligence for automated forms of marketing. When decisions cannot be based on data alone, the human decision maker may continue to play an important role, fueling an emerging dichotomy between more and less pronounced forms of automation in marketing processes (Van Bruggen and Wierenga, 2010).

Given the increased data processing capacity of machines, we can imagine that all decisions intended to be based on the use of data over time may be supported, if not assumed exclusively, by machines and artificial intelligence. Some questions ensue: What role remains for the human decision maker? What characteristics will human intervention in processes have? The human decision maker is likely to be concerned, rather than with information-based decisions, but with monitoring outcomes and the rules of thumb to be followed, in light of which to evaluate processes and decide when to "disconnect" the "autopilot". To do this, our thesis in this book is that a "heuristic decision making" should assume greater prominence, in particular by enhancing those decision-making modes that characterize the human decision maker and that are basically defined as "fast thinking" by Kahneman, or heuristics, seen as an element that can make decision makers smart (Gigerenzer, 2022).

In fact, heuristics are defined here as algorithms easily applicable with simplicity, robustness and transparency by the human actor. Automation assumes such prominence already today and even more so in the future that it represents a key differentiator within the marketing practice and the marketing studies. This is while other traditional differentiators tend to be less salient. For example, today the same platforms (as Adwords) are used by both consumer and business buyers, resulting in a convergence of some aspects of the buying process; many companies from business markets now also enter the consumer market, often with their own digital store, leading to an integration of business and consumer marketing expertise. Discussing these aspects, an emerging distinction is proposed related to the degree of "automation" present in the relationships between market players, which can be very high or lower, leveraging artificial intelligence and big data, or personal interaction and heuristics. These two components may integrate differently with implications for actor marketing.

Differences in approach also lead to a reconfiguration of competitive processes, which have always seen the evolution of technology as a powerful driver of change. Particularly relevant in this area today is the issue of artificial intelligence, which through its more advanced forms (machine learning, and in particular deep learning) supports an automation of decision-making processes, or at least of fundamental steps of these, not only for the collection and processing of information, but more generally for the formation of judgments and choices, and even for the elaboration of the models on the basis of which judgments and choices are made. This leads to the replacement of activities of human actors with automated marketing processes that absorb an increasing part of traditional marketing activities, both in the area of research, strategy, and marketing action itself (Huang and Rust, 2021). Especially but not only with "algorithm based" business models, where the use of the forms of automation related to the use of big data and artificial intelligence affect the marketing literature in terms that are more and more evident (Huang and Rust, 2021).

Relationships between actors grounded in potentially increasingly automated processes and the use of big data and automation result in the use of similar practices that are increasingly evolved and shoehorned into the potentially automatable marketing context. In fact, on the one hand, the greatest potential of automation is expressed precisely in the management of greater volumes of data and requiring greater efforts in terms of processing capacity. On the other hand, the future evolution in the direction of commoditization of decision-making processes based on the use of big data is associated with the growth in the value of decisions that are not automated for the time being. Activities that will remain the preserve of people may retain greater added value. The capabilities that remain with people also suggest relationships still based on the interaction between human actors and the use of simplified decision rules (heuristics), as their delegation to the machine is not considered effective (Guercini, 2020).

A proposition about the relation between automation and heuristics emerges: Automation does not lead to overcoming the marketers' use of heuristics, but is a new challenge for the adaptive toolbox, as it is managed by adapting the heuristics used and their scope.

Some tales from the business field put in evidence hypotheses and possible objects of discussion and future research (Guercini, 2023). One about the relationship between data and decisions appears reversed. While traditionally we have data on which decisions are based, here a situation would seem to emerge in which the use of systems requires the taking of decisions on which data depend, on which subsequent decisions should then be based. In this chain of decision-data-decisions, the role of heuristics can change remaining fundamental (Figure 5.3).

a. The traditional relation between data output and decision-making based on heuristics

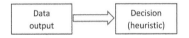

b. The new role of heuristics in decision making with the use of marketing automation systems

Source: Author's elaboration.

Figure 5.3   *The chain decision-data-decision and the role of heuristics*

REFERENCES

Agrawal, A., Gans, J., & Goldfarb, A. (2018). *Prediction machines. The simple economics of artificial intelligence*. Harvard Business Review Press, Boston, Mass.

Alpaydin, E. (2016). *Machine learning: the new AI*. MIT press, Cambridge, Mass.

Anwar, S. T. (2017). Alibaba: Entrepreneurial growth and global expansion in B2B/B2C markets. *Journal of International Entrepreneurship, 15*(4), 366–389.

Armstrong, J. S., Green, K. C., & Graefe, A. (2015). Golden rule of forecasting: Be conservative. *Journal of Business Research, 68*(8), 1717–1731.

Bagshaw, A. (2015). What is marketing automation? *Journal of Direct, Data and Digital Marketing Practice, 17*(2), 84–85.

Bainbridge, L. (1982). Ironies of automation. *IFAC Proceedings Volumes, 15*(6), 129–135.

Bell, M. L., & Emory, C. W. (1971). The faltering marketing concept. *Journal of Marketing, 35*(4), 37–42.

Benbasat, I., Goldstein, D. K., & Mead, M. (1987). The case research strategy in studies of information systems. *MIS Quarterly, 11*(3), 369–386.

Benhauer (2018). *Marketing automation. The definitive and ultimate guide to marketing automation.* Sales Manago Marketing Automation.

Biegel, B. (2009). The current view and outlook for the future of marketing automation. *Journal of Direct, Data and Digital Marketing Practice, 10*(3), 201–213.

Bostrom, N. (2014). *Superintelligence. Paths, Dangers, Strategies*, Oxford University Press, Oxford.

Bright, J. R. (1958). *Automation and management.* Harvard University: Division of Research, Graduate School of Business Administration, Boston.

Brock, J. K. U., & Von Wangenheim, F. (2019). Demystifying AI: What digital transformation leaders can teach you about realistic artificial intelligence. *California Management Review, 61*(4), 110–134.

Bucklin, R. E., Lattin, J. M., Ansari, S., Bell, D., Coupey, E., Gupta, A., Little, J.D.C., Mela, C., Montgomery, A., & Steckel, J. (2002). Choice and the Internet: From clickstream to research stream. *Marketing Letters, 13*(3), 245–258.

Bucklin, R., Lehmann, D., & Little, J. (1998). From decision support to decision automation: A 2020 vision. *Marketing Letters, 9*(3), 235–246.

Byrne, E. A., & Parasuraman, R. (1996). Psychophysiology and adaptive automation. *Biological psychology, 42*(3), 249–268.

Cavusgil, T., & Guercini, S. (2014). Trends in middle class as a driver for strategic marketing. *Mercati & Competitività, 10*(3), 7–10.

Colicev, A., Kumar, A., & O'Connor, P. (2019). Modeling the relationship between firm and user generated content and the stages of the marketing funnel. *International Journal of Research in Marketing, 36*(1), 100–116.

Cui, D., & Curry, D. (2005). Prediction in marketing using the support vector machine. *Marketing Science, 24*(4), 595–615.

Cummings, D., & Blitzer, A. (2010). *Think Outside the Inbox: B2B Marketing Automation Guide.* Leigh Walker Books, Atlanta.

Del Rowe, S. (2016). New Uses for Marketing Automation-The already effective technology will become even more valuable in the future. *Customer Relationship Management*, December, 24–27.

Frey, C. B., & Osborne, M. A. (2013). *The future of employment: How susceptible are jobs to computarisation?* Oxford University Press, Oxford.

Frey, C. B., & Osborne, M. A. (2017). The future of employment: How susceptible are jobs to computerisation? *Technological Forecasting and Social Change, 114*, 254–280.

Gigerenzer, G. (2022). *How to stay smart in a smart world: Why human intelligence still beats algorithms.* Penguin Books, London.

Goeldner, C. R. (1962). Automation in marketing. *Journal of Marketing, 26*(1), 53–56.

Grönroos, C. (1994). Quo vadis, marketing? Toward a relationship marketing paradigm. *Journal of marketing management, 10*(5), 347–360.

Guercini, S. (2020). The Actor or the Machine? The Strategic Marketing Decision-Maker Facing Digitalization. *Micro & Macro Marketing, 29*(1), 3–7.

Guercini, S. (2022). Scope of heuristics and digitalization: the case of marketing automation. *Mind & Society, 21*(2), 151–164.

Guercini, S. (2023) *Marketing automation and the scope of marketers heuristics*, Management Decision, https://doi.org/10.1108/MD-07-2022-0909.

Head, G. W. (1960). What does automation mean to the marketing man? *Journal of Marketing, 24*(4), 35–37.

Heimbach, I., Kostyra, D. S., & Hinz, O. (2015). Marketing automation. *Business & Information Systems Engineering, 57*(2), 129–133.

Hirt, M., & Willmott, P. (2014). Strategic principles for competing in the digital age. *McKinsey Quarterly, 5*(1), 1–13.

Hoejmose, S., Brammer, S., & Millington, A. (2012). "Green" supply chain management: The role of trust and top management in B2B and B2C markets. *Industrial Marketing Management, 41*(4), 609–620.

Huang, M. H., & Rust, R. T. (2021). A strategic framework for artificial intelligence in marketing. *Journal of the Academy of Marketing Science, 49*(1), 30–50.

Hubspot (2022). *What is marketing automation?* Available here: https://www.hubspot .com/marketing-automation-information.

Houston, F. S. (1986). The marketing concept: what it is and what it is not. *Journal of Marketing, 50*(2), 81–87.

Iankova, S., Davies, I., Archer-Brown, C., Marder, B., & Yau, A. (2019). A comparison of social media marketing between B2B, B2C and mixed business models. *Industrial Marketing Management, 81*, 169–179.

Järvinen, J., & Taiminen, H. (2016). Harnessing marketing automation for B2B content marketing. *Industrial Marketing Management, 54*, 164–175.

Jones, D. B., & Richardson, A. J. (2007). The myth of the marketing revolution. *Journal of Macromarketing, 27*(1), 15–24.

Kahneman, D. (2011). *Thinking, fast and slow*. Penguin Books, London.

Kaplan, J. (2017). *Artificial intelligence. What everyone needs to know*. Oxford University Press, Oxford.

Keith, R. J. (1960). The marketing revolution. *Journal of Marketing, 24*(3), 35–38.

Kelleher, J. D. (2019). *Deep learning*. MIT press, Cambridge, Mass.

Kotler, P. (1967). *Marketing management. Analysis, planning, and control*. Prentice-Hall, Inc. Englewood Cliffs, N.J.

Kotler, P. (1989). From mass marketing to mass customization. *Planning review, 17*(5), 10–47.

Lamont, J. (2015). Marketing automation: an accelerating solution. *KM World, 24*(2), 12–13.

Langeard, E., & Eiglier, P. (1987). Servuction: le marketing des services. McGraw-Hill, Paris.

Lazzeretti, L., Innocenti, N., Nannelli, M., & Oliva, S. (2023). The emergence of artificial intelligence in the regional sciences: a literature review. *European Planning Studies, 31*(7), 1304–1324.

Lee, T. Y., & Bradlow, E. T. (2011). Automated marketing research using online customer reviews. *Journal of Marketing Research, 48*(5), 881–894.

Leung, E., Paolacci, G., & Puntoni, S. (2018). Man versus machine: Resisting automation in identity-based consumer behavior. *Journal of Marketing Research, 55*(6), 818–831.

Little, J. D. (2001). Marketing automation on the internet. In *5th Invitational Choice Symposium*, June, 1–5.

Mero, J., Leinonen, M., Makkonen, H., & Karjaluoto, H. (2022). Agile logic for SaaS implementation: Capitalizing on marketing automation software in a start-up. *Journal of Business Research, 145*, 583–594.

Mero, J., Tarkiainen, A., & Tobon, J. (2020). Effectual and causal reasoning in the adoption of marketing automation. *Industrial Marketing Management, 86*, 212–222.

Miller, J. (2013). *The definitive guide to marketing automation*. [ebook] Creative director, Marketo.

Morgan, N. A., Jayachandran, S., Hulland, J., Kumar, B., Katsikeas, C., & Somosi, A. (2022). Marketing performance assessment and accountability: Process and outcomes. *International Journal of Research in Marketing, 39*(2), 462–481.

Müller, V. C., & Bostrom, N. (2016). Future Progress in Artificial Intelligence: A Survey of Expert Opinion. In Müller, V.C. (ed.), *Fundamental Issues of Artificial Intelligence*. Springer, Cham, Synthese Library, Berlin, 553–571.

Oracle (2016). *Marketing Automation Simplified – The small guide to big ideas*. E-book available at https://www.oracle.com/marketingcloud/content/documents/guides/marketing-automation-simplified-gad-oracle.pdf.

Paschen, J., Wilson, M., & Ferreira, J. J. (2020). Collaborative intelligence: How human and artificial intelligence create value along the B2B sales funnel. *Business Horizons, 63*(3), 403–414.

Porter, M. E., & Heppelmann, J. E. (2015). How smart, connected products are transforming companies. *Harvard Business Review, 93*(10), 96–114.

Ritter, T., & Pedersen, C. L. (2020). Digitization capability and the digitalization of business models in business-to-business firms: Past, present, and future. *Industrial Marketing Management, 86*, 180–190.

Rogers, E. M. (1995). Lessons for guidelines from the diffusion of innovations. *The Joint Commission Journal on Quality Improvement, 21*(7), 324–328.

Silverman, W. (1966). The economic and social effects of automation in an organization. *American Behavioral Scientist, 9*(10), 3–8.

Swani, K., Brown, B. P., & Milne, G. R. (2014). Should tweets differ for B2B and B2C? An analysis of Fortune 500 companies' Twitter communications. *Industrial Marketing Management, 43*(5), 873–881.

Świeczak, W. (2013). Marketing automation processes as a way to improve contemporary marketing of a company. *Marketing Instytucji Naukowych i Badawczych, 3*(9), 71–84.

Tagmark, M. (2017). *Life 3.0: Being human in the age of artificial intelligence*, Penguin Books, London.

Turing, A. M. (1950). Computing machinery and intelligence. *Mind. New Series, 59*(236), 433–460.

Tversky, A., & Kahneman, D. (1974). Judgment under Uncertainty: Heuristics and Biases: Biases in judgments reveal some heuristics of thinking under uncertainty. *Science, 185*(4157), 1124–1131.

Upadhyay, M. A., & Chitnis, P. (2022). *Modern marketing using AI. Leverage AI-enabled marketing automation and insights to drive customer journeys and maximize your brand equity*. BPB Publications, India.

Van Bruggen, G. H., & Wierenga, B. (2010). Marketing decision making and decision support: Challenges and perspectives for successful marketing management support systems. *Foundations and Trends® in Marketing, 4*(4), 209–332.

Van Bruggen, G. H., Smidts, A., & Wierenga, B. (2001). The powerful triangle of marketing data, managerial judgment, and marketing management support systems. *European Journal of Marketing, 35*(7/8), 796–814.

Vargo, S. L., & Lusch, R. F. (2008). Service-dominant logic: continuing the evolution. *Journal of the Academy of Marketing Science, 36*(1), 1–10.

Walsh, M. (2019). *The algorithmic leader. How to be smart when machines are smarter than you*. Page Two Books, Vancouver.

Wertenbroch, K. (2021). Marketing Automation: Marketing Utopia or Marketing Dystopia? *NIM Marketing Intelligence Review, 13*(1), 18–23.

Wiener, N. (1948). *Cybernetics or control and communication in the animal and the machine.* John Wiley & Sons, New York.

Wierenga, B. (2002). On academic marketing knowledge and marketing knowledge that marketing managers use for decision-making. *Marketing Theory, 2*(4), 355–362.

Wood, C. (2015). Marketing automation: Lessons learnt so far.... *Journal of Direct, Data and Digital Marketing Practice, 16*(4), 251–254.

6. Artificial intelligence and marketers' decisions in marketing automation

6.1 THE IMPACT OF ARTIFICIAL INTELLIGENCE ON MARKETING PROCESSES

Forms of artificial intelligence (AI) now affect various areas of business life and are also identified in marketing because of their configuration in terms of the ecosystem (Puntoni, Reczek, Giesler, and Botti, 2021, p. 132). The concept of AI is related to that of automation in that AI itself can be seen as an attempt to automate speculative-rational capabilities and human decision-making processes through computer algorithms (De Bruyn, Viswanathan, Beh, Brock, and von Wangenheim, 2020). The concept of AI is rooted in the human-machine relationship and its evolution both at the micro level (relationship between individual human actor and machine) and at the macro level (implications for society) (Lazzeretti, 2023). From a marketer's perspective, these systems represent an additional and qualitatively different step on a path of evolution of marketing decision support (Albers, 2012; Alexouda, 2005).

Machine learning (ML) "focuses on the design and evaluation of algorithms for extracting patterns from data" (Kelleher and Tierney, 2018, p. 1), achieving measurable performance that can improve with experience (Mitchell, 1997; Samuel, 1959). ML "is not just a database or programming problem; it is also a requirement" for AI (Alpaydin, 2016, p. 17). In ML the object of automation is the learning process itself (Jordan and Mitchell, 2015). In marketing, the potential of ML is related to the size and type of behavioral data available on users today. Particularly relevant in terms of quantity and quality of data is the contribution that comes from the use of mobile devices such as smartphones, which are evidently much more than phones and which follow the users, recording their location and being able to acquire information in relation to multiple uses (translator, watch, etc.). ML can thus help us detect associations or behavioral data in an increasingly complex world (Alpaydin, 2016, p. 145). The terms AI and ML are often used together and even interchangeably, although they have distinct meanings. AI also includes ML, but ML does not fully define AI, which in fact includes other processes as well (Alpaydin, 2016; Kaplan, 2017).

Despite this visibility and great growth in attention, the still exploratory character of the approach to AI is consequential to the progress of the technology in the making, the number and breadth of applications, and the pervasiveness of implications. This exploratory character is signaled in a broader literature by the uncertainty for the future of work (Jarrahi, 2018), to the dangers to humanity more broadly associated with the assertion of possible AI hegemony in a framework reminiscent of the dystopian component of science fiction literature (Bostrom, 2014; Shanahan, 2015; Tegmark, 2017). The issues posed by AI are of relevance to marketing, and marketing represents an area of application certainly of great interest to data science (Kelleher and Tierney, 2018).

In the marketing literature, AI and ML appear to be of interest from different perspectives and with different approaches. Perspectives from which to examine AI include that of marketers, with marketing planning activities (Huang and Rust, 2021), and that of consumers, with implications for marketers' actions (Puntoni, Reczek, Giesler, and Botti, 2021). AI then becomes relevant in a broader perspective including legal, ethical, and socio-economic aspects and having implications for society as a whole (Kaplan, 2017; Lazzeretti, 2023) and for its specific components (Nannelli, Capone and Lazzeretti, 2023).

Approaches to AI in marketing processes can be geared to grasp its potential and implications for marketers' tasks (Huang and Rust, 2021), considering both strengths and perceived issues in consumers' experiences (Puntoni, Reczek, Giesler, and Botti, 2021), or from the perspective of marketers (Kozinets and Gretzel, 2021). AI represents an element that supports the shift from traditional "inside out" marketing to an evolved and updated form of adoption of the marketing concept that is defined as "outside in" marketing, driven by data on customer interests and satisfaction (Rust, 2020).

This increasing focus on AI in marketing is confirmed by the trend in the number of publications. Just as an example, simply by querying the Scopus database about publications that contain "marketing" together with "artificial intelligence" ("marketing" AND "artificial intelligence") in the abstract, keywords and title, the products published in 2013 were 62, while those in 2022 were 513, with a steady growth over the years and overall more than eightfold over the decade. Despite this attention of the literature, the impact of AI in marketing does not yet appear to be configured in its outlines, suggesting that we are still at an exploratory stage. Experiences of using AI tools by marketers and consumers are growing. There are the cases of Amazon.com's Prime Air platforms or RedBallon's Albert's AI (Huang and Rust, 2021, p. 30) or Alibaba's Tmall Genie or Google Photo editing suggestions (Puntoni, Reczek, Giesler, and Botti, 2021, p. 131). The fields of application of AI are varied and very often clearly perceived by market actors, both marketers and consumers and customers, as in the case of AI-powered conversational agents, virtual assistants, or chatbots (Jeon, 2022; Pantano and Pizzi, 2020).

To frame the theme of the relationship between AI and marketing, it may be to recall the path from which AI emerges and develops. The origin of the phrase "artificial intelligence" is famously attributed to the choice of title for a lecture at Dartmouth College in Hanover, New Hampshire, in 1956 (McCarthy, Minsky, Rochester and Shannon, 2006). The role of machines in economic processes has been the focus of original contributions by leading economists (Marshall, 1994). However, it is one thing to imagine that machines can perform processing; it is quite another to imagine that human speculative-rational capacity can be automated. A few years before the coining of the term AI, in a famous article entitled "Computing, machinery and intelligence", Alan Turing (1950) wondered how the question "can machines think?" could be answered. Excluding that the answer could be given in direct form or on the basis of a survey, he formulated a key principle for defining AI that corresponded to the so-called "imitation game". Turing writes,

> Can machines think? is to be sought in a statistical survey such as a Gallup poll. But this is absurd. Instead of attempting such a definition I shall replace the question by another, which is closely related to it and is expressed in relatively unambiguous words. The new form of the problem can be described in terms of a game which we call the 'imitation game'. It is played with three people, a man (A), a woman (B), and an interrogator (C) who may be of either sex. The interrogator stays in a room apart from the other two. The object of the game for the interrogator is to determine which of the other two is the man and which is the woman. He knows them by labels X and Y, and at the end of the game he says either 'X is A and Y is B' or 'X is B and Y is A' ... We now ask the question, 'What will happen when a machine takes the part of A in this game?' Will the interrogator decide wrongly as often when the game is played like this as he does when the game is played between a man and a woman? These questions replace our original, 'Can machines think?' (Turing, 1950, pp. 433–434)

Turing's proposed redefinition of the question "can machines think?" suggests a key aspect of AI concept definition (McCarthy, Minsky, Rochester and Shannon, 2006) that may be relevant to the relationship between AI and marketing. The machine can think, in this sense be said to be intelligent, if it succeeds in being indistinguishable from a human operator in the experience of the interactant, thus if it passes the test implicit in the imitation game. Consumer marketing steps up research based on experiments and empirical testing, for example, comparing chatbots and human assistants. This way of defining AI overcomes the dilemma implicit in having to consider AI as an actor or as a resource available to actors, since what matters is the perception of other actors in the interaction. It matters not whether the machine can think and is actually intelligent, but that human actors can perceive it as such, in a view that puts the observer at the center in a manner similar to what happens in a radical constructivist view (Maturana and Varela, 1991; Guercini and Medlin, 2020; von Glasersfeld, 1995).

The importance and centrality of AI for marketing, goes hand in hand with an importance of marketing as a ground for AI. In fact, there is not only a large and growing interest in AI in the marketing literature, but also some interest in marketing in the data science and ML literature (Alpaydin, 2016, pp. 111ff.; Kelleher and Tierney, 2018, pp. 25–26, p. 152ff.), in which applications to marketing problems are among the most prevalent (Kaplan, 2017).

To talk about AI is to distinguish different types of intelligence and definitions of intelligence that have changed over time, highlighting for example the role of emotional intelligence versus social intelligence (Salovey and Mayer, 1990). Although there are many cases of the use of ML tools applied by firms to marketing problems, and although it has been pointed out that AI can substantially change the future of marketing (Rust, 2020; Wu and Monfort, 2023), still recently it is assessed that "academic marketing research to date provides insufficient guidance about how best to leverage the benefits of AI for marketing impact" (Huang and Rust, 2021, p. 30).

The relationship between AI and marketing is far-reaching and can be viewed from different perspectives. Huang and Rust (2021) examine the benefits that AI can bring to strategic marketing planning, distinguishing "mechanical", "thinking", and "feeling" aspects (Huang and Rust, 2021, p. 30). "Mechanical AI" refers to the automation of repetitive marketing functions and activities, such as in customer mailing systems in a database. "Thinking AI" refers to data processing to support decision making, such as in demand planning systems. "Feeling AI" refers to the analysis of human interactions and emotions, which can take a role in AI serving customer care such as in chatbot systems. To speak of AI is to avail oneself of a metaphor, and different forms of intelligence can also be recognized for human intelligence (Huang and Rust, 2021). The benefits of AI are relevant and related to the more general advancement of technology in the activities of marketers and consumers, particularly relevant in the relationship between marketing and AI in terms of benefits as well as limitations and risks (Wu and Monfort, 2023).

6.2   FORMS OF ARTIFICIAL INTELLIGENCE AND MARKETING DECISION MODELS

The change induced by new data-driven technologies on marketing activity has implications for the models for decision making adopted by marketers (Rust, 2020). Marketing is seeing profound changes as technology reconfigures its processes and challenges the established paradigm affecting digital environments and marketing activity as a whole. In this context, processes for automating both strategic and operational marketing tasks in a data-driven environment are increasingly making their way (Provost and Fawcet, 2013).

The term data-driven marketing refers to the development of marketing activities based on the use of data about the actions of actual or potential customers (Bleier, Goldfarb, and Tucker, 2020; Jabbar, Akhtar, and Dani, 2020; Krishen, Dwivedi, Bindu, and Kumar, 2021).

The impact of AI on marketing processes (Davenport, Guha, Grewnal, and Bressgott, 2020) is part of a more overall phenomenon that has also been referred to as "the technologizing of marketing" (Kozinets and Gretzel, 2021, p. 156). The latter also includes technologies other than those attributable to AI, such as tools for neuromarketing research (Guercini, 2020). Although there has been a lot of research on this topic for some years, the marketing literature often focuses on individual aspects (network listening, social media marketing, customer experiences, etc.) without providing a comprehensive approach. In fact, these new technologies have such major implications that we can envision a reorganization of the discipline that can challenge the characters of the paradigm as a whole and not just individual components. Huang and Rust (2021, p. 30) point out that academic marketing research has not yet established sufficient guidance about how best to leverage the benefits of AI for marketing activities. Four types of contributions in the marketing literature are identified: (1) AI algorithms for solving specific marketing problems (Dzyabura and Hauser, 2019); (2) customers' psychological reactions to AI (Luo, Tong, Fang, and Qu, 2019); (3) AI's effects on labor and society (Frey and Osborne, 2017); and (4) AI-related managerial and strategic issues (Huang and Rust, 2020; 2021).

The increased base of data available to decision makers has long characterized the marketing environment, at least since the 1990s when the "marketing information revolution" was talked about (Blattberg, Glazer, and Little, 1994). The phenomenon over the years has grown in scale so that behind the words we use today are potentials for producing and using data on a considerably larger scale. The effects have long been evident, at least at the potential level, on the kind of support that marketers can receive through an appropriate marketing decision support system (MDSS). The latter can enable decision makers to modify decision models that, as Van Bruggen, Smidts, and Wierenga (2001) pointed out, were otherwise strongly characterized by reliance on heuristics-based decision models, e.g., single-attribute decisions, habitual choice decision, or at random choice (Viswanathan, Rosa and Harris, 2005, p. 28).

The desire to use market opportunities arising from the new technological environment has implications for decision making. In particular, data are now available in volumes unthinkable in the past that offer new possibilities. Yet surprisingly, both consumers and entrepreneurs and managers perceive

Table 6.1   *Impact of AI forms and specific marketing activities*

	Mechanical AI	Thinking AI	Feeling AI
Marketing research	Data collection	Market analysis	Customer understanding
Marketing strategy	Segmentation	Targeting	Positioning
Marketing action	Standardization	Personalization	Relationalization

Source: Author's elaboration.

heightened uncertainty, attributable in large part to contingent events (health, geopolitical, etc.) but not always easily separated from more general conditions and trends.

The production of large volumes of data (big data) opens up important and changing prospects for marketing (Jabbar, Akhtar, and Dani, 2020). Data can provide value or even overwhelm marketers who find themselves confused in the absence of models for interpreting and converting them into judgments and choices. In addition, the change induced by new technologies and societal transformation may render obsolete experience, the value of which is related to the characteristics of human cognition (Simon, 1957; Augier and March, 2004).

From the combination of forms of AI and levels of marketing activity, it is possible to propose the grid for analyzing the effects of AI on marketing activities in Table 6.1, in which the areas of marketing activity affected by the impact of different forms of AI suggested by Huang and Rust (2021) are identified.

Taking the consumer perspective, Puntoni, Reczek, Giesler and Botti (2021) instead also see some problematic aspects of the consumer experience (Leung, Paolacci and Puntoni, 2018). These also assume relevance for the marketer, who is given some prescriptions to cope with them (Puntoni, Reczek, Giesler and Botti, 2021, pp. 134, 141, 144). The authors identify AI as an increasingly important tool to support businesses in providing benefits to consumers, but at the same time it highlights challenges at the societal and individual levels, examining sociological and psychological perspectives, respectively, on the implications of its deployment. In particular, Puntoni, Reczek, Giesler and Botti (2021) focus on the consumer side by identifying four types of experiences with AI: (1) data capture; (2) classification; (3) delegation; and (4) social. The study of these experiences from the consumer's perspective is also deemed important for marketers to consider the implications of these experiences. Thus, on the one hand, the benefits of AI for consumers are acknowledged, and on the other hand, the implications are suggested to scholars of the costs borne by consumers in their interaction with AI, which may cause them to resist automation (Leung, Paolacci and Puntoni, 2018). AI is proposed as

Table 6.2   *Experiences in AI: capabilities, sociological and*
                 psychological aspects

Experiences in AI	Users' capabilities	Sociological context	Psychological tension
Data capture	Listening	Surveillance society	Served versus exploited
Classification	Predicting	Unequal worlds	Understood versus misunderstood
Delegation	Producing	Trans-humanism	Empowered versus replaced
Social	Communicating	Humanized AI	Connected versus alienated

Source: Author's elaboration.

an ecosystem with four capabilities, which are: (1) listening; (2) predicting; (3) producing; and (4) communicating. An elaboration about the relationships among capabilities, consumer experiences, and emerging sociological and psychological issues is proposed in Table 6.2, where some key words emerging from the analysis proposed in the article by Puntoni, Reczek, Giesler and Botti (2021) are suggested.

Marketing studies are strongly attracted to the topic of AI, foregrounding the benefits generated for consumers and marketers, on which there is general agreement (Huang and Rust, 2021). Less generalized, however, is the consensus about the prominence of the cost implications of these benefits for consumers (Puntoni, Reczek, Giesler and Botti, 2021; Mariani, Perez-Vega and Wirtz, 2022) and marketers, some of which are widely acknowledged, however, such as limited transparency (Huang and Rust, 2021, p. 46; Kozinets and Gretzel, 2021). The topic of AI has strong peculiarities in many respects, but in others it is part of a longer-term trend encompassing more traditional forms of digitization and customer relationship management, which we defined in the previous chapter as marketing automation (De Bruyn, Viswanathan, Beh, Brock, and von Wangenheim, 2020).

Limitations of AI are highlighted from both the consumer and marketers' side, but some particularly relevant aspects are proposed in a commentary article proposed by Kozinets and Gretzel (2021). The degree of marketers' control over AI for Kozinets and Gretzel is very limited, in contrast to those who make recommendations to marketers in light of the problems consumers may face (Puntoni, Recker, Giesler and Botti, 2021). In essence, the ability of marketers to control AI appears limited for several reasons. First, many marketers with respect to the technologies underlying AI do not have very different skills from those of consumers, also presenting themselves as "consumers" of the services offered by large platforms (Kozinets and Gretzel, 2021, p. 156), so they experience the phase of "technologizing of marketing" in an "AI consumer" position. This is not to say that AI does not offer great benefits to marketers, but in many cases the degree of control is limited. The risk for marketers is to be subordinated to technologists without a sufficiently clear vision of the business. This leads marketers to experience the adoption of AI systems as market understanding personalities (De Bruyn, Viswanathan, Beh, Brock, and von Wangenheim, 2020). Indeed, in the absence of interpretation by marketers, one loses not only control but understanding of marketing activities. In this case, AI-based marketing would end up representing an incomprehensible black box (Kozinetz and Gretzel, 2021, p. 157). The loss of processing on the part of marketers in this case would bring benefits in the immediate and short-term as increased efficiency once the functionality is acquired by the new tools. In the long term, however, it could increase the vulnerability of marketers to changes in the AI system, since a perfected formula and business model with respect to the algorithms that intermediate the market would lose effectiveness if large players in the AI ecosystem made changes (Kozinets and Gretzel, 2021). In other words, the gain in effectiveness and efficiency achieved through the adoption of AI in marketing could translate into a loss of market understanding and expertise over time with increased vulnerability in relation to possible changes made to market intermediation algorithms by platforms that reason from a perspective not necessarily compatible with the interests of the individual marketer (Kozinets and Gretzel, 2021). Here it becomes crucial not to think in terms of automation as substitution but of automation as augmentation of marketers, with respect to which the adoption of decision-making models involving AI alongside the active presence of marketers becomes important. An application to the relationship between marketing decisions and automation of the decision models already proposed by Colson (2019) is proposed in Figure 6.1, where overcoming the traditional model (a) may lead to models (b) or (c), but compared to which model (d) is expected to yield superior results.

The risks of loss of control resulting from the retreat of the human component in decision-making models is documented by research in specific areas such as in automated forms of communication management (Mills, Pitt, and Ferguson, 2019). Differentiated approaches and perspectives that do not always converge emerge from these studies. A large part of the literature highlights the potential arising from the new tools made available to AI, such as in relation to the possibility of making predictions on which to base decisions (Agrawal, Gans and Goldfarb, 2018). At the same time, it assumes interest to assess the limitations of AI tools, such as errors due to components other than bias and underfitting of the data, for example, variance resulting in model flexibility and overfitting as the sensitivity of the model to noise in the data (Geman, Bienestock and Doursat, 1992; Gigerenzer, 2007). One approach we have already referred to in Chapter 2 is that decision making that can be activated by consumers and to some extent also by marketers takes on simplified but biased characters (usually referred to as heuristics) and that opens the

a. Decision model based on human judgement

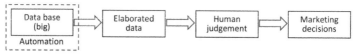

b. Decision model that imploys automated data elaboration

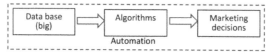

c. Fully automated decision model

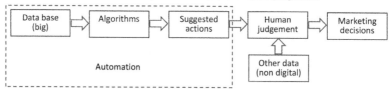

d. Decision model that combines the power of artificial and human judgement

Source: Author's elaboration.

Figure 6.1   Decision models

door to possible manipulation (even for good, as in nudges). The experience of social media suggests that, however much in a data-driven environment, people remain distinguishable from data (Gigerenzer, 2022, p. 26).

In the next sections, we try to delve into some areas of the new automated marketing by selecting three more specific topics, which are: (1) segmentation based on online customer behaviors; (2) recommendation systems that are in some way the consequential action of classifying a potential customer profile; and (3) the system of connecting marketers and media through the use of programmatic advertising that automatically defines the communication to be given to the individual customer on a site page (Busch, 2016).

AI-based marketing represents one of the most important application areas for data science, the impact of which on marketing activities is increasingly evident at the strategic and top management level as well as at the operational level (Jain, Baura and Barbate, 2022).

6.3   STRATEGIC MARKETING AND CLASSIFYING CUSTOMERS WITH ARTIFICIAL INTELLIGENCE

Segmentation represents a central theme in strategic marketing understood as a field of study and not only as a marketing strategy (Varadarajan, 2010). Research in the field of segmentation has been characterized by various evolutionary stages, from identification as an alternative strategy to differentiation (Smith, 1956), as a theoretical elaboration (Claycamp and Massy, 1968), to the deepening of techniques (Wind, 1978) to the identification of forms of finer segmentation (Kara and Kaynak, 1997). Segmentation represents the basis of the STP (segmentation-targeting-positioning) model, central to strategic marketing, where it confronts alternative archetypes such as community (Cova, Kozinets and Shankar, 2007) or fragments (Kara and Kaynak, 1997). Although cluster analysis has a focal position to define market segments through the use of data (Saunders, 1980), this procedure is not without its problems, one of which is the selection of variables on which to perform clustering (Punj and Stewart, 1983). Inaccurate selection of variables may offer little clustering information and lead to misleading results. To isolate these potentially "noisy" variables prior to clustering, Carmone, Kara, and Maxwell (1999) proposed the use of an algorithm referred to as the "Heuristic Identification of Noisy Variables" (HINoV), which demonstrated robustness in the context of a simulation with artificial data and for improving the quality of segmentation through cluster analysis (Carmone, Kara, and Maxwell, 1999, pp. 501ff.). This is not a unique case. For example, another approach for constructing market segments for particular applications (termed NORMCLUS), was introduced by DeSarbo and Grisaffe (1998).

The topic of segmentation changes some of its characteristics with data-driven AI, making greater use of individual personal profiles, so rather than market segmentation, it is accomplished through profile classification systems. This is not simply an automation of the traditional segmentation strategy, but a change of horizon that is well represented by the emergence of the "outside-in" marketing concept we referred to earlier (Rust, 2020). Already in microsegmentation, or finer segmentation, one was not limited to recognizing large clusters but could get to the individual buyer's market, according to an idea moreover already present in the concept of "complete marketing segmentation" recalled by Kotler (1967, p. 44). Profile classification is functional to the possibilities of matching with offers and proposals of products and services, realized almost simultaneously. Thus, individual needs can be linked to individual proposals without going through the aggregation in the segment, which had its own relevance anyway. It is possible to realize very fine levels in the treatment of market granularity, reaching the individual buyer at every single step of the buying process. On the other hand, however, unlike in microsegmentation (Claycamp and Massy, 1968, p. 391; Volkov, Maloletko and Kaurova, 2018), the data-driven system may not have profiling as its purpose, but the individual user's compliance with certain proposed classification criteria. In this case, it becomes central not so much to the segment, micro-segment, or even the individual buyer, but the responsiveness of a profile to certain characteristics whose relevance emerges independently of profiling, whereby the classification model (Katsikopoulos, Şimşek, Buckmann and Gigerenzer, 2020) becomes a strategic marketing theme.

Classification also gains importance among AI experiences from the consumer's perspective (Puntoni, Reczek, Giesler and Botti, 2021). Now, as has been well pointed out, in the face of AI systems even the marketers can assume the position of a "consumer" of the technologies that enable automation processes (Kozinets and Gretzel, 2021), and in this sense they too can experience AI/ML-based classification tools at least in two ways: (1) directly as an actor profiled by other actors; but also (2) as a marketer who benefits from the classification of their actual or potential customers by the AI/ML system. Classification is thus seen as the experience of receiving personalized ML-based predictions. Thus, this classification consists of leveraging AI's predictive ability to use sophisticated algorithms that can consider a large set of data, including characteristics of past and present customers, to identify recipients for an ultra-customized offer and to generate high engagement, relevance, and satisfaction (Kumar, Rajan, Venkatesan, Lecinski, 2019). Our perspective, however, is different from that of Puntoni, Reczek, Giesler and Botti (2021), in that we do not look at the consumer's experience, but at the classification understood as the lived experience of the marketer, albeit as a user/consumer of the ML platforms to which the AI system refers. From this perspective, the performance of the classification system becomes important for the marketer; this performance is defined in terms of matching customer's profile and the marketer's offer.

While the AI system enables in the short term a high fitting match between demand profile and supply, in the medium and long term it can be a separating element between marketer and its market context. It is in fact through AI/ML platforms that an understanding or misunderstanding of customers takes place in a kind of substitution and disintermediation process. This disintermediation can undermine the marketer's traditional understanding of the market, admittedly not without error, but nevertheless an important part of the marketer's activities, and one that can attribute to them the ability to adapt to change (Kozinets and Gretzel, 2021).

The shift from traditional segmentation to automatic classification based on AI and ML may imply a restructuring of the decision-making models adopted by the marketer (Colson, 2019). This affects not only operational decisions, but even more so strategic ones, as customer profiling and classification, and thus segmentation, is an essential object of the automation process. This interest of clustering and customer segmentation systems is so obvious that it assumes relevance not only for marketing scholars, but also for data scientists, if it is true that in machine learning manuals the "customer cluster" is given specific attention as an emblematic example of a particularly effective application of machine learning systems (Alpaydin, 2016, pp. 111ff; Upadhyay and Chitnis, 2022).

As a result of the emergence of marketing automation, the issues subject to decision making in relation to the STP process and strategic marketing may be profoundly changed. Customer classification activities will be automated as they are entrusted to the ML. Instead, choices related to the training and use of the database, the selection of the software and application, with possible choices with respect to the machine learning solution adopted at the level of training and subsequently inference based on the model extracted from the data, will assume importance. Strategic marketing will have to deal with the selection of the data and the part of the data to be considered in the training process of the AI system. We then move to decision-making models in which the human decision maker focuses on certain upstream and downstream steps in the processing but also in the identification of segments and targets that are instead automatically defined. This type of approach applies not only to the segmentation part, but also to the targeting part, and in principle also to positioning and operational marketing steps if deemed appropriate (Huang and Rust, 2021).

As we have said, in AI-driven automated marketing, the "classification" of individual profiles about which data are available becomes increasingly important. The most effective forms of classification, regardless of what models underlie them, represent newly relevant elements for marketing. Classification systems can be simple, robust and transparent, or more complex, data-sensitive (including the noise component), and opaque to the user themselves. Katsikopoulos, Şimşek, Buckmann and Gigerenzer (2020) describe fast and frugal trees and tallying heuristics that are shown to be effective and can become relevant in this new marketing context.

Automation insists on customer segmentation activities but also on that of targeting and operationally through recommendation systems. So let us see how to evaluate the performance of the classification system underlying the individuation of customer clusters and the fitting with possible business propositions. These are outcomes that any classification system achieves, whether simple or complex. Comparison about the performance of simpler or more complex decision-making models is therefore possible in this terrain (Chintalapati and Pandey, 2022; Krabuanrat and Phelps, 1998).

Customer profiling and the possibilities of AI and algorithm-based decision models imply a move beyond the traditional concept of the large segment that emerged historically after mass production (Claycamp and Massy, 1968). In fact, it is not so important to identify clusters, but to be able to classify against specific initiatives in the customer profile and make a proposal in relation to their individual characteristics. Large customer clusters are replaced by automatic and specific analyses against which individual customers can be viewed from a specific angle. The segment concept remains important for the marketer's strategic assessments and as a possible basis (like other archetypes, e.g., communities) for targeting and positioning, but they do not exhaust the potential of profiling in data-driven marketing. When analyzing data about a user/customer profile, classification is about assigning or not assigning it to the target audience we have set. This means making a prediction about the opportunity to reach the target with our actions. Thus, the AI system has data processing capabilities, however, it is not infallible, so the types of errors to which each test is subject and which are to be kept in mind when evaluating the performance of a classifier will be encountered (Katsikopoulos, Şimşek, Buckmann and Gigerenzer, 2020, pp. 38–39). The performance of the AI-based classification system, as with other classification systems, has four possible "outcomes": misses (or false negatives), hits (or true positives), correct rejections (or true negatives), and false alarms (or false positives). The possible outcomes of the relationship between prediction and recorded events are highlighted in Figure 6.3.

a. Prediction and errors in a binary classification (e.g., purchase/non-purchase)

the event ...	... occurs (+)	... does not occur (-)
... is predicted to occur (+)	(A) Hit (true-positive)	(C) False alarm (false-positive)
... is predicted not to occur (-)	(B) Miss (false-negative)	(D) Correct rejection (true-negative)

b. "Sensitivity" of the prediction system:

Sensitivity (hit rate) = (A) / [(A)+(B)]

c. "Specificity" of the prediction system

Specificity (correct rejection rate) = (C) / [(C)+(D)]

Source: Author's elaboration.

Figure 6.2   *Predictive machines and prediction errors*

Thus, the AI algorithm can be successful when it recognizes the presence or absence of a certain condition (cases A or D in Figure 6.2), while it is in error when it predicts something that later fails to come true, or fails to predict something that later comes true (cases B and C in Figure 6.2).

In the marketing technologizing process (Kozinets and Gretzel, 2021), segmentation is examined by Huang and Rust (2021, p. 34, pp. 37–38) as a field of application of mechanical AI within the STP model. Segmentation is considered in its traditional meaning of dividing "a market into pieces, with customers in each piece having unique needs and wants, for example using gender to slice the shoe market into male and female shoe segments" (Huang and Rust, 2021, p. 37). Examples of automatic categorization by different marketers are those on retail sectors (Dekimpe, 2020), mortgages by employing text-mining (Netzer, Lemaire, and Herznstein, 2019), and in the art market through text analysis and correspondence analysis (Pitt, Bal, and Plangger, 2020).

6.4   MARKETING AUTOMATION AND RECOMMENDATION SYSTEMS

Recommendation systems can be understood as systems for predicting customer behavior as an application of ML (Alpaydin 2016, p. 81). The starting point for the operation of recommendation systems is the availability of a large dataset on customer profile and behavior to which association rules of the form can be applied so that "people with profile A are also likely to do behavior B", for example, "people who buy X are also likely to buy Y" (Alpaydin, 2016, p. 118). The ML thus allows the right recommendations to be made to the right recipients at the right time, setting itself up as a "predictive machine" (Agrawal, Gans, and Goldfarb, 2018).

Marketers have long valued data about actual and potential customers. In fact, this data can be the basis for pursuing highly desirable goals, such as: best identifying one's target audience and defining strategy from data on current customers; pointing out attributes of our products or services that may meet consumer or user needs; improving management of stock levels in stores by offering promotions or managing customer waiting times; increasing revenue by suggesting to those who already buy some of our products or services what other products or services they might buy (cross-selling), adding additional and ancillary features to the products or services they already buy, or otherwise selling a higher-end product than they currently buy (up-selling). The position of what is referred to as "recommender systems" is largely aimed at more effective and efficient management of this online activity through forms of AI (Kelleher and Tierney, 2018, p. 25). This is a very important issue since production and distribution requires a more targeted approach to individual buyers, having shifted over the years from selling large amounts of a small number of items, to selling small amounts of a larger number of niche items (Anderson, 2006).

Recommendation systems imply a view of customer relationships increasingly immersed in data flows, both for specific actions and for the characteristics of their infrastructures even beyond specific actions, or in other words requiring no specific actions (Ansari, Essegarier, and Kohli, 2000; Isinkaye, Folajimi and Ojokoh, 2015). Let's take an example of a recommendation system in a specific action. An online consumer searches for a vacation in a tourist destination with a partner in July. After querying a few search engines and visiting a few online travel agencies, they leave this project on standby for a moment and return to other activities. However, the system has collected data on their searches and continues to offer recommendations. Let us now take an example of a recommendation system in a different context. A customer has purchased a monthly subscription that automatically renews when it expires. However, there are opportunities to make variations on the basic contract, to obtain additional services on terms reserved for those already in a program. There are also possibilities to match products that are often found to be purchased together with others; for example, if I am buying a book, one can report what other customers who have bought that book are buying together with it (Hardesty, 2019).

In a third example, someone is looking for a movie and registers with an online site that makes movie recommendations. To do this, the system can assign a numeric score that is a measure of how much we think that person will enjoy that particular movie. For example, the system can evaluate: (1) data on what the user has done in the past (historical principle); (2) data on what are the present characteristics of the user's profile (affinity principle); or (3) data on choices that have not yet been tried by the customer but might be interesting or convenient (experimentation principle). These are different principles that can result in even radically different recommendations (Ansari, Li and Zhang, 2018). In the case of movies, if the user has seen a lot of action movies, movies from this genre might be selected and recommended; if they have recently become a parent, movies might be proposed to watch with children; if, on the other hand, the user has never tried a genre but is believed to like to experiment, movies from a new genre might be proposed. Recommendation systems are strongly related to the theme of classification, where factors corresponding to segmentation bases (socio-demographic, psychographic, etc.) play a role in identifying the recipients of specific recommendations (Alpaydin, 2016, p. 119). Underlying the search system for profiles to target for recommendation may be hidden causes, e.g., "having a small child at home", which may convey recommendations on many different items (baby food, milk, diapers, etc.). Instead of learning the rules of association between two or more of these products, estimates can be made from hidden factors based on past purchases, which will stimulate an estimate of what may be needed but has not yet been bought (Behera, Gunasekaran, Gupta, Kamboj and Bala, 2020). In the movie example, several attributes of past purchases will be cross-referenced to make a selection of movie recommendations (Henning-Thurau, Marchand and Marx, 2012).

Even before the advent of the latest marketing automation systems, "decision-support systems" (DSS) could offer elaborations to help decision makers with complex tasks. Even then, managers were reluctant to use such systems: "even though system dynamics is an established management tool in many firms, it has not received the same level of acceptance as other management tools" (Otto, 2008, p. 1174). Among the reasons most often cited are: (1) a problem understanding the model inherent in the DSS; (2) a problem identifying when to use them; (3) an inability to extend the use of the DSS; and (4) an inability to explain the model or its output to others (Otto, 2008, p. 1173).

6.5   PROGRAMMATIC ADVERTISING IN MARKETING AUTOMATION

AI has a major impact in the communication and implementation of advertising campaigns. Online advertising (Evans, 2009) has grown over the years characterized by a number of trends including the orientation to mobile devices, the integration of advertising and e-commerce, and the rise of programmatic buying. In this area, there is increasing research focused on trend themes. For example, Miralles-Pechuán, Ponce, and Martínez-Viallaseñor (2018) propose a methodology for online advertising in small advertising networks using supervised ML and metaheuristic methods, with the intention of providing a tool to follow communication trends in online advertising focusing on small advertising networks, which are considered prospectively very useful in the years to come. Networks and relationships have importance from the moment that information reaches marketers as part of a marketing ecosystem (Zhang and Watson, 2020).

In communications, a significant aspect of the automation process affects advertising, where particularly relevant is the fast-growing phenomenon of programmatic advertising, which has achieved a majority share within digital advertising in recent years, which in turn has seen growth relative to other, more traditional forms of advertising (Busch, 2016).

Programmatic advertising (PA) refers to an automated, targeted process of buying and selling digital advertising space (Samuel, White, Thomas and Jones, 2021). Through PA, advertiser companies are able to reach a targeted and potentially more interested target audience in a way that improves the results of their campaigns and optimizes their online advertising investment

(Lee and Cho, 2020). Thus, PA is based on automation as well as market granularity in the context of changing effects of advertising in the digital environment (Turow, 2011). There is, however, a third basic characteristic of PA that is not dwelled on enough: the business network dimension (Guercini, 2023). PA functions through the interactions between actors who have primary needs, such as advertisers on the one hand and (digital) advertising media on the other, and by a number of actors who create and operate as intermediaries such as technology platforms and agencies. The interactions, relationships, and networks involving these actors are the PA business market, which can have customers as its end point, whether other companies or consumers (Alaimo, 2022). This network dimension emerges clearly from the representation of the network of roles we offer in Figure 6.2, which is the result of synthesizing diagrams available in the literature and on the websites of network actors. The importance of these relationships is confirmed by contracts with digital publicity operators, so as to cope with problems related to possible inefficiencies, even on terrain that is imagined as the strong point of digital communication, such as measurability of results (Porter, 2021).

PA is an emblematic case of AI-driven automated marketing. The automated nature of the processes of managing the exchange of advertising space between media/publishers and advertisers is evident from the above. The fact that important marketing activities are automated does not mean that there is simply a replacement of the human decision maker by an automated system. On the contrary, new tasks emerge and the work on relationships may become even more important for marketers to focus on having the processes of customer classification and price negotiation accomplished directly by automated systems now equipped with ML.

The use of computer-based technology in advertising management has precedents as far back as the 1980s, when interactive marketing models were set up that were made to improve the allocation of corporate advertising budgets among a company's individual brands (Basu and Batra, 1988). Also in the field of advertising, another form of automated marketing application is "profit optimizing search engine advertising" (PROSAD), a fully automated bidding decision support system developed by academics together with an online marketing agency (Skiera and Abou Nabout, 2013). The PROSAD system maximizes an advertisers' profit per keyword without the need for human intervention, based on a "cost-per-profit heuristic" that empowers advertisers to submit good bids even when there is significant noise in the data (Skiera and Abou Nabout, 2013, p. 213).

PA represents one of the terrains in which marketing automation has taken on a greater scale and importance (Busch, 2016; Chen, Xie, Dong, and Wang, 2019; McGuigan, 2019; Mills, Pitt, and Ferguson, 2019), highlighting the importance of managing issues and risks in terms of control and privacy

(Palos-Sanchez, Saura, and Martin-Velicia, 2019; Shehu, Abou Nabout and Clement, 2021).

The emergence of PA is linked to the great volatility with which marketers today have to deal in their connection with the interests of potential customers, fostered by the possibilities of media and in particular access to the Internet through mobile devices (Busch, 2016, p. v). A sense of volatility is perceived because of the relationship between the rapid evolution of technology and the psychology of human actors, both consumers and marketers, which evolves less quickly and may reject some implications of AI. "Programmatic" activity can be a tool for adapting to volatility in the technological society, corresponding to what, predominantly in the Anglo-American environment, is referred to as real-time bidding or RTB (Busch, 2016; Sayedi, 2018).

PA therefore is also called programmatic buying, as it proposes a form of automation in media space purchases for digital advertising campaigns, instead of purchases negotiated by publishers or media (Alaimo, 2022). It represents one of the most important technological developments in the field of marketing and communication, coming to consist of a form of AI-optimization and a form of marketing automation consisting of replacing human negotiations with ML. In other words, PA represents the automated system of buying digital advertising space, where ML is directed to optimize the contact of the advertiser marketer with publishers (Funk and About Nabout, 2016). PA consists of real-time auctions where advertising space is purchased the moment visitors load a website (Miralles-Pechuán, Quresh, & Namee, 2023; Malthouse, Hessary, Vakeel, Burke and Fudurić, 2019). Optimization occurs when, through PA, the advertiser buys advertising for the right consumer, at the right time and on the most appropriate channel, to show them ads that are most likely to meet their interests. This area of communication is assuming enormous proportions, having reached the vast majority of all digital advertising spending globally in recent years. As much as it represents a form of automation in marketing, while PA leads to the replacement of person-to-person negotiation with forms of ML such as optimizing AI, it also leads to the development of a network of relationships and connections between relevant actors (Puntoni, Reczek, Giesler, and Botti, 2021; Zhang and Watson, 2020). A representation of this network is shown in Figure 6.2 below, where advertising (AD) agency, advertising trade desk (ATD), demand side platform (DSP), supply side platform (SSP), advertising network, and advertising exchange are located between the marker/advertiser and publisher/media.

PA enables real-time, targeted, and efficient connection between the person searching online for the information they need versus the person who intends to convey messages (Shehu, Abou Nabout and Clement, 2021). Programmatic communication can also address relevant topics and issues in the relationship between marketers and other market actors (customers, but also suppliers,

a. Role network for programmatic advertising

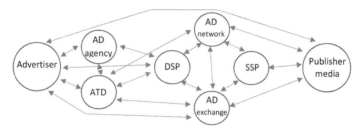

b. Example of channel of programmatic advertising in the advertiser's perspective

Source: Author's elaboration.

Figure 6.3   Programmatic advertising

influencers, etc.), in a way that can be, if handled appropriately, more confidential and personal (Deng, Tan, Wang and Pan, 2019). The PA system is
data-driven and uses a network of actors/platforms according to data classification mechanisms on users and media spaces (Jain, Barua and Barbate,
2022). For PA, rules on general data protection (GDPR) become crucial, which
can make relevant content and information reach election recipients without
spreading messages on a large scale and with relevant effectiveness effects
(Cooper, Yalcin, Nistor, Macrini, and Pehlivan, 2022). To do this, however, it
is necessary to develop in the company an organization capable of interfacing
with these tools, to be prepared to evaluate alternatives, and to implement
projects based on these new marketing technologies (Alaimo, 2022).

   The volatility that makes it important to operate in real time through PA
forms stems from the possibilities offered by technology, but also from the
societal change that characterizes consumer markets, the business environment, and thus in general, the marketing environment in recent years. It is
not simply digitization, but a version of it geared to meet the pace of changes
in the environment with flexibility and capacity for innovation. PA makes
use of marketing automation tools, and in particular evolved forms of AI, to
support advertiser purchases of advertising space in a way that improves the fit
between the subject of the ad and the audience reached. PA makes it possible
to keep up with the speed of changing trends (Zhang and Watson, 2020) and in
this way helps guide decision-making processes, in a context in which availa-

ble data and analytical tools have taken on characteristics not manageable by the human brain. PA is therefore an essential part of marketing automation. The McKinsey Global Institute, in one of its reports, defined the use of big data, ML and data-driven decision automation as the most important change in the coming years (Silberg and Manyika, 2019). PA is part of a process of data-driven marketing automation (Busch, 2016) taking on different names, such as "real time advertising" and "programmatic buying" and "automated trading" or "real-time bidding" (RTB). Some of these terms, such as RTB, emphasizes the ability to dynamically determine the prices of advertising space through auctions (Diwanji, Lee and Cortese, 2022). This is a new approach to advertising that is intended to provide more effective and efficient results and can become the basis for advertising and marketing at every level (Lee and Cho, 2020).

It has been many years now that Internet advertising has made it possible to measure the actual conversions of views or impressions into actions of potential customers, transforming what used to be advertising investment into something that at the limit tends to be assessable as a variable cost if not something akin to a sales commission (Guercini, 2009). More recently, digital advertising has evolved in the direction of seeking greater efficiency in the combination of supply and demand for advertising space, improving resource allocation as much as possible (Busch, 2016, p. 4). PA is the result of the simultaneous occurrence of a number of conditions over the past decade: (1) the immense computational power of computers, enabling the computation of complex data in milliseconds; (2) the limited cost of data storage; (3) the influx of new scientific expertise in marketing, such as mathematicians and quantum physicists; (4) the ability to form prices based on real-time supply and demand for each ad opportunity; (5) the globalization of advertising markets; (6) fast data connections to enhance the results of analysis of how to get the most out of individual impressions; and (7) driven personalization, whereby "real value comes with real identity" (Busch, 2016, p. 6). The interest in mathematical and scientific skills by the advertising and data-driven marketing industry has helped channel large resources to research fields useful for improving communication systems, to the point of being pointed to as one of the antecedents of PA development (Busch, 2016, p. 6).

In fact, however, PA is linked to forms of digitization and ML. Busch (2016, pp. 7–8) proposes that PA "should have as open a definition as possible in terms of its core characteristics, while also providing sufficient scope to allow affected marketing and marketing communication disciplines to get involved and experiment within their field of work". Given this openness, a number of principles underpinning PA are identified: (1) market granularity; (2) real-time trading; (3) real-time information; (4) real-time creation; and (5) automation. Again, in terms of definition, PA "describes the automated serving of digital ads in real time based on individual ad impression opportunities" (Busch, 2016, p. 8). Specifically, programmatic advertising is primarily based on two principles: (1) granularity; and (2) automation. Granularity refers to the difference between individuals in terms of impression opportunities to be selected, evaluated, and priced. Automation allows strong specificities in the way of looking at the individual and impression opportunities to be held together with extensive decision making (Guercini, 2022). In other words, automation of processes that were already accomplished manually in complex ways allows for efficiency and cost containment results while maintaining specificity of the ad campaign to its audience. This allows cost savings that should also be evaluated in light of the cost of the systems required to implement PA (Jain, Barua and Barbate, 2022).

The emergence of PA is then made possible by the adoption and promotion of these solutions by large players such as Facebook and Google, which have precisely adopted and promoted systems that provide millions of clients real-time, data-driven campaigns, made precisely primarily on Facebook and Google pages. These are joined by third-party PA technology providers, adopting principles of auction mechanisms, based on granularity and transparency (Qin, Yuan and Wang, 2017).

PA furthermore can be seen as the result of a business network essential to its realization, in which the media with their sales houses, provide the market for advertising with their real-time impressions. Typically, agency trade desks (ATDs) use multiple platforms to purchase an inventory of digital advertising space. Some of these interface with advertisers using their own application program interfaces (APIs), as Facebook or Google do, or demand side platforms (DSPs), which are the interface through which buyers (who are the advertisers directly or through their agencies) can participate in RTB auctions, allocating the budgets available to them to purchase ad space programmatically (Paulson, Luo and James, 2018). On the other hand, Supply Side Platforms (SSPs) consist of systems employed by those who offer advertising space or audience, e.g., website visitors, to buying companies, then selling them at the best possible price to be ticked off. Then we have Ad Exchanges, which are automated platforms that are connected to SSPs and DSPs to evaluate the real-time negotiation of advertising inventory that is being bought and sold (Alaimo and Kallinikos. 2018).

The mechanisms of PA operation represent a technological ecosystem within the marketing ecosystem. The schema depicted in Figure 6.2 can be supplemented by additional platforms or functions. For example, data management platforms (DMPs) that are points of contact between advertisers who are looking for impressions to buy through SDRs and publishers who are looking to place the spaces still available through the SSP, transforming data about users into actions for them that can be planned and delivered immediately (Jain, Barua and Barbate, 2022).

REFERENCES

Agrawal, A., Gans, J., & Goldfarb, A. (2018). *Prediction machines. The simple economics of artificial intelligence*. Harvard Business Review Press, Boston, Mass.

Alaimo, C., & Kallinikos, J. (2018). Objects, metrics and practices: An inquiry into the programmatic advertising ecosystem. In *Living with Monsters? Social Implications of Algorithmic Phenomena, Hybrid Agency, and the Performativity of Technology: IFIP WG 8.2 Working Conference on the Interaction of Information Systems and the Organization, IS&O 2018, San Francisco, CA, USA, December 11–12, 2018, Proceedings*. Springer International Publishing, Berlin, 110–123.

Alaimo, C. (2022). From people to objects: the digital transformation of fields. *Organization Studies*, *43*(7), 1091–1114.

Albers, S. (2012). Optimizable and implementable aggregate response modeling for marketing decision support. *International Journal of Research in Marketing*, *29*(2), 111–122.

Alexouda, G. (2005). A user-friendly marketing decision support system for the product line design using evolutionary algorithms. *Decision Support Systems*, *38*(4), 495–509.

Alpaydin, E. (2016). *Machine learning: the new AI*. MIT press, Cambridge, Mass.

Anderson, C. (2006). *The long tail: Why the future of business is selling less of more*. Hachette UK.

Ansari, A., Li, Y., & Zhang, J. Z. (2018). Probabilistic topic model for hybrid recommender systems: A stochastic variational Bayesian approach. *Marketing Science*, *37*(6), 987–1008.

Ansari, A., Essegaier, S., & Kohli, R. (2000). Internet recommendation systems. *Journal of Marketing Research*, *37*, 363–375.

Augier, M., & March, J. (2004). Herbert A. Simon, Scientist. In Augier M. & March, J. (eds.), *Models of a man: Essays in memory of Herbert A. Simon*, MIT Press, Cambridge, Mass, 3–32.

Basu, A. K., & Batra, R. (1988). ADSPLIT: a multi-brand advertising budget allocation model. *Journal of Advertising*, *17*(2), 44–51.

Behera, R. K., Gunasekaran, A., Gupta, S., Kamboj, S., & Bala, P. K. (2020). Personalized digital marketing recommender engine. *Journal of Retailing and Consumer Services*, *53*, 101799.

Blattberg, R. C., Glazer, R., & Little, J. D. (1994). *Marketing information revolution*. Harvard Business School Press, Cambridge, Mass.

Bleier, A., Goldfarb, A., & Tucker, C. (2020). Consumer privacy and the future of data-based innovation and marketing. *International Journal of Research in Marketing*, *37*(3), 466–480.

Bostrom, N. (2014). *Superintelligence. Paths, Dangers, Strategies*. Oxford University Press, Oxford.

Busch, O. (ed.) (2016). *Programmatic advertising. The Successful Transformation to Automated, Data-Driven Marketing in Real-Time*. Springer Nature, Berlin.

Carmone Jr, F. J., Kara, A., & Maxwell, S. (1999). HINoV: A new model to improve market segment definition by identifying noisy variables. *Journal of Marketing Research*, *36*(4), 501–509.

Chen, G., Xie, P., Dong, J., & Wang, T. (2019). Understanding programmatic creative: The role of AI. *Journal of Advertising, 48*(4), 347–355.

Chintalapati, S., & Pandey, S. K. (2022). Artificial intelligence in marketing: A systematic literature review. *International Journal of Market Research, 64*(1), 38–68.

Claycamp, H. J., & Massy, W. F. (1968). A theory of market segmentation. *Journal of Marketing Research, 5*(4), 388–394.

Colson, E. (2019). What AI-driven decision making looks like. *Harvard Business Review*, 8 July, 2–8.

Cooper, D. A., Yalcin, T., Nistor, C., Macrini, M., & Pehlivan, E. (2023). Privacy considerations for online advertising: a stakeholder's perspective to programmatic advertising. *Journal of Consumer Marketing, 40*(2), 235–247.

Cova, B., Kozinets, R. V., & Shankar, A. (2007). *Consumer tribes.* Routledge, New York.

Davenport, T., Guha, A., Grewal, D., & Bressgott, T. (2020). How artificial intelligence will change the future of marketing. *Journal of the Academy of Marketing Science, 48*, 24–42.

De Bruyn, A., Viswanathan, V., Beh, Y. S., Brock, J. K. U., & von Wangenheim, F. (2020). Artificial intelligence and marketing: Pitfalls and opportunities. *Journal of Interactive Marketing, 51*(1), 91–105.

Dekimpe, M. G. (2020). Retailing and retailing research in the age of big data analytics. *International Journal of Research in Marketing, 37*(1), 3–14.

Deng, S., Tan, C. W., Wang, W., & Pan, Y. (2019). Smart generation system of personalized advertising copy and its application to advertising practice and research. *Journal of Advertising, 48*(4), 356–365.

DeSarbo, W. S., & Grisaffe, D. (1998). Combinatorial optimization approaches to constrained market segmentation: An application to industrial market segmentation. *Marketing Letters, 9*, 115–134.

Diwanji, V. S., Lee, J., & Cortese, J. (2022). Deconstructing the role of artificial intelligence in programmatic advertising: at the intersection of automation and transparency. *Journal of Strategic Marketing*, https://doi.org/10.1080/0965254X.2022.2148269.

Dzyabura, D., & Hauser, J. R. (2019). Recommending products when consumers learn their preference weights. *Marketing Science, 38*(3), 417–441.

Evans, D. S. (2009). The online advertising industry: Economics, evolution, and privacy. *Journal of Economic Perspectives, 23*(3), 37–60.

Frey, C. B., & Osborne, M. A. (2017). The future of employment: How susceptible are jobs to computerisation? *Technological Forecasting and Social Change, 114*, 254–280.

Funk, B., & About Nabout, N. (2016). Cross-channel real-time response analysis. *Programmatic Advertising: The Successful Transformation to Automated, Data-Driven Marketing in Real-Time*, 141–151.

Geman, S., Bienenstock, E., & Doursat, R. (1992). Neural networks and the bias/variance dilemma. *Neural computation, 4*(1), 1–58.

Gigerenzer, G. (2007). *Gut feelings: The intelligence of the unconscious.* Penguin, London.

Gigerenzer, G. (2022). *How to stay smart in a smart world: Why human intelligence still beats algorithms.* Penguin, London.

Guercini, S., & Medlin, C. J. (2020). A radical constructivist approach to boundaries in business network research. *Industrial Marketing Management, 91*, 510–520.

Guercini, S. (2009). On Line Media Market and New Advertising Agencies: Analysis of an Italian Case. *Journal of Service Science and Management*, *2*(2), 117–128.

Guercini, S. (2020). The Actor or the Machine? The Strategic Marketing Decision-Maker Facing Digitalization. *Micro & Macro Marketing*, *29*(1), 3–7.

Guercini, S. (2022). Scope of heuristics and digitalization: the case of marketing automation. *Mind & Society*, *21*(2), 151–164.

Guercini, S. (2023). Marketing automation and the case of programmatic advertising. *Micro & Macro Marketing*, *32*(2), 239–247.

Hardesty, L. (2019). The history of Amazon's recommendation algorithm. *Amazon Science*, *22*, https://www.amazon.science.

Hennig-Thurau, T., Marchand, A., & Marx, P. (2012). Can automated group recommender systems help consumers make better choices? *Journal of Marketing*, *76*(5), 89–109.

Huang, M. H., & Rust, R. T. (2021). A strategic framework for artificial intelligence in marketing. *Journal of the Academy of Marketing Science*, *49*(1), 30–50.

Isinkaye, F. O., Folajimi, Y. O., & Ojokoh, B. A. (2015). Recommendation systems: Principles, methods and evaluation. *Egyptian informatics journal*, *16*(3), 261–273.

Jabbar, A., Akhtar, P., & Dani, S. (2020). Real-time big data processing for instantaneous marketing decisions: A problematization approach. *Industrial Marketing Management*, *90*, 558–569.

Jain, A., Barua, K., & Barbate, M. (2022). Role of Data Science in Programmatic Advertising. In *Data Science in Societal Applications: Concepts and Implications*. Springer Nature Singapore, Singapore, 33–46.

Jarrahi, M. H. (2018). Artificial intelligence and the future of work: Human-AI symbiosis in organizational decision making. *Business Horizons*, *61*(4), 577–586.

Jeon, J. (2022). Exploring AI chatbot affordances in the EFL classroom: Young learners' experiences and perspectives. *Computer Assisted Language Learning*, 1–26, https://doi.org/10.1080/09588221.2021.2021241.

Jordan, M. I., & Mitchell, T. M. (2015). Machine learning: Trends, perspectives, and prospects. *Science*, *349*(6245), 255–260.

Kaplan, J. (2017). *Artificial intelligence. What everyone needs to know*. Oxford University Press, Oxford.

Kara, A., & Kaynak, E. (1997). Markets of a single customer: exploiting conceptual developments in market segmentation. *European Journal of Marketing*, *31*(11/12), 873–895.

Katsikopoulos, K. V., Şimşek, O., Buckmann, M., & Gigerenzer, G. (2020). *Classification in the wild. The science and art of transparent decision making*. MIT Press, Cambridge, Mass.

Kelleher, J. D., & Tierney, B. (2018). *Data science*. MIT Press, Cambridge, Mass.

Kotler, P. (1967). *Marketing management. Analysis, planning, and control*. Prentice-Hall, Inc. Englewood Cliffs, N.J.

Kozinets, R. V., & Gretzel, U. (2021). Commentary: Artificial intelligence: The marketer's dilemma. *Journal of Marketing*, *85*(1), 156–159.

Krabuanrat, K., & Phelps, R. (1998). Heuristics and rationality in strategic decision making: An exploratory study. *Journal of Business Research*, *41*(1), 83–93.

Krishen, A. S., Dwivedi, Y. K., Bindu, N., & Kumar, K. S. (2021). A broad overview of interactive digital marketing: A bibliometric network analysis. *Journal of Business Research*, *131*, 183–195.

Kumar, V., Rajan, B., Venkatesan, R., & Lecinski, J. (2019). Understanding the role of artificial intelligence in personalized engagement marketing. *California Management Review*, *61*(4), 135–155.

Lazzeretti, L. (2023). *The Rise of Algorithmic Society and the Strategic Role of Arts and Culture*, Edward Elgar Publishing, Cheltenham.

Lee, H., & Cho, C. H. (2020). Digital advertising: present and future prospects. *International Journal of Advertising*, *39*(3), 332–341.

Leung, E., Paolacci, G., & Puntoni, S. (2018). Man versus machine: Resisting automation in identity-based consumer behavior. *Journal of Marketing Research*, *55*(6), 818–831.

Luo, X., Tong, S., Fang, Z., & Qu, Z. (2019). Frontiers: Machines vs. humans: The impact of artificial intelligence chatbot disclosure on customer purchases. *Marketing Science*, *38*(6), 937–947.

Malthouse, E. C., Hessary, Y. K., Vakeel, K. A., Burke, R., & Fudurić, M. (2019). An algorithm for allocating sponsored recommendations and content: Unifying programmatic advertising and recommender systems. *Journal of Advertising*, *48*(4), 366–379.

Mariani, M. M., Perez-Vega, R., & Wirtz, J. (2022). AI in marketing, consumer research and psychology: A systematic literature review and research agenda. *Psychology & Marketing*, *39*(4), 755–776.

Marshall, A. (1994). Ye machine. *Research in the History of Economic Thought and Methodology, Archival Supplement*, 4, 116–132.

Maturana, H. R., & Varela, F. J. (1991). *Autopoiesis and cognition: The realization of the living*. Springer Science & Business Media, Vol. 42.

McCarthy, J., Minsky, M. L., Rochester, N., & Shannon, C. E. (2006). A proposal for the Dartmouth Summer research project on artificial intelligence, August 31, 1955. *AI Magazine*, *27*(4), 12–12.

McGuigan, L. (2019). Automating the audience commodity: The unacknowledged ancestry of programmatic advertising. *New Media & Society*, *21*(11–12), 2366–2385.

Mills, A. J., Pitt, C., & Ferguson, S. L. (2019). The relationship between fake news and advertising: Brand management in the era of programmatic advertising and prolific falsehood. *Journal of Advertising Research*, *59*(1), 3–8.

Miralles-Pechuán, L., Ponce, H., & Martínez-Villaseñor, L. (2018). A novel methodology for optimizing display advertising campaigns using genetic algorithms. *Electronic Commerce Research and Applications*, *27*, 39–51.

Miralles-Pechuán, L., Qureshi, M. A., & Namee, B. M. (2023). Real-time bidding campaigns optimization using user profile settings. *Electronic Commerce Research*, *23*, 1297–1322.

Mitchell, T. M. (1997). Does machine learning really work? *AI Magazine*, *18*(3).

Nannelli, M., Capone, F., & Lazzeretti, L. (2023). Artificial intelligence in hospitality and tourism. State of the art and future research avenues. *European Planning Studies*, *31*(7), 1325–1344.

Netzer, O., Lemaire, A., & Herzenstein, M. (2019). When words sweat: Identifying signals for loan default in the text of loan applications. *Journal of Marketing Research*, *56*(6), 960–980.

Otto, P. (2008). A system dynamics model as a decision aid in evaluating and communicating complex market entry strategies. *Journal of Business Research*, *61*(11), 1173–1181.

Palos-Sanchez, P., Saura, J. R., & Martin-Velicia, F. (2019). A study of the effects of programmatic advertising on users' concerns about privacy overtime. *Journal of Business Research, 96*, 61–72.

Pantano, E., & Pizzi, G. (2020). Forecasting artificial intelligence on online customer assistance: Evidence from chatbot patents analysis. *Journal of Retailing and Consumer Services, 55*, 102096.

Paulson, C., Luo, L., & James, G. M. (2018). Efficient large-scale internet media selection optimization for online display advertising. *Journal of Marketing Research, 55*(4), 489–506.

Pitt, C. S., Bal, A. S., & Plangger, K. (2020). New approaches to psychographic consumer segmentation: exploring fine art collectors using artificial intelligence, automated text analysis and correspondence analysis. *European Journal of Marketing, 54*(2), 305–326.

Porter, J. (2021). Commentary: inefficiencies in digital advertising markets: evidence from the field. *Journal of Marketing, 85*(1), 30–34.

Provost, F., & Fawcett, T. (2013). Data science and its relationship to big data and data-driven decision making. *Big Data, 1*(1), 51–59.

Punj, G., & Stewart, D. W. (1983). Cluster analysis in marketing research: Review and suggestions for application. *Journal of Marketing Research, 20*(2), 134–148.

Puntoni, S., Reczek, R. W., Giesler, M., & Botti, S. (2021). Consumers and artificial intelligence: An experiential perspective. *Journal of Marketing, 85*(1), 131–151.

Qin, R., Yuan, Y., & Wang, F. Y. (2017). Exploring the optimal granularity for market segmentation in RTB advertising via computational experiment approach. *Electronic Commerce Research and Applications, 24*, 68–83.

Rust, R. T. (2020). The future of marketing. *International Journal of Research in Marketing, 37*(1), 15–26.

Salovey, P., & Mayer, J. D. (1990). Emotional intelligence. *Imagination, cognition and personality, 9*(3), 185–211.

Samuel, A. L. (1959). Some studies in machine learning using the game of checkers. *IBM Journal of Research and Development, 3*(3), 210–229.

Samuel, A., White, G. R., Thomas, R., & Jones, P. (2021). Programmatic advertising: An exegesis of consumer concerns. *Computers in Human Behavior, 116*, 106657.

Saunders, J. A. (1980). Cluster analysis for market segmentation. *European Journal of Marketing, 14*(7), 422–435.

Sayedi, A. (2018). Real-time bidding in online display advertising. *Marketing Science, 37*(4), 553–568.

Shanahan, M. (2015). *The technological singularity*. MIT Press, Cambridge, Mass.

Shehu, E., Abou Nabout, N., & Clement, M. (2021). The risk of programmatic advertising: Effects of website quality on advertising effectiveness. *International Journal of Research in Marketing, 38*(3), 663–677.

Silberg, J., & Manyika, J. (2019). Notes from the AI frontier: Tackling bias in AI (and in humans). *McKinsey Global Institute, 1*(6).

Simon, H. A. (1957). *Models of man; social and rational*. Wiley & Sons, New York.

Skiera, B., & Abou Nabout, N. (2013). Practice prize paper—PROSAD: A bidding decision support system for profit optimizing search engine advertising. *Marketing Science, 32*(2), 213–220.

Smith, W. R. (1956). Product differentiation and market segmentation as alternative marketing strategies. *Journal of Marketing, 21*(1), 3–8.

Tagmark, M. (2017). *Life 3.0: Being human in the age of artificial intelligence*, Penguin Books, London.

Turing, A. M. (1950). Computing machinery and intelligence. *Mind. New Series, 59*(236), 433–460.

Turow, J. (2011). *Media today: An introduction to mass communication.* Taylor & Francis, Hoboken.

Upadhyay, M. A., & Chitnis, P. (2022). *Modern marketing using AI. Leverage AI-enabled marketing automation and insights to drive customer journeys and maximize your brand equity.* BPB Publications, India.

Van Bruggen, G. H., Smidts, A., & Wierenga, B. (2001). The powerful triangle of marketing data, managerial judgment, and marketing management support systems. *European Journal of Marketing, 35*(7/8), 796–814.

Varadarajan, R. (2010). Strategic marketing and marketing strategy: domain, definition, fundamental issues and foundational premises. *Journal of the Academy of Marketing Science, 38,* 119–140.

Viswanathan, M., Rosa, J. A., & Harris, J. E. (2005). Decision making and coping of functionally illiterate consumers and some implications for marketing management. *Journal of Marketing, 69*(1), 15–31.

Volkov, D. V., Maloletko, A. N., & Kaurova, O. V. (2018). Formation of bounded consumers' rationality based on micro-segmentation. *European Research Studies, 21*(4), 754–762.

von Glasersfeld, E. (1995). *Radical constructivism: A way of knowing and learning.* Falmer Press, London.

Wind, Y. (1978). Issues and advances in segmentation research. *Journal of marketing research, 15*(3), 317–337.

Wu, C. W., & Monfort, A. (2023). Role of artificial intelligence in marketing strategies and performance. *Psychology & Marketing, 40*(3), 484–496.

Zhang, J. Z., & Watson IV, G. F. (2020). Marketing ecosystem: An outside-in view for sustainable advantage. *Industrial Marketing Management, 88,* 287–304.

7. Marketing automation and heuristics in marketers' experience

7.1 MARKETING AUTOMATION IN THE EXPERIENCE OF THE MARKETERS

This chapter examines the relationship between adoption of AI tools and decision making by marketers to take advantage of automation systems and maintain forms of control over marketing processes. Control can make use of various tools, most notably heuristics, to be integrated with decision-making models using the output of ML processes (Gigerenzer, 2022). To discuss this thesis, the chapter integrates the results of interviews conducted over the years with several dozen marketers (entrepreneurs, managers, or consultants). These interviews address the relationship between new marketing technologies and decision-making models adopted by marketers. Specifically, we selected from a larger database 27 interviews with entrepreneurs and managers who had the greatest affinity with the topic addressed. The interviews were conducted over a wide time span, namely from April 2019 to January 2023, placing them within the framework of a larger project (Guercini, 2022; 2023). In this chapter we report, in an emblematic rather than systematic way, some of the contents of the interviews about the relationship between the inclusion of automated forms and the use of new decision-making models, functional to our interest in the relationship between marketing automation and decision-making models. We present some data on the interviewees in Table 7.1.

Some useful themes emerge from these interviews that identify the impact of marketing automation in decision making. The marketers interviewed often confirmed the prevalence of marketing automation processes, and with that some relevant themes associated with the relationship between automation technologies and decision-making models. In this section we focus on marketing automation in the experience of marketers, while in the next section we examine the themes of marketers' "heuristics", contexts in which tasks for AI systems and marketers are implemented, respectively. In the successive two sections, task contexts and the scope and evolution of heuristics are examined, respectively.

Table 7.1   *Profile of interviewed managers and their organizations in in-depth interviews **

Name	Profile **	Position	Company	Size ***	Client
Marketer 1	male, 42 yo	country manager	food wine digital contents	Medium	consumer
Marketer 2	male,32 yo	head of users' acquisition	conglomerate services	Large	mixed
Marketer 3	male, 40 yo	market analysis director	conglomerate services	Small	business
Marketer 4	female, 37 yo	engagement manager	internet services	Large	mixed
Marketer 5	male, 37 yo	corporate digital manager	pharmaceutical	Medium	mixed
Marketer 6	male, 32 yo	digital marketing manager	online fashion retailer	Medium	consumer
Marketer 7	male, 38 yo	head of marketing	internet services	Small	consumer
Marketer 8	male, 35 yo	chief marketing officer	internet services	Medium	mixed
Marketer 9	male, 46 yo	marketing manager	financial services	Small	mixed
Marketer 10	male, 34 yo	head demand planning	tires manufacturer	Large	mixed
Marketer 11	male, 52 yo	chief financial officer	food chocolate	Large	consumer
Marketer 12	male, 59 yo	entrepreneur founder	marketing research	Small	business
Marketer 13	male, 38 yo	chief digital marketing	publisher	Medium	consumer
Marketer 14	female, 35 yo	IT sales senior manager	luxury fashion brand	Large	consumer
Marketer 15	male, 45 yo	digital sales director	eyewear	Large	consumer
Marketer 16	male, 45 yo	regional sales director	luxury fashion brand	Large	consumer
Marketer 17	male, 45 yo	marketing director	electromedical	Medium	business
Marketer 18	male, 39 yo	chief digital innovation	luxury fashion brand	Large	consumer
Marketer 19	male, 32 yo	IT and service manager	luxury fashion brand	Large	consumer
Marketer 20	male, 37 yo	chief marketing officer	digital platform	Small	mixed
Marketer 21	male, 40 yo	chief technology officer	luxury fashion brand	Large	consumer
Marketer 22	male, 41 yo	retail real estate director	specialty fashion brand	Large	consumer
Marketer 23	male, 50 yo	IT and entrepreneur	application developer	Small	mixed
Marketer 24	male, 33 yo	senior digital manager	division adv MNC	Large	business
Marketer 25	female, 35 yo	advertising trader	demand side platform	Medium	business

Name	Profile **	Position	Company	Size ***	Client
Marketer 26	female, 34 yo	manager network	Internet media observ.	Small	business
Marketer 27	female, 40 yo	digital marketing manager	mobile phone services	Large	mixed

Notes: * each contact was interviewed between April 2019 and January 2023; ** organization's size; the name of the company is hidden to ensure anomalousness for respondents; *** company size was defined on the basis of turnover and an assessment against known competitors.
Source: Author's elaboration.

The prevalence of the characteristics of heuristics in marketing tasks have long been the subject of attention (Guercini, 2012; Guercini, La Rocca, Runfola, and Snehota, 2014; 2015; Guercini and Freeman, 2023). In recent years, forms of automation have been examined for their impact on the characteristics of decision making in automated marketing processes (Guercini, 2019; 2022).

The interviews considered here highlight various aspects of the relationship between automation and managers' experience. A first emerging aspect is the widespread confidence in the affirmation and effectiveness of new technologies for marketing, and in particular the clear view of the automation process as a prospect for the future of marketing activities. Automation is seen as an ongoing phenomenon that will bring positive results. This positive view on the success of marketing automation, particularly AI-based marketing automation, is accompanied by a negative view on the future of humans and their possibilities in data-driven marketing processes. On the one hand, the importance of the human actor's participation in certain aspects of the marketing process is seen (e.g., the importance of the voice experience of interaction); on the other hand, an assessment emerges that humans will play an increasingly diminishing role because they are not as reliable as the machine. It is believed that "an artificial intelligence system will be more efficient than a human system. Humans themselves process on the basis of algorithms based on previous experience, but machines are more efficient at processing large masses of data" (Marketer 06).

Human input is perceived to remain central, not only for control but for key linkages within the automation process. In a company that trades wine, a mechanism for scoring products by users has been developed, based on which software is able to suggest wines based on the scoring mechanism. However, how can the recommendation be defined from the data about the user? For example, if a customer has already tried various wines of the same type, does it make more sense to suggest other wines of the same type or imagine that it is time to suggest a change? For an automated system to work, one must continue over time to teach the machine, for example, the meaning of terms. Why then is automation so important if at the same time it depends so much on real people? One theme that emerges is that "people do not feel like searching ... people want to be relieved of searching, if they trust it" (Marketer 01). Many "like to live in the age of automation, even when in fact the desire is to leave tasks to machines, no matter how much they perceive a loss of accuracy" (Marketer 02).

Marketing automation is not necessarily AI but is increasingly based on AI systems. A representation of the relationship between automated marketing, AI, ML and DL is given in Figure 7.1.

Note: The form corresponding to the smaller set is part of the larger one that includes it.
Source: Author's elaboration.

Figure 7.1   *The relation between forms of artificial intelligence applied to marketing automation*

Some marketers interviewed go so far as to point out that "for the future I cannot imagine marketing automation without machine learning" (Marketer 03). Yet there are cases in which ML applied to marketing automation has produced non-positive effects. A large pharmaceutical company had developed an AI system that started with a dataset of sick people to figure out what the best treatment was, but

> the algorithm proposed solutions that made the disease worse. The problem was that the dataset only included data about sick people, and that was a mistake, whereas it is now realized that the dataset should include both healthy and sick people. The fact is that a learning period is needed, so an error like this is trivial today, but it was not trivial in the early days of using these tools. A great algorithm without good data is useless. (Marketer 03)

Coupled with the confidence for the future is the idea that businesses are in many cases still lagging behind the adoption of AI-based marketing automation. When automation systems are more widespread, some loss of accuracy can be found in the face of less human intervention. Adoption of AI-based marketing automation is then not straightforward and "many companies are still very indifferent to these technologies" (Marketer 04). One emerging aspect is the need for an "onboarding period" (Marketer 03), meaning that automation systems in marketing are not immediately effective, requiring a period of adaptation of people to their use.

Automation can cover several activities in marketing, which are interrelated but distinguishable. Consider, for example, these activities emerging from the interviews as terrains of application of automated marketing: (1) email management with customers; (2) "abandoned cart" management in online purchases; (3) recommendation system for connected users; and (4) "cross-selling" actions. The first three activities are apparently distinct, but then in fact they are integrated: in fact, emails are used to make recommendations to those who initiated a purchase but then did not complete it (this is referred to by the concept of "abandoned cart"). The presence of decision heuristics is built into automation activities. For example, hiatus heuristics are used (Wübben and Wangenheim, 2008; Gigerenzer and Gaissmeier, 2011) for automation system that handle e-mails, whereby e-mail is automatically scheduled to be sent "after a predefined number of hours or days have elapsed since the creation of the shopping cart with the products whose purchase is not completed" (Marketer 06). Another area in which the use of automatic marketing is accompanied in the surveyed experiences with the use of heuristics by marketers is related, for example, to the case of "cross-selling" (Marketer 07), an activity that integrates with that of recommendation systems. Cross-selling is a long-standing policy in marketing and is strongly linked to, for example, direct marketing processes. Having defined a database of customers, each of whom has bought some of my products, marketers interviewed try to increase their sales by proposing to each customer some of the other products that they might buy. A decision will have to be made as to the most appropriate criterion for identifying products to recommend to individual customers. For example, it might be judged that the products that can most easily cross-sell are those that other customers have already bought together with others, so the recommendation aimed at cross-selling might consist of pointing out to the customer that those who have bought product A have in many cases also bought product B. However, it is only one of the possible criteria, for example, as we have seen in the case of the wine e-commerce site (Marketer 01), wherby a customer scoring system was constructed and it was planned to recommend for cross-selling purposes those products that had criteria in line with the ratings expressed by individual customers, regardless of whether other customers had purchased those products together or not. The judgment formation rule can be integrated with automation systems by deriving different types of integration between automated systems and human decision making, even when these automated systems were not ML-based.

A major advantage for marketers who incorporate marketing automation systems is the time gained from being able to free themselves from many tasks previously done manually and directly. Marketing automation tools have evolved a great deal and allow staff to address issues such as managing standardized customer communications, profiling users in the digital environment, managing interrupted buying processes, and cross-selling. There are broad areas such as demand planning and programmatic advertising that can be addressed through data-driven, AI-based marketing automation systems. This also includes the management of promotional campaigns: "a campaign that works is one that uses data in an automated way. Five years ago we did not have AI applied to marketing; today it is fundamental to our company. We apply it ... through recommendation systems" (Marketer 08).

Campaigns using AI can perform better because they are more responsive, but if there is poor quality data or changes in the target context, the results can be negative. In fact, with AI and ML, "one downside is that you lose a little bit of control, you no longer put your hand on the data and the model at the moment when the machine logic is foreign to us" (Marketer 08). Then there are "sectors with small numbers, such as many SMEs in business-to-business, for example, that have less advantage in using automation systems based on artificial intelligence, since a good algorithm if it works on little data is less correct" (Marketer 08). A manager of an electro-medical company basically reiterates this point, adding further:

> There are sectors, particularly in business to business, in which the numbers of operations, machines and customers are very low and consequently the data base does not assume such large proportions as to create a suitable ground for the application of big data analysis techniques. Another element to consider is the time at which the decision is made, which can have enormous weight. The sales part is one element within the big world of marketing. The marketing man is comparable in the theater to the author and the impresario; the salesman is comparable to the actor. In the world of our enterprise, which is the world of medical devices, forms of automation from data do not have great effectiveness ... On the one hand in the world there is a strong scientific society that states that the needle of a device must be retractable. A company that makes the device with a non-retractable needle loses a whole slice of the market but gains another slice because the device is still being misused but widely used. No algorithm can detect these dynamics, but they become relevant to individual firms. In my experience, what I can say is that we rely only on the large numbers there are always trivial variations that affect the prediction of the machine. They affect so much the conditions of the moment when the decision is made. (Marketer 17)

Automation capabilities are critical because "the customer's life is simplified if we anticipate the customer's needs. The customer may desire not having to think (don't let me think). First the data then creativity is developed. Creativity is enhanced by the data base developed by marketing automation" (Marketer 09). To do this, however,

> input information management is critical. Having information about general market movements can help our AI make predictions. The problem is that very difficult to get forecast data. We have historical data, and that is the basis for developing models to estimate the future. Another way is to work in partnership with other companies by integrating information systems so that we know what is happening to the customer before they even realize it. (Marketer 10)

> A mix of various tools is used to address the limitations of AI. In our forecast, the baseline (the product mix) is formed by AI. Then for the total volume other tools come into play, for example, data from previous years and long-term trends, to complete the forecast. The data suggested by AI is integrated with the human element that evaluates what to accept and what to discard. (Marketer 10)

The possibilities of AI in marketing automation are contingent on convenience and opportunity evaluations in dealing with marketers, as "it can be disturbing to these customers to go into their pockets using even a technological system that is difficult to explain. You always try to surround AI with understandable key performance indicators. Even internally, the decision trees that our MLs put up are not easy to explain" (Marketer 20).

An interesting case emerges in the demand planning of a multinational tire company.

> The company is geared to use preventive systems and 'touchless' planning, without human intervention but emerging from the system automatically. However, I wouldn't know how I would behave if the AI told me that a snow cyclone is coming in a week and so now you have to tell production to make extra snow tires. I would not move in that direction by exposing myself: if then the prediction turns out to be wrong I put my career at risk. AI is one component but it is not the only one. Right now it is perceived as one of the ten inputs at the table, but it is definitely not the absolute benchmark for forecasting, it is just one of the benchmarks. If the AI predicts 100 and we are at 98, then that is fine, because it confirms some anchoring. However, if the AI predicts 100 and we expected 85, we would go and try to get a better understanding of what the AI sees that we do not see. Then the policy adopted with respect to forecasting also matters. We are generally a little more conservative, or we make estimates based on policy assessments as well." In 2020, "health events all came to a halt, and also for technical reasons because there was a cut in spending, and these projects on AI also had to be postponed. (Marketer 10)

These mixed forms of AI adaptation in automated marketing invoke elaboration processes that are based on "anchoring" systems, a term used as a label for one of the heuristics and biases program heuristics (Tversky and Kahneman, 1974), or with the approach to forecasting that expresses being conservative as a "golden rule" (Armstrong, Green and Graefe, 2015).

Listening to the network is an interesting terrain in which AI and ML forms can be employed. "Our company has a proprietary platform for listening. It started from this consideration: regardless of the development of technology, there is always a need for substantial human intervention" (Marketer 12).

Automation requires more planning in the organization's marketing activities. "These systems are becoming more and more user friendly, and it is no longer necessary to have technical expertise. The organization for this has to equip itself less and less with technicians and more and more with marketing figures; the technical aspect is better bought from outside than developed internally" (Marketer 13).

7.2 MARKETERS' ADAPTIVE TOOLBOX IN THE MARKETING AUTOMATION PROCESSES

From the interviews presented earlier, there is evidence of the prevalence of some decision rules involving forms of integration between AI-based and human decision making. The adoption of AI- and ML-based automated marketing tools on topics examined in the previous chapter, such as new forms of customer classification, new recommender systems, and forms of PA, enter marketing processes (when this occurs) confronting, from the marketer's point of view, existing tools. From the marketers' point of view this evolution must find justification. Thus, there is a comparison, for example, between "algorithmic driven" and "rules driven" recommendation systems (Lee, 2023). The attitude of the marketer also becomes relevant to the defining of the behavior model when choosing the decision model, as evidenced by research (Christen, Boulding and Staelin, 2009). How do the inclusion of these new AI-based marketing technologies and determining marketing automation compare with pre-existing approaches in marketing activities? This question may appear theoretical, but in reality it is experienced practically and operationally by all marketers who are introducing and before that are considering the adoption of AI-based tools. It is a question related to the very definition of marketing automation that we dealt with specifically in Chapter 5 above. It could also be defined in these terms: how does the inclusion of these tools impact the market enterprise interface management model and, I would say more broadly, the business model? To what extent can I rely on these tools, and in what ways should I complement them with tools for monitoring and comparing the results given by new technologies with those originating from other sources?

Let us examine the perspective of marketers, which is moreover similar to that of consumers in terms of technology users (Kozinets and Giesler 2021). Research on decision making has highlighted the natural prevalence of heuristics in the decision-making models of experts in particular. Even though a debate is open on a prescriptive level, even at times highly polarized, about the accuracy of heuristics, the fact that they correspond to the most widely and naturally diffused decision making adopted by human decision makers is a point on which different actors largely agree, from Gigerenzer to Kahneman, from Thaler to Klein. Let us try to adopt Kahneman's view of system 1 and system 2: is AI better able to replace the former or the latter? Probably everything that comes to translate into forms of computation, the new tools will have clear margins of superiority over the human actor's ability to evaluate. Consider the management of advertising space made available online through PA versus other traditional forms. At the same time, the very case of PA highlights the presence of risks, and consequently the need to resort to empirical insights and evaluations of alternative possibilities for control over processes that, through automation and ML, may escape the awareness of the same data scientists and programmers who set them up. This is where heuristics can take on a new role as a verification and control system, the use of which marketers need to be educated in just as marketing automation is gaining momentum.

The literature proves that total error is composed not only of bias, but also of variance (see Geman, Bienenstock and Doursat, 1992), as indeed admitted by Kahneman himself in his book on "noise" (Kahneman, Sibony and Sustein, 2021). There is ample research showing that variance error can outweigh bias error, and it is pointed out by Gigerenzer and colleagues that in many situations heuristics can outperform less simple decision models in terms of accuracy (see for example Gigerenzer and Brighton, 2009). This is why it is important to take a more comprehensive view that takes into account the possibilities of error in the decision model and thus the possibilities of heuristics. This is basically the reason behind the perspective of "positive heuristics" (Guercini and Lechner, 2021).

Managers resort to intuitive heuristics instead of statistical prediction methods (Parikh, Lank and Neubauer, 1994; Patterson, Quinn, and Baron, 2012). This is on the descriptive level, that is, of observing managers' actual behaviors. But the comparison between heuristics and more complex prediction methods is also brought to the prescriptive level. The use of hiatus heuristic in interrupted procurement management activity represents a hybridization between human and AI decision-making models. Furthermore, hiatus heuristic compared to more complex models might be more accurate (Gigerenzer and Gaissmaier, 2011; Wübben and Wangenheim, 2008). This is true both in action-dependent classification processes for the future and directly in forecasting processes (Parikh, Lank and Neubauer, 1994).

As early as the 1990s, some authors were examining a number of computer-based heuristic methods that had been successfully applied to problems outside the field of marketing. These methods included "simulated annealing", "genetic algorithms", "branch-and-bound", and "tabu search", assuming a concept of heuristics that is quite different from rule-of-thumb and assumed to be precisely adoptable with the aid of computers (Coates, Doherty, and French, 1994, p. 210ff.). There were relatively few instances of the use of these methods as applications in marketing, but their possibility of use and application to large marketing databases was a subject of discussion (Coates, Doherty, and French, 1994). More recently, heuristic algorithms also based on the use of many variables are being examined for their use in the management of relationship marketing programs (Daukseviciute and Simkin, 2016).

Jeon (2022) examines the influence that job titles assigned to AI agents can have on customer perceptions and marketing outcomes such as customer satisfaction, brand attitude and intention to buy. The paper uses three experimental studies from this perspective using a scenario or a combination of scenarios and a real AI chatbot to study consumer perceptions about the AI representative and the human manager. Customer behavior is examined in light of the heuristics-and-biases approach, referred to by the author as the "Heuristic Judgement Model", with reference essentially to Kahneman (2011), without a comparison with alternative approaches such as, for example, the fast-and-frugal approach (Gigerenzer and colleagues) or the simple-rule approach (Eisenhardt and colleagues) or the use of nudges by a choice architect (Thaler and colleagues). This corresponds in many ways to the mainstream but excludes a priori some of the assumptions present in the debate about the role of heuristics in decision making. On the marketer's side, "this study provides evidence for a simple but effective tactic that can increase the effectiveness in using AI agents for marketing: assigning human job title to AI agents" (Jeon, 2022, p. 900). This is a supportable conclusion but it is unclear whether it can be based on emotional deception, where the short-term effect detected in the study should be verified against its long-term effects through longitudinal studies.

Thus, the change in marketing related to automation has an impact on the behaviors of marketers, whose decisions first require new skills to understand and use the characteristics of these new tools, and second require new awareness about the characteristics of the decision-making processes adopted. The impact of tools that enable data-driven processes is important for decision-making processes because they change their timing and subject matter. With respect to timing, these tools replace marketers in some tasks, requiring processing of large volumes of data in a short time and in many cases even with actions directly derived from the result of the processing (Ameen, Sharma, Tarba, Rao and Chopra, 2022). Consequently, with respect to the object of the decision, the marketer is increasingly asked to decide not from the results of processing, but in selecting the data and the type of tools (software, systems, platforms, etc.) to be used, how to control and integrate the work of these systems. In addressing these issues, we question the role of the forms of problem solving used by marketers, and this is where our focus is on heuristics (Guercini, 2022).

Marketing activities in companies have been changing for years now as a result of new technologies. This is evident in both operational and strategic marketing activities. These technologies include not only, but primarily technologies related to the digital environment. These are not the only technologies relevant to marketing change, for example there are electromedical technologies that have a major impact at the level of tools for neuromarketing research that is different in nature for the type of technology involved (Marketer 17). The digital part, however, has an obvious prominence.

The individual heuristics adopted by the observed actors can be categorized at different levels. For example, the "multipliers" we considered in chapter 4 are a general category that includes more specific categories, such as the "mark-up" adopted for setting sales prices from purchase prices, or the calculation of costs. But there are also other decision models, adopted for the formulation of estimates and forecasts, for example on sales volumes or costs to be included in the next budget. At least three levels are identified in this example: the level of the individual heuristic (mark-up for pricing), the specific type (mark-up), and the general type (multiplier). The scope changes depending on the level considered: a certain mark-up (e.g., 1.5) can be used to define the price of a product, while its scope is narrower when considering mark-ups in general. In some cases rules adopted correspond to a general heuristic, while at other times individual rules may appear to be unrelated to more general types.

7.3   MARKETERS' TASKS AND DECISION CONTEXTS

The decision context is a determinant of the performance of the automated marketing process. This context can take on specific characteristics depending on several factors, including the type of organization and industry, as well as for the technology that enables marketing automation. The application of AI as an element underlying the marketing automation process is realized within a context identified with an ecosystem (Puntoni, Reczek, Giesler and Botti, 2021; Kozinets and Gretzel, 2021). Automated marketing systems are realized in the context of a business network in which actor's bonds, resource ties and activity links are created (Håkansson, Ford, Gadde, Snehota and Waluszewski, 2009). These approaches are relevant for reading the context in which decisions are made with respect to the automated marketing process (Mero, Tarkiainen and Tobon, 2020).

As much as automation invokes a theme of replacing the human element, in the reality of automated marketing processes the relational dimension between actors is crucial to build and keep active and lead to an evolution of the network for the realization of processes. Let us take the example of PA seen in the previous chapter. The PA context is different from the more traditional "direct advertising" context. The PA context is automated and works in real time. All exchanges take place in fractions of a second, with inevitable consequences for the kind of control that can be exercised, and consequently the kind of risk one is confronted with. From an operational point of view, PA is characterized by processes of automation of the advertising process in a digital context. This context, however, is still the result of relationships and interactions between actors who have to solve problems and develop opportunities and are also for this reason, if possible, even more vital than in traditional advertising networks. The operational flow, however, is no longer carried out by people but by technological systems and essentially forms of AI (ML, DL) that carry out the process in real time, joining advertiser with publisher and thus the user. The platforms between demand side and supply side of PA are operated by actors who realize negotiation processes that regulate how to address and improve the accuracy of the automated process. Personal contacts and relationality among these actors are critical to managing the most important level of negotiation (Busch, 2016).

PA represents an important case for our analysis for several reasons. First, as we have seen, it is undoubtedly a marketing automation system that has been very successful and widespread. Second, the context of programmatic advertising presents an evolved scope among those characterizing automated marketing, which allows us to highlight the kind of opportunities but also problems faced by marketers in the automation process.

PA is a marketing process that realizes the exchange of advertising space in a digital context and has these characteristics: (1) it is based on an automated system; (2) it operates in real time; and (3) it is targeted user-oriented. We see PA at work directly in our experience every time we enter the webpage of an online newspaper and find a different advertisement than another who enters the same page of the same newspaper at the same time. This is no small difference from advertising in traditional print newspapers, where each of us, regardless of our profile, found the same advertisement. In other words, PA "essentially means automation of the advertising space exchange process. However, it is not the only feature. Another fundamental and related one is the fact that the processes happen in real time. However, there are also risks ..." for PA,

> because direct has characteristics of lower risk in some respects. One element of
> greater safety of direct compared to programmatic is the possibility, in case of an

image crisis of your business, to continue to use direct while it is not the case to use programmatic. This is because, if there is bad news about your business and articles are circulating about it, you want to avoid advertising for your products on pages that give bad news about your business or even your own products. You can't be selective about that using programmatic. (Marketer 24)

Programmatic has become or is becoming, depending on the market, a majority in the management of digital advertising, but it does not monopolize digital advertising and is not likely to totally exhaust it. In fact, digital advertising includes forms such as advertising delivered directly from search engines (typically, that which we find on Google response pages) or directly in social media (advertising presented directly on social media pages or in influencer blogs linked to evaluation on the overall public/community character of the social media or blogger). Digital advertising managed in direct mode is called "in reservation" (Marketer 25). The element in fact that characterizes PA is primarily the different object of exchange compared to traditional advertising systems. In PA, the advertising market does not exchange advertising space, but essentially exchanges targeted users. The system is in real time, which requires a buying program. Advertising space on a site's page is exchanged with reference to the moment the user "lands" on the page. The exchange therefore takes place in real time with respect to that event, and for this to happen there needs to be a program that defines the purchases (demand side), hence the expression "programmatic buying" (Marketer 26).

PA requires, as we have seen, collaboration among a number of actors, and extensive use of heuristics by marketers occurs precisely within the processes of interaction among these actors (Guercini, La Rocca and Snehota, 2022). In fact, PA is an ecosystem of actors and is produced with reference to a network of service providers and customers:

> There are agreements between actors in the network that generates programmatic advertising. It is not just an ecosystem that develops. There are relevant interactions in a business network with agreements that are aimed at achieving results, in terms of business arrangements between individual actors, not between species of organizations. In other words, it interacts firm A which is a publisher with firm B which operates an SSP," at the personal level not automatic operation. (Marketer 27)

7.4   MARKETERS' HEURISTICS SCOPE AND EVOLUTION

The interviews we conducted with entrepreneurs and managers address the topic of marketing automation in the experiences of the marketers interviewed, examining the process of marketing automation. A positive view and perceived fears and limitations coexist in the marketers' narratives. In particular, the positive view relates to the possibilities realized and achievable in the future through marketing automation in some specific areas (customer profiling, recommendation systems for sales completion and cross-selling, just to name a few examples). The most positive assessments are of the future possibilities of AI in marketing processes. As evident in PA, automation generates new AI actors and networks in which marketing activities are developed. AI-based marketing automation also has limitations that insist particularly on the problems of control and risk management, as well as the awareness that has emerged from some experiences of the need for networks of relationships between actors in order to be able to improve data quality and control over results. The heuristic rules adopted by marketers are found precisely to address these problems, but they are the crucial ones where AI cannot be left alone. The workings of the most advanced online advertising processes show how the uncertainty and difficulties in the operation of AI can result from interactions and agreements through which the actors who determine the link between advertisers and publishers address the problems, both technical and business, that can be had in the operation and performance of the system. The human decision maker and the heuristics they use are the enablers for overcoming these nodes and building the context that enables the AI-driven automated marketing process to work.

The decision models that best deal with the condition of uncertainty are those that have the attribute of robustness. This is defined as the characteristic of a model to be generalizable to novel situations (Katsikopoulos, Şimşek, Buckmann and Gigerenzer, 2020). Robustness is a characteristic of heuristics understood as models for decision-making, along with others such as speed, frugality, and transparency. Heuristics are fast in the sense that they can offer solutions to a problem very quickly; they are frugal in that they require little information to apply; they are transparent in that they can be understood and taught quickly even to novices (Katsikopoulos, Şimşek, Buckmann and Gigerenzer, 2020). These characteristics make the use of heuristics in many cases as indispensable to break out of deadlocks, since "when optimal solutions are out of reach, we are not paralyzed to inaction or doomed to failure. We can use heuristics to discover good solutions" (Gigerenzer, 2004, p. 63).

Applying research on a number of managers, we showed the contexts in which this integration between AI systems and human decision-making models can occur. Many different heuristic rules followed in business-market relationships emerge in organizations (Guercini, 2019). Recurrent for example is the use of coefficients or multipliers to make estimates or solve decision-making problems, among which recurrent are the multiplier, threshold, and calends heuristics already anticipated in Chapter Four and that emerged in several situations in interviews with marketers.

"Multiplier heuristics" as a basis for heuristics are found whenever an estimate that is often important or necessary for future planning is determined by applying a multiplier factor to actual recorded data. For example, the event of trade show attendance is an opportunity to contact customers and observe competitors, but also an essential basis for making estimates and forecasts from data collected at trade shows by applying multipliers, for example, multiplying orders collected at trade shows by a coefficient in order to estimate next year's sales. Another example of a multiplier, perhaps the most widely used, is the "mark-up" for pricing. Marketers define the sales price by applying, precisely, a coefficient, the mark-up (e.g., 1.5 to 2 depending on the product category or sales format) to the purchase price, defining the price for selling to the end customer. The term "mark-up" can refer to the entire procedure or to the specific coefficient applied.

Multipliers can be described in terms of three "building blocks" (Gigerenzer and Brighton, 2009), as anticipated in Chapter 4: (1) "search rule", which indicates to search for input data (e.g., collected orders or purchase price); (2) "stopping rule", which indicates to stop when such data has been acquired; and (3) "decision rule", which consists in this case of applying an expected coefficient. Here the problem of scope emerges at two levels: the procedure as a whole; the second is the numerical value of the coefficient. Not surprisingly, as we have said, the term "mark-up" can refer to both levels.

"Threshold heuristics" was previously introduced as a model for forming a judgment or choice from the outcome of verifying that a certain predetermined or otherwise definable threshold is reached based on the judgment or choice. The threshold is not only used in satisficing (Artinger, Gigerenzer and Jacobs, 2022), but also in other heuristics. For example, a rule applied to sales to individual foreign markets directed at containing a specific uncertainty condition was found in textile companies, namely that exports to a single foreign country were to be contained within a certain threshold (10 percent in one specific case) of annual company sales (Guercini and Runfola, 2021). This rule was justified by the need to contain risks to countries by distributing it among several countries, and the entrepreneurs adopting it considered it so important that the company's founder had passed it on to his children, who had adhered to it during their years of management. As anticipated in Chapter 4, threshold heuristics have the following "building blocks": (1) "search rule" is to search for input data (the current level of sales in a country in total sales); (2) "stopping rule" is to stop when you have acquired (percentage to total sales, or absolute value); (3) "decision rule" is to contain sales achieved within the threshold, which may vary depending on the context.

As with multipliers, for thresholds the problem of scope arises at two levels: the procedure as a whole; the numerical value of the threshold.

The "caldends heuristics" emerges when applying certain dates/days identified in a calendar, which define the time at which to define a judgment and/or choice, from some input data referable to those dates. For example, in a company engaged in purchasing expensive raw materials produced in distant countries and at certain seasons of the year (such as cashmere for the production of luxury garments) certain weeks or days in the calendar year are identified on which to observe commodity price trends in order to form an estimate of price trends in the following year. The case at hand is particularly interesting. The decision is a very delicate one because making the mistake of buying means either running out of raw material to process later in the year, or paying additional costs that can eliminate profit margins considering the impact of raw material costs on the price of sales. These dates were kept confidential by entrepreneurs, even if they were known in the industry, because their knowledge was still considered a competitive factor and the heuristics of the kalends applied by one company might differ slightly from those applied by another company.

In the pre-industrial world, calends are dates in the period between December and January when weather observation is the basis for forecasting the weather season in the following months, if not throughout the entire year. The "building blocks" of the calends anticipated in Chapter Four are: (1) "search rule" is acquiring an input data on a specific day, such as it could be the price level of a specific commodity on some specific days of the year, either given directly or calculated indirectly; (2) "stopping rule" is stopping when the input data has been acquired (e.g., the absolute value and/or price trend on those days); and (3) "decision rule" is the activation or non-activation of an action related to the date or calendas (e.g., concluding contracts). A representation of the scope of these three rules is offered in Table 7.2.

These heuristics emerging from narratives are not new phenomena to the management literature (Guercini, 2019; 2022). "Multipliers" can be found in the literature whenever the topic of mark-up is identified (Akçay, Natarajan and Xu, 2010; Arcelus and Srinivasa, 1987; Shafahi and Haghani, 2014; Takano, Ishii and Muraki, 2014), as well as when discussing methods for decision making (Cotterill and Putsis, 2001; Greenbank, 1999; Vilcassim and Chintagunta, 1995). "Thresholds" are present in other cases (Bhaskaran, Ramachandran and Semple 2010; Deshpande, Cohen and Donohue, 2003), such as whenever a watershed level is defined, at which judgment changes and a change in behavior is expected. What we call "heuristics" are rules

Table 7.2   *Three emerging types of heuristics rules*

Heuristics	Definition	Scope of the rule	Scope of the factor	Examples
Multipliers	Applying a multiplier factor to an actually recorded datum to estimate or forecast	Tasks where the operation of multiplying is used	Tasks where a certain value of the multiplier is used	Mark-up in pricing – Budget forecasts
Thresholds	Verifying the achievement of a threshold (pre-established or otherwise definable) for judgment or choice	Tasks where a threshold is applied	Tasks where a numerical value of the threshold is used	Satisficing Limits in negotiation
Calends	Identifying days in a calendar (or hours in a day) as the moment in which to define a judgment and/or a choice	Tasks where to consider the calends	Tasks where a certain day (or other time units) is used	Seasonal product launch – Budget calendar

Source: Author's elaboration.

based on identifying the appropriate time to behave, e.g., gathering information and making a judgment or choice (Jagannathan, Marakani, Takehara and Wang, 2012; Useem, 2006); they can be related to the literature dealing with issues such as seasonality in new product launches (Bruce, Daly and Kahn, 2007; Radas and Shugan, 1998) and planning or promoting at the right time (Borle, Singh and Jain, 2008; Malhotra, Morgan and Zhu, 2018; Rajagopalan and Swaminathan, 2001). The categories of heuristics identified are examples of more general decision-making models that are widely present in decision-making and decision-maker behavior in many companies, which may also have room for integration into decision-making models in marketing automation.

REFERENCES

Akçay, Y., Natarajan, H. P., & Xu, S. H. (2010). Joint dynamic pricing of multiple perishable products under consumer choice. *Management Science*, 56(8), 1345–1361.

Ameen, N., Sharma, G. D., Tarba, S., Rao, A., & Chopra, R. (2022). Toward advancing theory on creativity in marketing and artificial intelligence. *Psychology & Marketing*, 39(9), 1802–1825.

Arcelus, F. J., & Srinivasan, G. (1987). Inventory policies under various optimizing criteria and variable markup rates. *Management Science*, 33(6), 756–762.

Armstrong, J. S., Green, K. C., & Graefe, A. (2015). Golden rule of forecasting: Be conservative, *Journal of Business Research*, 68(8), 1717–1731.

Artinger, F. M., Gigerenzer, G., & Jacobs, P. (2022). Satisficing: Integrating two traditions. *Journal of Economic Literature, 60*(2), 598–635.

Bhaskaran, S., Ramachandran, K., & Semple, J. (2010). A dynamic inventory model with the
right of refusal. *Management Science, 56*(12), 2265–2281.

Borle, S., Singh, S. S., & Jain, D. C. (2008). Customer lifetime value measurement. *Management
Science, 54*(1), 100–112.

Bruce, M., Daly, L., & Kahn, K. B. (2007). Delineating design factors that influence the global
product launch process. *Journal of Product Innovation Management, 24*(5), 456–470.

Busch, O. (ed.) (2016). *Programmatic Advertising. The Successful Transformation to Automated,
Data-Driven Marketing in Real-Time.* Springer Nature, Berlin.

Christen, M., Boulding, W., & Staelin, R. (2009). Optimal market intelligence strategy when
management attention is scarce. *Management Science, 55*(4), 526–538.

Coates, D., Doherty, N., & French, A. (1994). The new multivariate jungle: Computer intensive
methods in database marketing. *Journal of Marketing Management, 10*(1–3), 207–220.

Cotterill, R. W., & Putsis Jr, W. P. (2001). Do models of vertical strategic interaction for national
and store brands meet the market test? *Journal of Retailing, 77*(1), 83–109.

Daukseviciute, I., & Simkin, L. (2016). Optimising relationship marketing programmes: a holistic approach. *Journal of Strategic Marketing, 24*(6), 500–518.

Deshpande, V., Cohen, M. A., & Donohue, K. (2003). A threshold inventory rationing policy for
service-differentiated demand classes. *Management Science, 49*(6), 683–703.

Geman, S., Bienenstock, E., & Doursat, R. (1992). Neural networks and the bias/variance
dilemma. *Neural Computation, 4*(1), 1–58.

Gigerenzer, G., & Gaissmaier, W. (2011). Heuristic decision making. *Annual Review of
Psychology, 62*, 451–482.

Gigerenzer, G. (2004). Fast and frugal heuristics: The tools of bounded rationality. In Koehler,
D. & Harvey, N. (eds.), *Blackwell handbook of judgment and decision making.* Blackwell,
Oxford, UK, 62–88.

Gigerenzer, G. (2022). *How to stay smart in a smart world: Why human intelligence still beats
algorithms.* Penguin, London.

Gigerenzer, G., & Brighton, H. (2009). Homo heuristicus: why biased minds make better inferences. *Topics in Cognitive Science, 1*, 107–43.

Greenbank, P. (1999). The pricing decision in the micro-business: a study of accountants, builders and printers. *International Small Business Journal, 17*(3), 60–73.

Guercini, S., & Freeman, S. M. (2023). How international marketers make decisions: exploring
approaches to learning and using heuristics. *International Marketing Review, 40*(3), 429–451.

Guercini, S., & Lechner, C. (2021). New challenges for business actors and positive heuristics. *Management Decision, 59*(7), 1585–1597.

Guercini, S. (2012). New approaches to heuristic processes and entrepreneurial cognition of the
market. *Journal of Research in Marketing and Entrepreneurship, 14*(2), 199–213.

Guercini, S. (2019). Heuristics as tales from the field: the problem of scope. *Mind &
Society, 18*(2), 191–205.

Guercini, S. (2022). Scope of heuristics and digitalization: the case of marketing automation. *Mind & Society, 21*(2), 151–164.

Guercini, S. (2023). Marketing automation and the case of programmatic advertising. *Micro &
Macro Marketing, 32*(2), 261–270.

Guercini, S., La Rocca, A., & Snehota, I. (2022). Decisions when interacting in customer-supplier
relationships. *Industrial Marketing Management, 105*, 380–387.

Guercini, S., & Runfola, A. (2021). Heuristics in decision-making by exporting textiles
SMEs. *Journal of Global Fashion Marketing, 12*(1), 1–15.

Guercini, S., La Rocca, A., Runfola, A., & Snehota, I. (2014). Interaction behaviors in business relationships and heuristics: Issues for management and research agenda. *Industrial Marketing Management, 43*(6), 929–937.

Guercini, S., La Rocca, A., Runfola, A., & Snehota, I. (2015). Heuristics in customer-supplier interaction. *Industrial Marketing Management, 48*, 26–37.

Håkansson, H., Ford, D., Gadde, L. E., Snehota, I., & Waluszewski, A. (2009). *Business in networks*. John Wiley & Sons, Chichester.

Jagannathan, R., Marakani, S., Takehara, H., & Wang, Y. (2012). Calendar cycles, infrequent decisions, and the cross section of stock returns. *Management Science, 58*(3), 507–522.

Jeon, Y. A. (2022). Let me transfer you to our AI-based manager: Impact of manager-level job titles assigned to AI-based agents on marketing outcomes. *Journal of Business Research, 145*, 892–904.

Kahneman, D. (2011). *Thinking, fast and slow*. Penguin Books, London.

Kahneman, D., Sibony, O., & Sunstein, C. R. (2021). *Noise: a flaw in human judgment*. Hachette, London.

Katsikopoulos, K. V., Şimşek, O., Buckmann, M., & Gigerenzer, G. (2020). *Classification in the wild. The science and art of transparent decision making*. MIT Press, Cambridge, Mass.

Kozinets, R. V., & Gretzel, U. (2021). Commentary: Artificial intelligence: The marketer's dilemma. *Journal of Marketing, 85*(1), 156–159.

Lee, M. (2023). *Algorithm-driven vs. Rule-driven Recommendations in E-Commerce*. https://www.bloomreach.com/en/blog/2023/algorithm-driven-vs.-rule-driven-recommendations-in-e-commerce.

Malhotra, S., Morgan, H. M., & Zhu, P. (2018). Sticky decisions: Anchoring and equity stakes in international acquisitions. *Journal of Management, 44*(8), 3200–3230.

Mero, J., Tarkiainen, A., & Tobon, J. (2020). Effectual and causal reasoning in the adoption of marketing automation. *Industrial Marketing Management, 86*, 212–222.

Parikh, J., Lank, A., & Neubauer, F. (1994). *Intuition: The new frontier of management*. John Wiley & Sons, Chichester.

Patterson, A., Quinn, L., & Baron, S. (2012). The power of intuitive thinking: a devalued heuristic of strategic marketing. *Journal of Strategic Marketing, 20*(1), 35–44.

Puntoni, S., Reczek, R. W., Giesler, M., & Botti, S. (2021). Consumers and artificial intelligence: An experiential perspective. *Journal of Marketing, 85*(1), 131–151.

Radas, S., & Shugan, S. M. (1998). Seasonal marketing and timing new product introductions. *Journal of Marketing Research, 35*(3), 296–315.

Rajagopalan, S., & Swaminathan, J. M. (2001). A coordinated production planning model with capacity expansion and inventory management. *Management Science, 47*(11), 1562–1580.

Shafahi, A., & Haghani, A. (2014). Modeling contractors' project selection and markup decisions influenced by eminence. *International Journal of Project Management, 32*(8), 1481–1493.

Takano, Y., Ishii, N., & Muraki, M. (2014). A sequential competitive bidding strategy considering inaccurate cost estimates. *Omega, 42*(1), 132–140.

Tversky, A., & Kahneman, D. (1974). Judgment under uncertainty: Heuristics and biases. *Science, 185*(4157), 1124–1131.

Useem, M. (2006). How well-run boards make decisions. *Harvard Business Review, 84*(11), 130–136.

Vilcassim, N. J., & Chintagunta, P. K. (1995). Investigating retailer product category pricing from household scanner panel data. *Journal of Retailing, 71*(2), 103–128.

Wübben, M., & Wangenheim, F. V. (2008). Instant customer base analysis: Managerial heuristics often "get it right". *Journal of Marketing, 72*(3), 82–93.

8. Conclusion and implications to *Marketing Automation and Decision Making*

In the introductory chapter we presented the thesis, later developed in the volume, that the emergence of marketing automation and in particular the use of AI tools in marketing processes requires greater awareness and legitimization of the use of heuristics by marketers. At the end of this journey, we can draw some conclusions. Some marketing activities, such as customer clustering or programmatic buying, see automation made possible by the most advanced forms of AI and in particular ML. As pointed out by one of the managers interviewed (Chapter 7), machines can talk to each other on the basis of data and models they form and evolve through data-driven learning. From these processes marketers as decision makers may be substantially excluded, and the same computer scientists who set up the system may then lose vision of its learning path. In this case, as has been noted, the position of marketers is not very different from that of consumers (Kozinets and Gretzel, 2021). The development of automation offers great opportunities and is the main technology-driven perspective of transformation of marketing and business more generally. However, this does not mean that the new systems that operate marketing processes are error-free and potentially cannot also lead to negative effects on business. Their use poses problems in terms of transparency and consequently control for marketers themselves. The relationship between the new tools and marketers also comes through the view we have of the role of human intelligence with respect to their use, and that view cannot fail to consider the space and type of use we can make of heuristics in decision-making models, enabling the avoidance of the effects of AI accidents that could be avoided through processes simple to the human mind (Gigerenzer, 2022).

The perspective of marketers and business must first take into account the performance of decision-making models in terms of effectiveness (results achieved) and efficiency (ratio of results to means employed). In light of this reflection, automation of marketing processes offers important new perspectives (Guercini, 2022). However, the point of view should not be that of an uncritical belief that automated processes are by definition superior to models that include interventions of human intelligence in key steps of marketing activities (Colson, 2019). Today, as we have seen for example in the case of PA, the role of AI in marketing processes can be really crucial and precisely why it makes it realistic and important to reflect on the transparency and possibility of control of AI systems.

The trend toward automation is a fundamental trend in contemporary marketing. Marketing is one of the terrains of choice for new AI technologies where they are most evident in their applications and implications. In the comparison between human intelligence and AI, the latter emerges first as an imitator (think of the Turing test) and then as a challenger to human decision making, or so it appears. This is a challenge that is hardly confined to the field of marketing and naturally takes on a more general value, stimulating the formulation of hypotheses that from science fiction have become the subject of attention by scholars from various disciplines, such as that concerning the so-called "singularity" (Shanahan, 2015) or "superintelligence" (Bostrom, 2014) and thus the relationship to the evolution of human intelligence (Tegmark, 2017) or its possibilities (Gigerenzer, 2022).

In a managerial and entrepreneurial view, new systems should not be embraced uncritically because of their superior processing capacity, but because of an assessment of the positive and negative effects they may have for human actors and for functioning in the system in the short and long term. Technological systems then can propose new errors and problems. One entrepreneur interviewed highlighted how, when faced with a problem in a computer system, the solution may be to work on the system or to reset it. When a computer is no longer processing efficiently, "turning off the power" is a heuristic solution that can always be viable and can solve problems or errors in the machine. When driving an automatic car using an AI system, when the driver's hands rest on the steering wheel, the system can be set up to give priority to the driver, highlighting an example of integration between human intelligence and AI.

The idea we presented is that the very challenges posed by the increasing presence of AI and automation in marketing require an integration of these capabilities with extensive use of heuristics by operators. Not only challenges to maintain forms of control, but also challenges to make AI effective in the most complex operating processes that require the development of networks of actors (Guercini, La Rocca and Snehota, 2022) who are responsible for defining the data that must feed the system and the type of parameters that can be shared with some actors and not with others. This makes some already realized terrain of development of AI to marketing processes, such as PA, a context in which relationships between business actors and the processes of interaction and networking take on fundamental importance (Guercini, 2023; Håkansson and Snehota, 2017).

The widespread tendency to see AI-based automation as the superior solution to the use of human components in decision making is grounded in the advantages of an automated system that can seize opportunities in real time and generate more efficient and less costly processes. There is no doubt that these systems have strengths that are already making them irreplaceable and an essential basis of competitive advantage for adopters, if not defining an entire business model (Huang and Rust, 2021). Marketers, however, must also evaluate technology for the risks involved and how crises generated by changes and to control over marketing activities in such circumstances can be managed. This is precisely the logic of making things work and getting results, posing security problems to be answered by integrating systems and decision-making models of a different nature. The integration of different systems and models basically arises whenever a higher standard of security needs to be achieved. This opens up new perspectives to a conscious use of heuristic decision models, which, moreover, demonstrate earlier performance that can be superior to less simple models, complexity not having to be understood as a guarantee of greater effectiveness (Gigerenzer and Gaissmaier, 2011). To do this, and to make AI work, in several systems, technologies are integrated with heuristic reasoning that allow marketing processes to be put in place as we have seen in Chapters 6 and 7 above. Heuristics therefore need to be evaluated for their actual presence and the results they enable. This kind of position has implications: massive plans for training in the informed use of heuristics by those who must use AI in marketing probably need to be careful.

Automation has been seen as replacement, but it can also be seen as augmentation, in the sense discussed in Chapter 5 above. Automation comes to marketing in the form of the grafting of new skills that, for marketing, result in an increasingly deep and significant restructuring, to the point of prospectively framing a new paradigm. In fact, similar to the development of the mainstream marketing paradigm in the 1950s–60s, the change in technologies (mass production, mass media, etc.) leads to a configuration of marketing activities and thus also of the paradigm of reference, so new technologies (digitization, possibility of personalization, interaction, automation) leads to new possibilities for paradigm change (see Chapter 2 of this volume).

Marketing research on this topic is careful seeing in particular aspects of the impact on consumer behavior (Puntoni, Reczek, Giesler and Botti, 2021). These are fundamental aspects, but from specific components, an overall view needs to be developed that offers perspectives to marketers called upon to respond to consumer needs and, above all, an overview of the impact of the phenomenon on the relevant marketing model (see Chapters 3 and 4 of this volume).

There are some major paradigms around which research programs are formulated and conducted in different disciplines. This is also the case for marketing, a discipline that has been undergoing a long transition for some decades now between foundational paradigms that still represent the basic frame in educational processes (think of the basic marketing or introduction to marketing courses taught in universities around the world) and the trends of evolution that often lead to a "splitting" with marketing being associated with a new area (service marketing, industrial marketing, but also digital marketing) according to the field of application, sectoral or technological, in which it finds application. These major areas of marketing have been harbingers of implications for the evolution of the discipline as a whole, suggesting useful models even for domains other than those in which they were generated, for example when they proposed dominant logics from the evolution of the context and their heuristic effectiveness (Vargo and Lusch, 2004).

Automation pre-dates AI and does not coincide with it, but certainly automated marketing is increasingly driven by the adoption of AI systems. Automation affects activities that in the past had the character of relevant decision-making processes assumed by managers, where now managers are still managing decision-making processes but upstream and downstream from automated activities (Chapter 5).

Often linked to digitization, however, automated marketing poses a different perspective concerning a broad paradigm. What can the use of heuristics yield? Integrating decision models that consider a lot of data with very robust models can better handle an overall security problem of decision models. As we have seen in previous chapters (particularly Chapters 6 and 7), the automation of marketing processes is particularly conspicuous in specific fields, such as PA, which now uses AI and ML to interact with DDPs and SSPs and implement automated auctions, making it easier for brands to show their specific target audience advertising (Kietzmann, Paschen and Treen, 2018).

Marketing is one of the areas in which the implications of AI adoption can attract the most attention, not only from insiders but from the general public. All users of the Internet may perceive the presence of advertisements, are exposed to the subject of providing or accessing data, may look for products to buy and in some cases even to sell. In other words, there is widespread experience of digital marketing processes, and one can easily imagine the application of AI to such processes. In fact, AI is already widely used on the Web with marketing implications as well. Just think of the use of the common Google search engine to check for products or services that may represent purchase alternatives. As we have seen, we are in a data-driven marketing automation context.

The connection between heuristics and automation emerges as early as Simon and Newell's (1965) studies of the heuristic compiler, before the emergence of the term artificial intelligence. These studies spoke of "heuristic programming ... used as a tool of psychological research, by constructing programs that simulate, in as much detail as possible, the behavior of human being ..." (Simon and Newell, 1965, p. 28). After more than 60 years of research and advances in computer technologies and about 30 years of Internet development, we return to the confrontation between human heuristics and digital tools. This is enough to make them worthy of attention even in the face of the tools we can equip ourselves with, including artificial intelligence. This is for two reasons. The first, because we should not underestimate the reasons why our minds work the way they do, the solutions that evolution has provided have stood the tests of context on many occasions, and research programs that compare different models of decision making are certainly useful in capturing the effectiveness that heuristics can achieve in many contexts (Gigerenzer, 2007; Todd and Gigerenzer, 2012). The second reason is that, even when they may produce less effective outcomes than more complex decision models, heuristics are a fundamental feature of the way people form judgments and make choices. This makes them relevant even when at the source of bias. For example, if the state of risk aversion is perceived, even if it is excessive, it is still an element that may make the purchase of insurance solutions worthy of attention, because our nature is such that people live better when provided with patterns that give them the perception of protection. In other words, heuristics are worthy of attention for the very fact that they are a feature of human beings and as such cannot be considered something to be overcome or overlooked. Our activities and programs, however, must put humans and their cultural needs at the center of behavior research and thus also of decision-making patterns (Lawrence and Nohria, 2001; Pirson and Lawrence, 2010).

Heuristic rules offer a solution to the cognitive limit problem. Heuristics represent algorithms that, because of their characteristics, are particularly congenial to human memory and processing capacity. The adoption of heuristics by marketers does not simply represent the activation of procedures to solve specific problems, but can represent a real strategy, since it makes it possible to break out of the impasse of cognitive limit or illusion of control. The discussion of heuristics is important because it allows awareness to be pushed forward about the characteristics of an element that is central to understanding and human behavior in general. This function is particularly evident in the context of marketing activities.

Finally, there are some areas on which future research on marketing automation and decision making by marketers can be exercised. Heuristics is a topic of discussion and debate among different approaches and also presents itself as a definitional problem, not least in relation to the possibility of competitively testing their accuracy and general performance against alternative models. As we have seen (Chapters 6 and 7) heuristics can be located on different levels of the decision-making models adopted by marketers, for example, one can have heuristics that represent components of other heuristics (e.g., solving through a heuristic the source data search problem). Then within heuristics that are more articulated or more specific to a problem (e.g., to estimate sales to customers in the next year) one can have more basic and more general rules (counting some elements or multiplying by a coefficient dictated by experience). This articulation by levels may play a role in the forms of integration of human intelligence with AI in decision-making models adopted by marketers.

One of the earliest and most important tools for evaluating and to some extent defining AI is the Turing test, which we recalled earlier (in particular, see Chapter 6) that is a test of a machine's ability to exhibit intelligent behavior indistinguishable from that of a human (Turing, 1950). Widespread consideration about the potential of AI could lead to a reversed logic from that of the Turing test, whereby the intelligence of human actors is assessed for their ability to imitate AI. Heuristics, already considered in the past to make AI smart, can be still be a basis for making decision makers smart in general (Gigerenzer, 2022) and marketers in particular.

Automated marketing is evolving and has already developed in some areas, such as those we examined in the preceding capitols (user clustering, recommender systems, programmatic communication), and will develop further in the near future. Since they are all data-driven elements, these areas of automation are connected to each other and feeding off each other, requesting and producing data, so there will be systems integration in the future. The idea we have proposed concerns the relationship of these integration processes with elements of human decision making based on transparent, robust and controllable systems, even as simple as they may be precisely heuristic-type models (such as tallying and fast and frugal tree in Katsikopoulos, Şimşek, Buckmann and Gigerenzer, 2020).

Ultimately, anything that can emerge from large databases can be processed quickly by machines, and if computational capabilities can be accessed, the role of simple and transparent decision-making models may prove to be a key element as a tool for differentiation and advantage in marketers' decision-making processes. This is an important issue not only for marketing but for society, which will require continuous research in parallel with the evolution of technology and its applications in marketing processes.

REFERENCES

Bostrom, N. (2014). *Superintelligence. Paths, Dangers, Strategies*, Oxford University Press, Oxford.

Colson, E. (2019). What AI-driven decision making looks like. *Harvard Business Review*, 8 July, 2–8.

Gigerenzer, G., & Gaissmaier, W. (2011). Heuristic decision making. *Annual Review of Psychology, 62*, 451–482.

Gigerenzer, G. (2007). *Gut feelings: The intelligence of the unconscious.* Penguin Books, London.

Gigerenzer, G. (2022). *How to stay smart in a smart world: Why human intelligence still beats algorithms.* Penguin Books, London.

Guercini, S. (2022). Scope of heuristics and digitalization: the case of marketing automation. *Mind & Society, 21*(2), 151–164.

Guercini, S. (2023). Marketing automation and the case of programmatic advertising. *Micro & Macro Marketing, 32*(2), 261–270.

Guercini, S., La Rocca, A., & Snehota, I. (2022). Decisions when interacting in customer-supplier relationships. *Industrial Marketing Management, 105,* 380–387.

Håkansson, H., & Snehota, I. (2017). *No business is an island: Making sense of the interactive business world.* Emerald Group Publishing, Bingley.

Huang, M. H., & Rust, R. T. (2021). A strategic framework for artificial intelligence in marketing. *Journal of the Academy of Marketing Science, 49*(1), 30–50.

Katsikopoulos, K. V., Şimşek, O., Buckmann, M., & Gigerenzer, G. (2020). *Classification in the wild. The science and art of transparent decision making.* MIT Press, Cambridge, Mass.

Kietzmann, J., Paschen, J., & Treen, E. (2018). Artificial intelligence in advertising: How marketers can leverage artificial intelligence along the consumer journey. *Journal of Advertising Research, 58*(3), 263–267.

Kozinets, R. V., & Gretzel, U. (2021). Commentary: Artificial intelligence: The marketer's dilemma. *Journal of Marketing, 85*(1), 156–159.

Lawrence, P., & Nohria, N. (2001). *Driven: How human nature shapes organizations.* Harvard Business School, Boston, MA.

Pirson, M. A., & Lawrence, P. R. (2010). Humanism in business–towards a paradigm shift? *Journal of Business Ethics, 93*(4), 553–565.

Puntoni, S., Reczek, R. W., Giesler, M., & Botti, S. (2021). Consumers and artificial intelligence: An experiential perspective. *Journal of Marketing, 85*(1), 131–151.

Shanahan, M. (2015). *The technological singularity.* MIT Press, Cambridge, Mass.

Simon, H. A., & Newell, A. (1965). *Heuristic problem solving by computer.* Carnegie Institute of Technology, Pittsburgh.

Tagmark, M. (2017). *Life 3.0: Being human in the age of artificial intelligence.* Penguin Books, London.

Todd, P. M., & Gigerenzer, G. E. (2012). *Ecological rationality: Intelligence in the world.* Oxford University Press, Oxford.

Turing, A. M. (1950). Computing machinery and intelligence. *Mind. New Series, 59*(236), 433–460.

Vargo, S. L., & Lusch, R. F. (2004). Evolving to a new dominant logic for marketing. *Journal of Marketing, 68*(1), 1–17.

Index